Victory Without Peace

Victory Without Peace

by Roger Burlingame
and Alden Stevens

Harcourt, Brace and Company, New York

24862

A WARTIME BOOK

*This complete edition is produced in full
compliance with the government's regulations for conserving paper and other
essential materials.*

Contents

Victory Without Peace

1. A New Kind of War

THE end of the Great War was not yet in sight. Yet the days of peril and despair were over. Victory, though it might still be many months away and would still take many lives, no longer seemed a dream or an illusion. There was growing sureness about the outcome of the war. It was time to think about what would follow.

The new year broke on Washington with bitter cold. Over the vast spaces, down the broad avenues, the wind swept like an enemy. Crowds of government workers braced themselves against it, coats held close as they scurried across the dusty streets or huddled beside temporary buildings waiting for the packed streetcars. Small-town and city girls recruited from every corner of the country to run government typewriters spent days and weeks looking for lodgings which must almost certainly be cold, for the fuel shortage was acute. They had not expected so harsh a climate, and were unprepared. Overworked restaurant owners struggled to feed the hungry thousands. Uncertain jitney buses chugged and wheezed along routes selected by their drivers, routes which might change at any time without notice, carrying white-collar workers to the barren half-heated hall rooms they called home. Once there, they had nothing to do but shiver. Friends were far away, movies were few, plays were expensive, and high rents and food prices absorbed almost the whole of their civil-service pay checks.

More coming always. All day, every day, trains brought into the Union Station from all directions new faces: typists, clerks, executives, job-seekers, profiteers, lobbyists, secret agents, promoters, and patriots coming to do what could be done in Washington in war time. They stood in line to telephone; they searched the full hotels looking for sleeping space; they pestered Congressmen and busy government executives.

From abroad came news. News first of the deadlock on the front in France, then news of a probable offensive by the armies of the Kaiser in the spring. Hope that with the American help now streaming across the Atlantic the Allies would hold, and later, as the endless mass of reinforcements from the New World multiplied and shaped new armies, would overwhelm the hordes of Ludendorff and Hindenburg. From Russia came word of the new Bolshevik government which, good or bad, proved that this was a new kind of war which bred new ideas, which pitted whole peoples against governments, which challenged the old order as it had never been challenged before.

It was hard to tell what was really happening over there in Europe. Reports were so confused—it was so difficult to sift the prejudices and the propaganda from the fact; so impossible at this distance to estimate the forces and the personalities and the new groups. It made it hard to estimate the war itself, hard to judge where we stood in this new dark and shifty morass, hard to know America's part and place.

Into this doubting, wondering, seething city of Washington came a man just back from Europe, a slight, graying man wearing a precise pepper-and-salt business suit under a sleek chesterfield, a man with a well-made soft felt hat and high-topped black kid shoes. From one of the parlor cars on an incoming train he stepped, and was whisked by waiting automobile to a white house with a dignified portico.

"The President's waitin' for you, Colonel," said the colored doorman who opened the car door. "He said to bring you to his study the minute you got here."

Colonel House stepped out of the car and walked through the great front door, taking off his hat and coat as an usher went to announce him.

President Woodrow Wilson strode forward from behind the great desk as his friend entered the room. He took House's hand in both of his and shook it.

"My dear fellow," he said with warmth and eagerness, "I'm delighted to have you back! Tell me all about everything!" He made a sweeping gesture with his right hand and led the way to a divan.

"In one word?" asked House, smiling.

"In as many as you like." To the servant disappearing behind a softly closing door he called: "Have them bring up some coffee right away. You've had something to eat, I suppose?"

House nodded. The two men sat down, and Wilson's mobile face turned expectantly to his friend, but House waited cautiously until the servant had closed the door before he spoke.

"To begin with," House said, "Europe is exhausted. The people don't seem to care any more. And they are beginning to ask what the devil it is all about anyway."

Wilson nodded. "That's true in England as well as on the continent?" he asked.

"Absolutely." Then lowering his voice in a very confidential tone, House said: "It hasn't been reported in the press, but the trade-unions are simply howling for action. Four million workers went out on strike in England in 1917—as against a quarter of a million in 1916. They had eight separate government commissions investigating strikes and their causes. The Labor Party has worked out a program for postwar England that is nothing short of a revolution, and they're pressing Lloyd George for a statement. And it had better be a good one!"

"What do they want him to say?"

"Mostly they want assurances that this is not just an old-fashioned war of conquest. Arthur Henderson particularly insists that the British working-class must get some tangible social progress out of it—and Henderson is a pretty strong figure right now."

Wilson looked thoughtful. This was important. But there were other immediately important matters too.

"What about the front?" he asked. "What's the real situation?"

"Neither good nor bad at the moment," House said. "To some extent the Allies might almost be said to be fighting each other. Off the record, General Bliss and Admiral Benson both say co-operation between the French and British is sporadic and uncertain. Sometimes it's good enough, other times a man on one side or the other isn't willing to give up anything, or is angry because something went wrong last week, or just doesn't like the man he's talking to. They can't count on each other."

"How is it good, then?"

"The only good element is the fact that American troops are coming in—and that peps up both the French and English. And they see more coming in all the time, and it gives them hope. They can see a possibility of winning now."

"You mean the average British soldier had given up hope before we—"

House nodded gravely.

"The collapse of Russia left the Allies in a really desperate state. Every Tommy knew that it was only a matter of time before the Germans would clean up the Eastern Front and send their eastern forces west. Some of them have already shown up in France. And they couldn't see how the

Allies were going to overcome the advantage, where they were going to get reserves. Now it's true that the American troops have done no real fighting yet. But they're there. The British and French troops feel that there is an inexhaustible reservoir of reserves coming in. They feel backed up."

"We've had some encouraging reports about the Bolsheviki here," said Wilson. "There are indications that they may not be the irresponsible rabble we thought at first. What's your impression—is there any chance of bringing Russia back into the war?"

House shrugged his shoulders. "Our friends the British have no use for Lenin and his crowd. One reason may be that they aren't getting the straight news. There is something there—vague, perhaps, but real. I don't know what it is. The Russians seem to have found themselves after being buried under oppression for—oh, God knows how long—centuries. They've overthrown Kerensky and got Lenin—nobody knows what Lenin will do. A wild agitator, perhaps. Yet there the will of the people is expressing itself—and what is the result? They've quit the war because they say it's just imperialism."

Wilson rose and walked slowly to his desk. He picked up a carved ivory letter-opener and tapped it idly on the polished surface. Then he dropped it and spoke with decision.

"We've got to make clear that it isn't imperialism," he said. "This is a new kind of war, not the same old conflict of kings and prime ministers and powers. The Russians have to be shown that. And not only the Russians—the people of all nations. The Inter-allied Conference—"

"That was a terrible disappointment to me," House interrupted. "Of course, we should have planned an integrated diplomatic offensive right there. I couldn't get 'em to do it. Between you and me and the graveyard I think they're scared to death of Russia and they don't quite trust us. And a manifesto on war aims that might bind 'em afterward is the last thing they want."

Wilson listened and nodded. This was a sore point of long standing, and a discouraging one to the President, who knew that America, to fight well, must have strong convictions of the rightness of the moral issues in the war. Nothing had changed this, nor would it ever.

But diplomatic unity had not yet been brought about, and now as he heard Colonel House's report on Europe it became clearer and clearer to President Wilson that he himself would have to show the way. House had more to say about the unsuccessful Inter-allied Conference.

"We should," he said, "have formulated a policy as broad, as far-reaching, and as effective as the co-ordination of our military, naval, and economic resources had been. It should have been a world-appealing policy and one which would have shaken Germany behind the lines."

And now the Manchester *Guardian* had published the texts of the secret treaties released by the impolite Bolsheviki who cared nothing for the blushes of capitalist statesmen. There must be a counterattack on the diplomatic front; the Germans had scored on the publicity given the treaties.

Colonel House knew that President Wilson was watched expectantly by liberal and labor circles all over the world. Millions had come to regard him as the moral leader, the man who represented the long view and who saw the war not merely as a means of changing boundaries but of pushing forward social frontiers.

"I can't get them to see it," said the President, thoughtfully pounding his right fist in the palm of his left hand as he paced back and forth. "They don't understand it. Why do they think I asked long ago for a statement of war aims— and said that, as far as I could see then, both sides had the same aims?"

"That made the English angrier than anything you ever said."

"It didn't make them angry enough to answer my questions. Yes, they made a statement. About defense, reparations, guarantees, based on the old game of balance of power. But it didn't tell us why their men should be expected to give their lives. It didn't tell us what their victory would do for humanity. It didn't tell us about a peace guaranteed by all the peoples of the world working not against one another but in concert."

"I doubt," said House, "if even now they would agree on those answers."

"We've got to agree—unless we mean to lose the war. As you say, just as we have had to agree on strategy and supplies and munitions, we've got to agree on what we're fighting for. And it's got to be an agreement of peoples, not of governments. What I said a year ago, I still say, that the only peace which can endure is a peace made secure by the organized major force of mankind. There must be, not a balance of power, but a community of power; not organized rivalries, but an organized common peace."

"I didn't hear much of that at the conference," said House. "I think England and France still feel bound by the secret treaties."

But the President did not seem to be listening. He had sat down at his desk and pulled the little old Hammond typewriter that always stood there, toward him. He was staring at the keys. He turned suddenly to speak again:

"I think the soldiers understand," he said. "I think the men and women in the factories know, the people on the farms. . . . If someone spoke the truth, I think they would recognize it."

He began to write then, and Colonel House knew that he would talk no more.

2

In every town and city lines were forming, lines of young men whose numbers had been called. Some of them understood the words President Wilson had spoken. Some were going forth to save the world, to save democracy, to rescue the France that once helped America free herself. Some were off for a great adventure and for nothing else. Many others stood sullen and unhappy. "Why should we go?" they asked. "What have we got against the Germans? Wilson was supposed to keep us out of war—why didn't he?"

There were gashes all over America where trees had been hacked away and all else that was green uprooted; scars in the red and brown and yellow American earth now flecked with snow. Training camps were being built, and munitions factories, and dams on great unharnessed rivers like the Tennessee. There were barracks for construction workers, and tents for the overflow. "Making so much money I don't know what to do with it!" they said over a thousand poker games at night.

But beyond, in the bleak, leafless winter woods were tents and flimsy shacks where a few wives of carpenters and steel workers and steam fitters made shift to live. Their unkempt children, bundled into all the clothes they owned, dashed about the camps or stood with red faces and running noses, silent, cold, and bored before their temporary homes. And the wives said to the men when they came back from the day's work: "What are we staying here for? What good is it? We can't keep warm, the kids are sick, it's awful. Let's go home."

The towns nearby were swamped by the wave of newcomers; there were strangers sleeping in spare rooms, living rooms, chicken houses, garages, on front porches and in tents in the back yards. The townsfolk on Saturday night stayed home because there were more construction workers than there were old residents; and they were men determined to spend their money on satisfying pent-up nervous urges in saloons and in the brothels that had suddenly come into being. "This town's ruined," many said, "and what's the good of it?"

In Chicago and Detroit and Toledo and other northern cities men both black and white came from the farms and mountains of the South to get the unbelievable wages that had never existed before, wages so high they could hardly believe they were real. Men who had not seen three hundred dollars in a whole year now made that much in a month. Yet with prices shooting up they had gained little, and there were other causes of dissatisfaction. Living conditions were bad, many workers resented the speed-up, old resident workers resented the newcomers and saw them as a threat to their jobs after the war was over. "These damned niggers!" some said, and went out with clubs looking for men whose skins were black.

In the timber and wheat lands of the Pacific Coast the Industrial Workers of the World were singing a song of class and revolution. The rich, they said, kept the war going for their profits, and as always the workers got the short end. To them as to the Russians it was an imperialist war and not a war to free mankind from tyranny. "Solidarity!" they cried. "One big union!" Their weapons were strikes, sabotage, fire, and calm, cold disdain for all capitalist authority.

"Food will win the war," said the government, and farmers planted all their fields, and in the West broke new land, bought tractors, plows, and disks on time, worked day and night to make wheat grow where grass had grown before. For $2.25 wheat was gold, and grass was only grass. Let the oldsters shake their heads and say it was against nature; the plains had seen poverty and hardship too long to resist their only chance at riches. "Food will win the war—and war will lift the mortgage."

The coal and iron and copper and silver mines disgorged their ore and smelters poured smoke skyward and gangue upon the nearby slopes, while prospectors with burros sought new mines. Sweating, swearing men drilled wells for oil wherever there was any hope of finding it. Potash, sulphur, salt, and the new steel-making metals—vanadium, tungsten, and molybdenum—were hunted, found, and ripped from the earth for the uses of war.

To the men and women doing all this work it was not one war but many. To a few it meant fabulous new wealth, sometimes honest, sometimes not. To many it meant higher wages—and with them higher living costs. To most the war as they saw it was the war as it affected them. The larger vision was far from clear, though many believed deeply that it was not the German people we were fighting but the German system, that we were fighting not for power and glory for ourselves but for humanity, freedom, and a better world. Perhaps the largest group of Americans who believed in the war and its aims were those who believed in Woodrow Wilson. They remembered his rise and his record—a record of social advance that had been breath-taking at first and a little shocking, but a record rooted in the needs of ordinary Americans and not aimed to increase the wealth of a few.

3

Seven years earlier, when the New Jersey political bosses, Jim Smith and his son-in-law Jim Nugent, had stood, hats in hand, and knocked at the front door of the president's mansion at Princeton University, they had foreseen no such devotion to the people's cause. For their machine, backed by

many of the large corporations which in the New Jersey of
1910 could do as they pleased, represented the most reactionary elements of the Democratic party. They thought Wilson
would be tractable, and they were sure that his name and
prestige would win them support from the substantial businessmen and wealthy backers they wanted so badly.

Woodrow Wilson received them cordially and talked with
them freely that night in Princeton. Although he had never
been in politics before, he clearly knew why they were there
and he was glad they had come. Perhaps one reason was that
he was tired of wrangling with the university trustees over
matters which seemed to him perfectly obvious and simple.
Would he consent to run for governor if nominated? Yes,
but he would not seek the nomination—did Messrs. Smith
and Nugent think he could be nominated? They did indeed.
So did Colonel George Brinton McClellan Harvey, publisher
of *Harper's Weekly,* who had once unsuccessfully pushed
the good Dr. Wilson for United States senator. But in New
Jersey at that time governors were elected directly, and senators were not.

Smith and Nugent, delighted with their talk with Dr.
Wilson, began to work out their strategy. When the convention met, hardly any of the delegates had ever seen Wilson,
but it mattered little, for Smith and Nugent controlled
enough votes to nominate him in spite of Progressive opposition.

The sweating delegates in the old Taylor opera house on
that scorching, exhausting day, nearly half of whom were
disgruntled over the result, awaited announcement of the
figures on the final vote, though all knew who had won it.
The Progressives milled about at the back of the hall wondering what this sphinxlike amateur politician they had failed to
beat would do. Suddenly the clerk of the convention, per-

haps under the direction of that wily stage-manager, Colonel George Harvey, announced:

"We have just received word that Mr. Wilson, the candidate for the governorship, *and the next President of the United States*, has received word of his nomination, has left Princeton, and is now on his way to the convention!"

The band played lustily as the next Governor of New Jersey and the next President of the United States drove at breakneck speed the eleven miles from Princeton to Trenton. And the dramatic device of George Harvey and the Jersey bosses was an outstanding success. Wilson, vigorous, cool, and poised, strode to the platform and spoke words which must have made Smith, Nugent, and the others who had forced through his nomination gulp, yet strictly the words were true:

"I did not seek this nomination, I have made no pledge and have given no promises. If elected, I am left absolutely free to serve you with all singleness of purpose. It is a new era when these things can be said. . . . The future is not for parties 'playing politics' but for measures conceived in the largest spirit, pushed by parties whose leaders are statesmen, not demagogues, who love not their offices but their duty and their opportunity for service. . . ."

Joseph P. Tumulty, one of the Progressives who had entered the hall bitterly opposed to Wilson, said that the crowd was transported. He himself was from that moment Dr. Wilson's, heart and soul. So were most of those who heard the speech.

Jim Smith found Woodrow Wilson President of Princeton and left him Governor of New Jersey. Wilson found Smith in control of New Jersey politics and left him a helpless, sputtering ex-politician. Let the cast-off boss complain that Woodrow Wilson was an ingrate who broke promises to the friends who had put him into office if he would; New

Jersey's independent newspapers and New Jersey's people could see that the new governor was nobody's fool and nobody's tool, and they gave evidence that they were for him. If he had thrown out the bosses, so much the better.

It was, as the convention clerk had surmised, Governor Wilson in 1910; President Wilson in 1912. He became president not because of overwhelming public support—in fact he drew only 6,294,000 votes against a total of 7,603,000 for his divided opposition.

Woodrow Wilson began his first term as president with at least the tacit approval of many newspapers, and with a good share of Congress either actively on his side or willing to give him a fair chance.

Among the senators inclined to be friendly was Theodore Roosevelt's close friend, Senator Henry Cabot Lodge, who called on the new president soon after the inauguration. Wilson saw a distinguished-looking Boston Brahmin with a carefully groomed short beard and mustache, an average-size man with a rather small face and deep-set eyes, with a brow deeply, perhaps perpetually furrowed as though he never ceased to worry about the world and its troubles.

"You do not, of course, remember me, Mr. President," the Senator said, "but I had the pleasure of sitting next to you at the alumni dinner at a Harvard commencement."

"Senator," said Wilson, "it is not necessary to recall our meeting at Cambridge, because a man never forgets the first editor who accepts one of his articles. You were the first editor who accepted an article written by me."

Lodge was surprised, and Wilson explained that when Lodge was an editor of the *International Review*, thirty-three years earlier, he had accepted Wilson's article on "Cabinet Government in the United States." Only a few weeks later Mr. Lodge made an impassioned speech in the Senate supporting the President on the matter of the Panama Canal tolls—one of the first important items on Wilson's legislative program.

So helpful was Mr. Lodge's speech that the President telephoned his appreciation, and a few days later, following a strong criticism of administration policy by Senator Bristow, Mr. Lodge made another speech on the floor of the Senate, saying:

"When he [the President] is dealing with foreign relations, in some respects of a most perilous and difficult character, if he says, on his high responsibility, to the Congress of the United States that a certain step in foreign relations is necessary to the good name and possibly to the security of the United States . . . I think it becomes the duty of all men, who look upon foreign relations as I do, not to try to block his path but to give him such aid and assistance in our humble way as we are conscientiously able to give."

Senator Clark of Wyoming jumped up to demand whether that meant that Mr. Lodge intended to back the President regardless of whether he agreed with administration policies or not. In other words, was Senator Lodge abandoning the Republican party?

Mr. Lodge clarified his position:

"I certainly should not support the President in any policy which I believed to be wrong," he said, "or which went against my conscience; but where I have no policy to substitute, and he is engaged in a difficult situation, I am ready at least not to throw obstacles in his way, and so far as I honestly and conscientiously can, I am going to give my support."

Woodrow Wilson, reading the speech in the White House study the following day, felt a warm glow of confidence and appreciation. So he could count on this influential member of the Foreign Relations Committee of the Senate—who was, by seniority of service, in line to be its next chairman. A close friend of Theodore Roosevelt's, a key senator, and one with much prestige. A man to be counted upon for aid in a tight spot! Wilson pulled his Hammond typewriter over to him, for the habit of writing his own notes was one he kept long after he went to the White House:

My dear Senator, [he wrote] May I not express my sincere appreciation of your generous action yesterday in replying as you did to the criticisms of Senator Bristow. I feel honoured by your confidence and your general comprehension of my motives.

4

The early months of Wilson's administration had been full of triumphs. He had enough support in Congress to put through the things he most wanted. Westerners cheered his Underwood Tariff Bill and applauded when he charged that a "tariff lobby" was obstructing it because rich manufacturers intent on keeping prices high did not want even modifications in the protective tariff policies.

All over the country the small businessman (and many leaders of big business too) approved the establishment of the Federal Reserve Board which stabilized the nation's banking and went far to prevent bank failures. They could see that the new board, together with the new currency regulations, worked against speculators and manipulators and in favor of the average citizen. And when the opposition had threatened a filibuster to prevent passage of this bill many new friends had rallied to the President's side and more ground had been cut from under Republican leadership.

Farmers watched almost with gaping mouths the Wilson farm program: the Federal Farm Loan Act, the improved marketing machinery, the establishment of grain and cotton standards, the better roads which made the automobile no longer a rich man's toy but a poor man's tool, the better schools, and last but far from least, the great extension program—the county agent system. So far as the average farmer could see, all this favored him and only occasionally and incidentally helped the big operators. And none of it was Wall Street stuff. This fellow in the White House may have been a college professor, but he seemed to know something about the real problems farmers had to face.

The working trade-unionists in the American Federation of Labor gave Mr. Wilson and his administration credit for the Clayton Act which specifically provided that the anti-trust laws could not be construed to forbid organization of labor unions and could not be used to restrict their legitimate activities. It had not been Wilson's fault that the Supreme Court had nullified two excellent child-labor acts and they gave him credit for trying. The eight-hour day for railroad workers was established and the Railway Brotherhoods were won. The American Federation of Labor, which before Wilson became president had had less than 2,000,000 members, had 2,773,000 by 1916 and 3,500,000 by 1918. When war came, President Samuel Gompers of the federation knew that workingmen were behind him when he gave his pledge of steadfast support to Mr. Wilson.

The income-tax law and the establishment of the Federal Trade Commission drew bitter criticism from large corporations and the rich, and this criticism was itself reason enough for thousands of average Americans to applaud these acts.

Organized labor—farmers—businessmen—all felt tangibly benefited by Wilson's domestic program. The President knew this, and was sure he could count on all these groups if he could make his purposes and America's aims in the war clear to them. Yet he knew that these things were not clear, and it was perhaps even more important to keep informed the millions of Americans who had showed their trust in him, than it was to keep the Congress informed. He owed the American people a clear and specific statement of what this war was all about. And he knew that others not in America would be listening to what he said.

5

Billy Sunday arrived in Washington on January 6th, 1918. He preached in his new Tabernacle on "The Need for Revival," and other subjects. He deplored "frizzle-headed, manicured fingernailed mothers." He ranted against the "Bacchus Specials" that took thirsty Washingtonians to Baltimore to escape the local prohibition laws. He promised to go to Camp Meade and "chase the devil out of camp."

On January 8th Woodrow Wilson, who reminded many of a Scotch Presbyterian minister, preached in the House of Representatives on another subject. The day dawned clear and moderately cold. It was not until the middle of the morning that the House and Senate had any intimation that the President intended to speak to them that day. They had no idea what he would talk about. Twelve-thirty had been set as the time for the address, and there was much to be done.

Meeting at noon, the members listened to a prayer by the Chaplain, approved the previous day's journal after a brief wrangle over a point of no quorum mistakenly attributed to Mr. Cooper of Wisconsin when it was Mr. Gillett of Massachusetts who had actually made it, and granted an extension of the time for the completion of the municipal bridge at St. Louis.

Mr. Flood of Virginia now asked unanimous consent to postpone a previously arranged recess for a Serbian commission until after the President's speech. Mr. Gillett demanded the reason for this sudden and unseemly alteration of the schedule, saying this was the first he'd heard of any such thing.

With some show of patience the Speaker explained that the President had only that morning notified them of his desire to speak, and this apparently satisfied Mr. Gillett, who sat down.

Now a concurrent resolution (which the Senate had already passed) had to be put through to authorize the joint session to hear the President. It went through without a hitch, and this heavy and exhausting business settled, the House recessed for fifteen minutes.

At 12:25 precisely Doorkeeper Joseph J. Sinnott announced the Vice-President and the senators, and the House politely rose as Mr. Marshall took the chair at the Speaker's right and the senators filed into the chamber and found seats.

The Speaker now appointed Representatives Flood, Sherley, Webb, Pou, Gillett, and Campbell to wait upon the President; the Vice-President selected Senators Martin, Stone, Simmons, Overman, Gallinger, Lodge, and Warren for the same arduous task, and the assemblage settled down to await the hour of 12:30 and the President.

Senator Lodge, with his associates assigned to "wait upon" the President, speculated on the characteristic dry humor of Vice-President Marshall in choosing him as one of the group.

At 12:30 precisely the President arrived, and Lodge, together with the other members of the House and Senate selected for the function, escorted him into the hall.

The President took his place at the Clerk's desk. The Speaker was brief: "Gentlemen of the Sixty-fifth Congress," he said, "I present the President of the United States."

"Gentlemen of the Congress," said the President, "once more, as repeatedly before, the spokesmen of the Central Empires have indicated their desires to discuss the objects of the war and the possible basis of a general peace. Parleys have been in progress at Brest-Litovsk between Russian representatives and representatives of the Central Powers to which the attention of all the belligerents have been invited for the purpose of ascertaining whether it may be possible to extend these parleys into a general conference with regard to terms of peace and settlement."

Senator Lodge coughed slightly and wondered what the President was driving at. He had found Wilson disconcertingly unpredictable ever since the President had flatly called him a liar on the matter of the *Lusitania* note. On that occasion Senator Lodge had charged Wilson with bad faith and with not really meaning what he said in his note to the German government holding that government to "strict accountability" for American loss of life when the *Lusitania* had been sunk by a submarine. It had been a most embarrassing experience for Senator Lodge, and he had felt that the President had been unfair and shifty in denying the charge by simply saying that it was untrue. Later the President had refused to speak on the same program with Mr. Lodge. And since that time there had been no cordial relations between the two men.

The galleries, half-empty because no advance notice of the speech had been given, seemed only moderately interested. Most of the representatives were paying polite inattention as the President went on to say that the Russian representatives, sincere and in earnest, had broken off the negotiations because of the evident intention of Germany to demand large slices of Russian territory and other impossible terms.

"There is, moreover, a voice calling for these definitions of principle and purpose which is, it seems to me, more thrilling and more compelling than any of the many moving voices with which the troubled air of the world is filled." He paused a moment, and with a vibrant emphasis, said, "It is the voice of the Russian people!"

Senator Lodge winced slightly at the tremendous burst of applause. "Bravo!" shouted the two Socialist representatives. There was the suggestion of a smile on Lodge's face as he heard the President continue with a pledge of the United States to aid the Russian people in the attainment of "their utmost hope of liberty and ordered peace." But many others applauded.

The words that followed, words of peace, words telling of justice and fair dealing, of a better life to come out of the war, led to the recital of a definite program of fourteen points. The President read them off with careful emphasis and with a pause after each:

"I. Open covenants of peace, openly arrived at, after which there shall be no private international understandings of any kind, but diplomacy shall proceed always frankly and in the public view.

"II. Absolute freedom of navigation upon the seas, outside territorial waters, alike in peace and in war, except as the seas may be closed in whole or in part by international action for the enforcement of international covenants.

"III. The removal, so far as possible, of all economic barriers and the establishment of an equality of trade conditions among all the nations consenting to the peace and associating themselves for its maintenance."

Lodge looked about the hall quickly. He heard applause, but there was consternation too. No Republican cared to accept a point which sounded like an attack on all protective tariffs.

"IV. Adequate guarantees given and taken that national armaments will be reduced to the lowest point consistent with domestic safety.

"V. A free, open-minded and absolutely impartial adjustment of all colonial claims, based upon a strict observance of the principle that in determining all such questions of sovereignty the interests of the populations concerned must have equal weight with the equitable claims of the Government whose title is to be determined.

"VI. The evacuation of all Russian territory and such a settlement of all questions affecting Russia as will secure the best and freest co-operation of the other nations of the world in obtaining for her an unhampered and unembarrassed opportunity for the independent determination of her own political development and national policy—[Applause interrupted the President, who continued quickly, cutting it off.]—and assure her of a sincere welcome into the society of free nations under institutions of her own choosing; and more than a welcome, assistance also of every kind that she may need and may herself desire. [More applause, but the President continued.] The treatment accorded Russia by her sister nations will be the acid test of their good will, of their comprehension of her needs as distinguished from their own interests and of their intelligent and unselfish sympathy."

The audience seemed to believe that it was listening to a great and important speech. Coughing and sneezing had stopped. Senator Lodge was no longer smiling as the President, warming with his audience, went on:

"VII. Belgium, the whole world will agree, must be evacuated and restored, [There was strong applause here.] without any attempt to limit the sovereignty which she enjoys in common with all other free nations. . . .

"VIII. All French territory should be freed and the invaded portions restored, and the wrong done to France by Prussia in 1871 in the matter of Alsace-Lorraine, which has unsettled the peace of the world for nearly fifty years, should be righted, in order that peace may once more be made secure in the interest of all."

The Congress rose as one man, cheering and applauding, and the galleries went wild! There could be no mistaking the enthusiasm now—enthusiasm for the ally, France, yes, but perhaps even more enthusiasm for the President who was speaking the national opinion in magnificent terms. This was the most spontaneous applause before the end of the speech, and the most prolonged.

The next five points dealt with the frontiers and boundaries of European states. They evidently did not seem very important to most of the audience. Mr. Lodge lost the thread. He cared little how these matters were settled. His mind kept going back to the free-trade statement, and the overgenerous handout to Russia—

The President read his last point:

"XIV. A general association of nations must be formed under specific covenants for the purpose of affording mutual guarantees of political independence and territorial integrity to great and small states alike."

There was loud and prolonged applause for the League of Nations idea, including some from the Republican members.

"An evident principle runs through the whole program I have outlined. It is the principle of justice to all peoples and nationalities and their right to live on equal terms of liberty and safety with one another, whether they be strong or weak. . . . The moral climax of this, the culminating and final war for human liberty, has come, and the people of the United States are ready to put their own strength, their own highest purpose, their own integrity and devotion to the test."

The speech was over. The applause had just begun, the long, thunderous applause that meant the speech was a success. But when a man has called you a liar and insulted you by refusing to speak on the same program with you, what he says is unlikely to carry you away. Senator Lodge was already thinking of the implications of some of the things President Wilson had said. And the furrows in his brow were deeper than usual as he left the chamber with the rest of the senators.

2. Words Across Nomansland

THE bitter winter which was a surprise in Washington was a chronic business in the north of Russia. There was no grumbling or astonishment at the cold. The discontent, piling through the centuries like the ice on a glacier, had other causes. In 1917 the avalanche had come. In November it had swept all before it—the meanness and the corruption, the tyranny and the fear, along with many of the beauties of an old civilization. What would follow no one, in the uncertain midwinter, could know. To many millions there was such a dawning of hope as had never before brightened the Russian sky. But to others, in all parts of the world, there was only the promise of new disaster: of anarchy, savagery, chaos, which might well sweep on over the whole of Europe.

In Petrograd, the arctic capital of this vast, mysterious land, there were many frightened or wondering foreigners. There were Americans. The Americans, as always, felt more detached, safer. The whole thing was too strange to their own tradition and experience to seem real. Their homes were far away—too far for this shadow to reach. So, however they might discuss its good or evil or shake their heads over its portents, they did not feel, as Frenchmen and Englishmen did, the direct touch of its icy fingers.

Some of the Americans had watched the whole movement of the avalanche from the day when Imperial Russia had been called invincible, inexhaustible—the great "steam roller," certain to crush Germany. Had not her resources been infinite, her man power drawn from a population of a hundred and fifty million? Then the Americans had learned that men, no matter how many, cannot fight against even a small trained, equipped army with their bare fists. When the gossip came through that there was only one rifle to six men, that enormous stores of munitions lay rotting on the wharves of Murmansk and Archangel, that trains were being sidetracked and sent to the wrong places, and that many such things happened not only through bungling but to enrich profiteers, they had smelt the decay at the heart of the Empire.

Then came the gossip that German intrigue was working in ministries and government offices, playing with the jealousies of the bureaucrats, juggling the orders; that the final arbiter, the Most High, Nicholas, Czar of All the Russias, played dominoes and walked among his roses while a million soldiers died and, at last, that the control had passed into the hands of his superstitious wife who in turn had come under the hypnotic spell of Rasputin, the libertine "monk" from Siberia.

To those who had troubled to look into Russian history over half a century these things were not surprising. The surprise was that a hundred and fifty million people could have been suppressed so long in a modern world—hounded, beaten, impoverished, deprived of land, food, and education for the benefit of a handful of landlords and a resplendent imperial court. In 1905, at the end of the Russo-Japanese war, the lid of this stinking, steaming caldron had almost blown off. There was a revolution then, led—like many revolutions—by students and intellectuals. In the capital they had roused the people and right under the Czar's nose an ominous mushroom called a soviet had grown up overnight. A soviet was a workers' council, independent of all parliaments, for revolution. Why had the soviet failed? In America the question had puzzled people whose history books had taught them that when a government becomes destructive of the rights of life, liberty, and the pursuit of happiness, it becomes the right of the people to alter or abolish it.

But Americans in Russia felt the darkness of the land. In a country where only twenty of every hundred persons are literate, organization is difficult. In a country where some 80 per cent of the people are peasants scattered over an area three times as large as the United States—peasants for the most part unable to move from their thatched, chimneyless houses in which family and livestock live together in one room—numbers do not count. And the Czar's police and soldiery were strong in December, 1905, and could be used at home. So the soviet of October, 1905, lasted less than two months. In 1906 the leaders were shipped a thousand miles east to exile in Siberia, bands of Cossacks were sent over the countryside on errands of slaughter and the revolutionary forces were driven underground. So the imperialist government gained new strength, the peasants grew hungrier and in their misery drank so much vodka that the Czar's treasury which held the monopoly on alcohol was able to balance its budget.

But in 1906 Russia had been at peace. The war with Japan was over. In 1917 she was still at war. In 1917 millions of the scattered peasants had been brought together into armies. In 1906 the Czar's armies were on hand, equipped for the home job of stopping revolutions. In 1917 they were away at the front, where they had suffered years of defeat, hunger, and betrayal by a corrupt war office. The professional soldiers had been stubbornly loyal while they had kept their faith in the Little Father. But now their loyalty was weakened on two sides: by the mass of the conscripted peasants who, in the face of defeat, had begun the cry for Peace, Bread, and Land, and by a divided government at home which had lost faith in itself.

So the Americans in Petrograd had learned that war time is the time for revolution.

Long before spring thawed the ice of the Neva in 1917, the demonstrations of the people began. The Little Father was away at staff headquarters where he had made himself Supreme Commander and performed his duties by playing dominoes with his generals. At night he wrote pale love letters to his wife. His wife answered that she had "put on the trousers" and was running the country from her splendid country palace at Tsarskoye Selo. She ran the country by firing such bureaucrats and ministers as she personally disliked or who had whispered against Rasputin (now dead from a prince's bullet).

In March the police and soldiery, ordered to disband the crowds, were refusing to fire and, often, falling into the people's arms. Deserters from the front, bringing back their rifles, joined the people's side. When such things happened, the Czar's own friends knew that the jig was up and advised him to abdicate. The Czar, looking up from his game with his strange, cold, feeble eyes, named his brother, the Grand Duke, Michael, in his place. He showed no emotion. All he really wanted was to get back to his roses.

But Michael, too, was unacceptable to the people. So a Temporary Government was patched up, with a liberal— Prince Lvoff—at its head. It issued some fine, democratic proclamations. The people went wild. They poured into the streets embracing and weeping. The government leaders did not tell them that they meant only to stave off revolution. For the people, revolution was in full swing, warming their hearts against the age-long cold. Now there would be Peace and Bread and, for the peasants, Land.

A mushroom soviet had appeared again in March. The Temporary Government could not oppose it so they humored it. They let it organize other soviets all over Russia. They had no choice. But they hoped, always, to lead the soviets to moderation and to persuade them that the war must go on.

This had been the point of the wedge, dividing the people from the new government. The people wanted peace. The government still felt the burden of the Czar's obligations to Imperial Russia's allies against Germany. Their opponents said that the government only wanted Constantinople, promised to Russia in a secret treaty with England and France, and that the people refused to die for Constantinople.

For a while it had seemed as if the new government would win out. The soviets were wobbly. One of the new ministers, Alexander Kerensky, was persuasive with his speeches. He himself was a leftist; he called himself a "people's man." Many American observers thought him the savior of Russia. They scorched the cables with the news that this empire which had once been an autocracy as bad as Germany was now a democracy like ourselves. And there were those who thought that this news had overcome the last of Wilson's scruples and cleared the way for America's entry into the war to "make the world safe for democracy."

What would have happened had Kerensky been allowed uninterruptedly to continue his persuasion, these Americans, thinking back in November, could not say. In November most of them put the blame for what had happened on the arrival in Russia of a special train on a night in April—a train which had crossed Germany from Switzerland under German protection.

Off the train had stepped a short, carelessly dressed man, an unimpressive man with a big, bald head and an untrimmed beard. His impassive face gave no sign of the flame in his heart. He did not look like a veteran revolutionary. There was nothing in his appearance to show that for ten years of exile he had thought and dreamed only of two things: first the liberation of the Russian people, second the liberation of all workers through world revolution. His name was Vladimir Ilyich Ulyanoff; his friends called him Lenin.

From that moment everything had seemed to change. Lenin had talked, written, circulated his words through the whole underground of Russia. This is not revolution, he said. This is not Peace, Bread, and Land. This is the old regime in disguise. It is worse than the old, because it fools the people. The Tauride Palace where it holds its meetings smells to heaven of aristocrats, landlords, bourgeois capitalists. Who is this premier, Prince Lvoff? Not a proletarian, certainly! Kerensky is only the tool of men who want to hold their property, keep the peasants down, continue the war for imperialistic gain.

Through the summer Lenin's words spread like fire to every corner of the immense land. Soldiers heard them, deserted in droves, came home, packing the roads, riding on the tops of trains—lest they be too late for the distribution of the land. The soviets crystallized their thought, purged themselves of moderates and weaklings, and the party of the extreme left, the old Bolshevik party of 1903, became strong. Kerensky, thrown off balance, kept moving from left to right and back again to keep his power.

Yet even in July Kerensky was able to launch one last attack against the outside enemy. The Galician offensive started brilliantly enough against the already cracking Austrians. For a brief interval the news of victory fought the growing influence of Lenin. If the people could win victory and revolution both. . . . But Lenin never swerved. He was sure that the Germans would come in to save their Austrian allies. In August they came. The Russian army was sent into full flight and the Germans would have marched into Petrograd but that they had other jobs on their hands. So they left a static front (too close to the capital for the comfort of the foreigners there) and the remnants of the Russian armies, loyal to individual officers, remained to hold it.

From then on, nothing could stop the full revolution. Kerensky forced Lenin into hiding across the Finnish border but he could not stop the echo of his words. "Peace, Bread, and Land!" They were simple words, gigantic in their strength. In September Kerensky proclaimed a "republic" and assumed full power himself, but it was hardly more than a gesture. The soviets, reinforced by thousands of factory workers and hundreds of thousands of ex-peasant soldier deserters, grew stronger than the government. Then the call which Lenin had sent across the border from Finland grew into a slogan: "All Power to the Soviets!"

In the first week in November Kerensky called out the Petrograd garrison to defend his government. The old, loyal garrison refused. Instead, they helped the Bolsheviki seize the palaces, the arsenals, the telephone exchanges. On the 6th Lenin came back. On the 7th Kerensky disappeared to recruit an army somewhere else. On the 8th Lenin addressed the All-Russian Congress of Soviets assembled in Smolny Institute in a suburb of Petrograd.

Smolny Institute had been a finishing school for the daughters of noblemen, founded by Catherine the Great. In it, generations of gently bred girls had learned the etiquette and languages of the imperial court. In its great ballroom, where Lenin spoke on the night of November 8, 1917, they had studied the complex courtesies which set them apart from the common man. Tonight the common man was spitting on the floor. Hundreds of him stood in silence before their Messiah. The acrid transpiration of their sweat filled every tapestry-hung corner.

All day Lenin had argued with soviet committees, persuading the minority compromisers of the necessity of immediate peace. His hard logic convinced them. So, in the evening, he could explain his formula to a unanimous, cheering throng.

His formula was simple. The workers and peasants of Russia had liberated themselves from the tyranny of both Czarist and bourgeois-capitalist governments. The German workers and peasants were ready to overthrow their government and would overthrow it if they believed that peace would result. So, also, would the war-weary masses in England and France. They needed only this great example of the Russian workers whose soviets had taken the full power into their hands. They already knew that the war was being fought for the benefit of the rich landlords and capitalists— for territory, for indemnities which could bring no solace to the masses who bore the burden of the fighting.

Based on this logic was the first Decree of the Soviet Government, which Lenin read:

"The Government considers it to be the greatest crime against humanity to continue the war for the sake of dividing among the powerful and rich nations the weaker nationalities which were seized by them, and the Government solemnly states its readiness to sign immediately the terms of peace which will end this war, on the basis of the above-stated conditions, equally just for all nationalities without exception."

The conditions were "no annexations, no indemnities, and the principle of self-determination."

Lenin went on to explain the easy steps by which this world peace would be effected. First there would be an armistice between Russia and her enemies, Germany, Austria-Hungary, Turkey, and Bulgaria, of not less than three months' duration. This would be time enough for peace negotiations. Meanwhile appeals would be made to the "three most advanced nations of mankind . . . England, France, and Germany." The appeals would be made, not to the governments of these nations but *over the governments' heads* "to the class-conscious workers."

A thunder of cheers met Lenin's speech. His face did not change. He did not smirk or bow to his frenzied audience. He did not thank them for their devotion. Always his eyes seemed focused on something beyond the moment—on the next move. When quiet came he asked for a vote. It was unanimous.

No one in the great room seems to have doubted that, once these appeals were launched, the workers in each enlightened nation, especially Germany, would instantly (within three months) overthrow any government which wanted to go on with the war. Why not? The Russians had done it in eight months. . . . And events were moving faster now.

In the Smolny ballroom, listening that night to Lenin, was an American. He was neither a peasant nor a factory worker. He had been gently bred, educated at the best private schools and at Harvard; his father was in a lucrative business in Portland, Oregon, his brother was in the United States Army. Did he suppose that his country, which seven months before had entered this war on the very basis on which Lenin wanted to sue for peace—no annexations or indemnities and self-determination of peoples—would also withdraw if an appeal were made to her workers?

John Reed was a writer. Even in his school days his verse had been vigorous and beautiful; later his prose had grown sure, direct; it had flamed too with passion. His heart had gone out to the oppressed. Breaking from his tory environment, he had mixed with labor, taking its part in strikes.

He had come to Europe as a war correspondent. He had toured both Allied and German trenches before America came in, so he had learned of the war from both sides. He was not sure that the millions of dead had known why they must die. Now, in Russia, he was finding the end and clarification of a long, uncertain dream. It was not a dream of battalions and guns. It was a dream of peoples and peace.

Tonight the Russian dream obscured the reality of the homeland. It dimmed the simple truth that American workers in factories and fields had not suffered and would never suffer as Russian workers and peasants had suffered. It hid, for the moment, the vision of a land where government was still by the clear consent of the governed and of a land whose people's representatives had voted their country into this war with the definite intent of bringing that same consent of the governed to the peoples of the world.

John Reed could not take part in the Smolny meeting. He could not raise his hand for Lenin's peace. He could only listen and report. But he reported that "great Russia was in travail, bearing a new world."

2

The other Americans in Petrograd differed from John Reed and from one another. Ambassador Francis, a politician from Missouri who gloried in his prestige and his silk hat, became so angry and alarmed that he closed the doors of his embassy to the new government. Before either interpreting the situation to Washington or receiving Washington's advice, he simply refused to speak to Bolsheviki. Yet as long as an embassy remained in Petrograd, it was essential that business be done with some Russian government and only the soviets headed by Lenin and his lately arrived partner Leon Trotsky remained. In addition to being criminals and traitors, neither of these persons looked to Mr. Francis like a responsible official. Neither wore a cutaway nor owned a silk hat.

So communication was engineered through Raymond Robins of the American Red Cross mission. Robins was not—

in November at least—a true Bolshevik sympathizer. But Robins was deeply interested in the revolution. So he undertook an off-the-record liaison between the American embassy and Lenin's headquarters in Smolny Institute. As time went on and he grew intimate with Lenin and Trotsky, he hoped that he could establish better relations between the new Russia and the United States.

Late in November, a shrewd, energetic American journalist arrived in Petrograd with two letters in his pocket. One was to Kerensky. Edgar Sisson had not come as a reporter. Yet as he got off the train which had brought him from Sweden across Finland and saw about him the riffraff of people which always collects in railway stations in uncertain times, he knew that he would need all the training which prepares newsmen for the unexpected.

He had learned at the frontier that there was no Kerensky for his letter. He had learned too that in Kerensky's place was a man who had been branded in London and Paris as a traitor. So, in the cold bleakness of his hotel bedroom in Petrograd he brought out the second letter and reread it.

"We want nothing for ourselves . . ."

The words warmed him. How many of the Allies could write this truth about their own aspirations? At that very moment Trotsky was publishing in the Bolshevik papers, *Pravda* and *Izvestia*, the texts of secret treaties made early in the war between Czarist Russia, England, France, and Italy. It was treasonable of Trotsky to bring out these skeletons from the war's diplomatic closet. But the treaties themselves . . . There was the Treaty of London, for instance, the Allies' bribe to Italy to enter the war in 1915. It promised Italy great chunks of territory which by all rights of self-determination should go to the Jugoslavs. There was a secret agreement which gave Turkey's Constantinople to Russia. There was a bribe to Rumania giving her slices of

Hungarian land. There were very secret memoranda awarding the Arabs' Syria to France and certain other territory to England. Trotsky was revealing these things to the world to show what a sordid war it was. Millions of poor soldiers were being killed, not for principles, but for loot—the loot of imperialistic governments. But in addition, some of these so-called Allies were actually cutting one another's throats.

Trotsky, of course, had forgotten to mention Germany's rape of Belgium, her frightful devastation in France following a sneak attack. He only published the incidents of the war which were hangovers of the old diplomacy. Yet the documents were damaging. . . . In America's archives, there were no such ghosts.

We want nothing for ourselves and this very unselfishness carries with it an obligation of open dealing. Wherever the principles of Russian freedom are at stake we stand ready to render such aid as lies in our power, but I want this helpfulness based upon request and not upon offer. Guard particularly against any effect of officious intrusion or meddling and try to express the disinterested friendship that is our sole impulse.

The letter woke a sharp memory in Edgar Sisson. Closing his eyes, he could see the White House room, the President walking up and down as he talked of the Russian people. Later, characteristically he had written this letter—for Wilson must always write as well as speak—but it was the strength of his face and voice, the confidence of the pacing step in that tense room, which seemed to hold a microcosm of the world that stuck in the mind of the American journalist.

So Sisson knew that the presence or absence of Kerensky had no effect upon his job. His job was with the Russian people. It was to help them when fundamental principles of freedom were at stake—if they wanted help. It was to tell them about American ways and American freedom, for their guidance. Now that he had learned what was going on, he knew that he must also tell them why America was in the war—"wanting nothing for ourselves." Would that keep them fighting after their disillusionment about the other Allies? It was a tenuous hope, for the Bolshevists were already asking for an armistice, but it was part of Sisson's job.

Officially Sisson was on George Creel's Committee on Public Information (usually shortened to "C.P.I."). Americans still stammered over the word "propaganda." They were willing to distribute "information" or even publicity among their allies and, when possible, more darkly among their enemies. Sisson's instructions from Creel were to develop, in the Petrograd office of the C.P.I., all the machinery of publicity, to search the city for every available translator, interpreter, stenographer, printer, and billposter; to get out placards and pamphlets; to extend services to every newspaper editor; and to get before the Russian public in one way or another every item of heartening American truth.

In the first weeks Sisson and his assistant Arthur Bullard read the papers and studied the complexity of political colorings, talked with the editors. Bolshevik propaganda in *Pravda* and *Izvestia* was getting into its stride. It plugged the theme that all the belligerent governments were imperialistic in their aims. It made no exception for the United States. Wilson was a "hypocrite." His "empty phrases" did not disguise his imperialism.

Yet in this early phase Petrograd was still diverse, reflecting a nation in transition. Performances of the opera and the ballet went on. Champagne was drunk, gay kept women were in evidence, the signs of privilege and wealth had not vanished. The opposition press and opposition placards were still printed and, even at Smolny, opposition voices were still heard. So when Sisson sent contradictions to the papers which had vilified Wilson, the papers printed them too. It was a strange world with liberty and dictatorship side by side in a grotesque parade.

But in December the C.P.I. saw the vision of an even bigger job. On the 15th, the armistice was signed between the Bolsheviki and Germany at the German staff headquarters in the dreary, battered town of Brest-Litovsk in what had once been Russian Poland.

The armistice was not precisely what Lenin and Trotsky had hoped. It would last not three months or six, but twenty-eight days. Major General Hoffmann, Chief of Staff of the German Eastern Command, smiled at the soviets' delegates when they talked about "no annexations." It was a noble idea, of course. It would be considered in the peace negotiations following the armistice. But the Russian delegates had asked that the Germans immediately evacuate the Russian territory which they had occupied in the Riga gulf. Did these comrades believe, then, that Russia had won the war?

Hoffmann agreed not to transfer any of his troops away to other fronts during the armistice period—not, at least, any whose transfer had not already been arranged for. As all arrangements had been made and enormous bodies of troops were already on their way to France, this was not significant. The agreement would satisfy the Bolsheviki who were, at the moment, sending out feelers to Russia's former allies.

This was important. Trotsky had sent out a wireless message from Petrograd addressed "to the world." It contained Lenin's appeal to the workers of the Allies over the heads of their governments. He had followed it by a request through neutral ambassadors to the governments themselves that they all, like Russia, conclude an armistice with Germany and bring this atrocious war to an end. No Ally had answered by December 15. So the separate armistice with the Bolsheviki was signed. But Hoffmann was cautious. Suppose, he thought, Trotsky's appeal worked? Then there would be a peace while Germany was still winning. The request for it would come from the enemy!

So the armistice was tough but not too tough. Yet what struck the Americans of the C.P.I was neither its toughness nor its gentleness but a single clause which, for some inscrutable reason, had slipped through the fingers of the shrewd German commander. For Sisson and Bullard this clause was the very blueprint of the C.P.I.'s job.

Article IV of the armistice provided for "intercourse" between troops in prescribed centers of the neutralized area between the lines. Twenty-five unarmed persons from both sides might get together at certain times and by conversation strengthen "the friendly relations between the contracting parties." The exchange of newspapers and letters would be permitted.

A lawn party in nomansland!

It did not take long for the Americans at the C.P.I. to find out what full advantage the Russians were taking of this loophole. From the day of the armistice, every printing press in Petrograd was working overtime printing newspapers, pamphlets, handbills in German. To Lenin and Trotsky this was not a novel activity. To them the effect of underground propaganda was an old story. Yet when had it been possible on such a scale?

Lenin's large aim had been the brotherhood of the workers —the proletarians—of the world. He did not limit it to Germans. Americans—or, for that matter, British, French, and Italians—in government circles were not attracted by the idea of seeing this applied to their own people. But to apply it to Germans would be to weaken German fighting power. If the Bolsheviki did this it would be next best to fighting the enemy with guns. And now the way was opened.

But the men at the C.P.I. were not immediately concerned

with weakening Germans with soviet lures. Their concern was to show the German people that America had come into this war not for conquest but to make a better world. That American soldiers were fighting not merely in defense of their country but to end tyranny everywhere and to end the source of wars. That the President of the United States was not aiming at the total destruction of Germany but only at the end of a monstrous government which sought to bring the free peoples of the world under the dominion of the German despotism. The Americans wanted these words to reach not merely industrial workers or peasants. They wanted them to echo in the Reichstag, in meetings of the Social Democrats, in the shops and city streets, in the homes of the bourgeoisie. The words bore no tag of socialism, no trademark of any political party or economic theory. They were the simple truth. And America could say these things without fear or afterthought. There were no secrets to catch up with such words from behind. In this way, the United States stood unique among the Allies.

But who was America? A few men in the C.P.I. at Petrograd? Would their signatures carry such words into a hostile camp? How far would anonymous messages get?

On January 3rd, Edgar Sisson cabled to George Creel in Washington:

If President will restate anti-imperialistic war aims and democratic peace requisites of America thousand words or less, short almost placard paragraphs, short sentences, I can get it fed into Germany in great quantities in German translation and can utilize Russian version potently in army and everywhere. . . . Need is for internal evidence that President is thinking of the Russian and German common folk in their situation of this moment. . . .

A week later, the word came back over the wire. It was not a message to Germany or to Russia. It was a message to the Congress of the United States. But as the Americans in Petrograd read it they knew that it had been spoken over the heads of all governments to the tired people of the world.

It told not of war but of the end of war. It told not of conquest but of self-determination. It told of open dealings, of the open arrival, not at agreements, but at covenants. It told of the equality of large and small nations in a democratic world society.

Edgar Sisson saw that the message was the product, not of his suggestion, but of years of thought. These words had been only just below the surface during Sisson's October interview at the White House. Yet throughout them ran a current of awareness about Russia which—whether or not his cable had inspired it—made the message as immediate for the Russian people as for the Germans.

It began, indeed, with Brest-Litovsk. It expressed the sense of confusion in the news which must be felt in America. But, as it showed the confusion there, it showed too the confusion in the minds of the negotiators. Again the President seemed to see a pattern beneath all the little tactics of intellectuals and politicians—the pattern of his own long thought—the pattern of a trend which none of the negotiators could alter or control. Again the President was using his old device—forcing the parties of the dispute to clarify it for themselves and, if they failed, forcing the peoples to clarify it for them. This seemed to be Wilson's function—to make the war clear to its fighters.

"The issues of life and death hang upon these definitions. No statesman who has the least conception of his responsibility ought for a moment to permit himself to continue this tragical and appalling outpouring of blood and treasure unless he is sure beyond a peradventure that the objects of the vital sacrifice are part and parcel of the very life of Society and that the people for whom he speaks think them right and imperative as he does."

Then, instantly vital to the Creel Committee in Petrograd, came this praise of the Russian people:

"Their power, apparently, is shattered. And yet their soul is not subservient. They will not yield either in principle or in action. Their conception of what is right, of what is humane and honorable for them to accept, has been stated with a frankness, a largeness of view, a generosity of spirit and a universal human sympathy which must challenge the admiration of every friend of mankind. . . ."

The men behind the closed doors of the embassy were startled. Was the President in ignorance, then? Had no one told him of the Smolny traitors? How could he fail to know that, at the moment he was speaking these words to the Congress, Lenin's own editors were calling him "hypocrite"?

These thoughts did not trouble Edgar Sisson. To him the message was a quick, burning tool for his own work. His work reached beyond Petrograd. It reached beyond Brest-Litovsk where, in the new year, the postarmistice peace negotiations were beginning.

His translators worked continuously. On January 12th, he took the finished Russian script directly to Lenin. Lenin ran with it to the telegraph operator who sent it, entire, to Trotsky at Brest-Litovsk. Sisson did not attempt to fathom Lenin's mind. It was enough for the moment, that the message had crossed the border. Next he printed 100,000 placards in Russian and got them posted through the city so that the people might ponder the "hypocrite's" words. Then he had a million copies printed in German and started them on their long underground journey.

In the sad months that followed, the words of the President seemed, along with many people—workers, peasants, bourgeois, and princes—to perish in the Russian winter. By

March, when the Russian hopes came to an end at Brest-Litovsk, few Americans believed that Wilson's thought had persisted in the dark reaches of Europe or that it could rise again from the silence to block a tragic destiny.

3

There were Americans in London. Many of them had been there through the dark summer of 1917. There were officers of the Army and the Navy, war planners, supply planners, Red Cross workers, C.P.I. Outposters, members of the embassy staff, men who had fought as volunteers in British armies and were getting transferred to their own. In the winter when the green fog closed in and little hopeful news seeped through, these people in the fringe of America at war had one bright moment to look back on.

On the 4th of July, London had celebrated. For the first time in history, the American flag had flown beside the Union Jack on Victoria Tower of the Palace of Westminster. From windows in Whitechapel and Chelsea little starred flags had hung. All the solemn town had grown festive; the people had crowded about the embassies and the statues of Washington and Lincoln to show their joy in the new friendship with an old enemy and in the wind of hope blowing so bravely from the west.

On the 5th, the London *Times* had printed an editorial which many Americans had clipped.

It should never be forgotten [said the *Times*] that the average American has been brought up to believe that Europe has one set of interests and his own country another; and that nothing could possibly run more counter to American history or cut more sharply across the accepted traditions of American policy than to find the United States at war with a European Power and committed to fighting on European soil for a cause which involves, so far as he can see, no obvious and tangible interest. . . . Moreover, the Americans have entered the arena with hardly one of the impulses that normally drive a nation to arms and sustain it through the stresses of a prolonged conflict. They do not hate Germany, nor do they fear her. . . . They do not believe for a moment that Germany can in any way imperil them. They covet nothing she possesses and the lure of military glory moves them not at all. The war from their standpoint is not a fight for existence, for trade, for territory, for conquest, for the enforcement of national policies or even for any universally recognized motive of self-defense. . . . They have been summoned to it to "make the world safe for democracy"; and they are probably the only people to whom such a summons could be addressed or who could have found in themselves the imagination or the idealism to respond to it. . . . The political balance of the universe shifted when General Pershing's troops landed in France, and America, in entering the war, has also entered the world—to play in it . . . a vigorous and inspiring part. . . .

Here was the whole plot of the story. Here were the reasons for staying out and the reasons for coming in. One nameless Briton had seen it crystal clear, and he had told other Britons that it "should never be forgotten."

But by the end of the year, it was in danger of being forgotten.

In October the brave Ypres offensive, begun in July, bogged down in the swamps of Passchendaele under the pitiless German machine guns.

In October the Austrians, led and heavily reinforced by Germans transferred from Russia, broke the Italian line at Caporetto and the retreat which followed was a rout with Italian soldiers throwing away their rifles and announcing that they were going home.

In November came the bitter news from Russia, and in November too the brilliant tank attack of the British Third Army at Cambrai faded out from lack of reserves.

In December came the certainty that enormous German forces were moving west from Russia to prepare a spring offensive which might well end the war.

In December the man in the London street and the man in the Manchester factory were told by Trotsky that Britain, as well as France and dead Imperial Russia, was covered with the cobwebs of secret entanglements and that his comrades in arms had died not for eternal peace or a better world for the common man but for Constantinople, Syria, and Dalmatia (of which they had never heard).

In December the tonnage sunk by German submarines under the nose of the proud British navy was reported to be not only in excess of present shipbuilding but of projected shipbuilding for 1918 and that if the Atlantic lifeline to America should be cut Britain would meet starvation in five weeks.

In December British military leaders were saying that, unless America could double her present promises, "the Allied cause was lost."

Yet by the 1st of January, only four American divisions had landed in Europe and only one had gone into the line.

So when, on January 8th, the west wind blew again, Englishmen had lost their festive July mood. There was controversy over the message which came on that wind. The *Times*, which in July had stated America's position with such fervor, saw in the speech of the Fourteen Points only a "lofty flight to the ideal" which seemed "not to take sufficient account of certain hard realities," and added that "we should all rejoice to see some such splendid vision . . . actually clothed in flesh and blood." And the *Times*, which since July had dwelt with unusual ferocity on the criminality of Lenin, doubted that Mr. Wilson "entirely appreciated the actual situation in Russia."

But British labor read the President's words in another

light. To the worker, shocked by the secret treaties revealed in Russia, the war must have a longer aim than Constantinople and Syria or else it would be better to lay down arms now. Lenin and Trotsky were appealing to British workers to insist on an end to this vicious war. But now, suddenly, in the midwinter despair, came the word that the war was no longer vicious, that it was no longer a quarrel of national governments but a revolution of people seeking a better world. Its aim did not stop with victory but went on into the long peace which these Points would make secure for all men. "What we demand in this war . . . is that the world be made fit and safe to live in. . . . *All the peoples of the world are in effect partners in this interest. . . .*"

So Wilson was not reviling Lenin and Russia as Winston Churchill and the *Times* had done. He even echoed Lenin's words, condemning secret treaties, promising that "diplomacy shall proceed always frankly and in the public view." And he spoke of the "thrilling" voice of the Russian people calling for definitions of principle and purpose which would justify the "tragical and appalling outpouring of blood and treasure." The difference was that Lenin had not found these definitions and so had abandoned the fight, but Wilson had found them and in them a reason for fighting to a finish. To the sturdy common man of Britain, the Wilson concept—in spite of all the weariness and suffering—was more appealing. So British labor in London hailed the message as "one of the classic utterances of Allied statesmanship during the war."

To the Americans, chilled by the London darkness, there came new hope. To them the message was like the flash of a lighthouse in a storm. It was not so much the Fourteen Points which moved them. It was the fact that in this hour of disaster, athwart all the somber news, this man across the sea had dared to talk not of war but of peace after victory. Never, for an instant, had the vision of failure distracted his eyes. His thought had leapt over the bombs and bayonets, the gas and the flame, to the ordered world beyond, a world built by the democracies on the ruins of an old order and maintained by a concert of free peoples.

"Here is the program," he had said quietly above the howl of the tempest. "It is time to think about it."

4

There were more Americans in Paris than in London. They too had a July Fourth to remember. It had been a mystical day like an interval in a cathedral where a miracle was in progress. To Frenchmen, what was happening was so irrational that it must be the work of Our Lady of Victory.

An American, waiting for the traffic on his way to the fête, overheard a conversation between a priest and a colonel.

"But it is strange," said the colonel, "for this army of theirs to come five thousand kilometers—for what?"

"Their president has said," answered the priest, "it was to make the world safe . . ."

"He has said that, but America is already safe."

"For liberty . . ."

"But America is free. The Boche has not attacked America."

"I have talked with an American, my colonel. He said that they were fighting for democracy."

"Men do not fight for words, Father."

"The Americans say they fight for principles, my colonel. The Boche, they say, has broken his word. He invaded Belgium and France. He has cut off the hands of children."

"But they were not American children."

"It is curious, my colonel. But perhaps we have no right to question the impulse God has given to these people. You remember Ribot said after the President had asked his parliament to declare war, that it was an event beyond the power of man. Ribot, a man of the world, said that."

"Ribot is a fool. National governments are cynical, Father. They are not moved by religious impulses. They make war for defense or for gain."

"Ah," said the priest. "Has my colonel forgotten the holy Crusades?"

So a good many of the people made the sign of the cross as the troops went by on their long march to Picpus Cemetery.

There was only a handful of them. The Americans who watched thought them not well drilled. It was hardly an impressive sight. . . . Yet the people of Paris were impressed.

When the column turned away from the more decorous streets, the women and children ran out with flowers and small flags. They wept and threw their arms about the soldiers, breaking the rhythm. They mingled in the ranks and lifted their children to ride on the shoulders of the marching men. They hung wreaths round the soldiers' necks. Little aproned gamins ran along the gutter. "Sammee," they shouted and "boyee." And French poilus, standing all along the line of march, cheered America and Wilson and, turning to each other, said, "C'est la victoire, quand même." Then, at the cemetery, before the tomb of the young French general who had once brought more than a handful of French soldiers to Rhode Island, the colonel of the battalion's regiment answered all the questions at once.

"Nous voici, Lafayette," he said.

So the Americans in Paris, men of the embassy, officers of the army's staff, engineers, transport planners, women of the Red Cross, knew that the battalion had done what it had come for and that thousands of Frenchmen all over France, hearing of their coming, would breathe again.

But that was in July.

Since then, a complete house cleaning had become necessary in the French Army because of the spring mutinies which had affected sixteen army corps.

In August the French success on the Chemin des Dames had been won, the British said, six months too late.

In August Painlevé, the French War Minister had begged the British to let a generalissimo be appointed over the Allied forces and the British had refused.

In October the French front had been weakened by the transfer of six French divisions to Italy to help stop the disaster there.

In October President Wilson had insistently urged unity of command but the only result was the feeble Supreme War Council established in November at Rapallo.

In November the Inter-allied Conference at Paris had bogged down with the results which Colonel House reported to Wilson in January.

In December the stiff-backed, poker-faced American general whose headquarters at 27, rue Constantine, were besieged by newspaper reporters and other buzzards of catastrophe, sent a desperate demand to Washington for a million men by June.

Thus the Americans in Paris, so near the battling armies, needed, in the winter, even more assurance than those in London. They needed the news from the First Division at Gondrecourt. They needed the stories of the immense plans and achievements of the American engineers at the ports of Brest and Saint-Nazaire where a million soldiers from the homeland were to come ashore. They needed the tales of the Signal Corps which already had strung its wires clean across the north of France.

But most of all they needed the message of January 8th from their undisturbed Commander-in-Chief to tell them that "the program of the world's peace is our program," and that to the vindication of the principle beneath that program, the people of the United States stood "ready to devote their lives, their honor, and everything they possess."

5

There were few Americans in Rome. Yet all over Italy stood the houses which Italians called the *case degli americani*, houses built by men who had lived and worked half their lives in the United States and gone home to buy new land with the proceeds and to build upon it. In the Italian army there were few who could not name a cousin who had enlisted or would soon enlist in that other army overseas—a man they might one day meet if the war lasted long enough and if they could hold their stand on the Piave after Caporetto.

Yet there were few Americans in Rome—outside the Red Cross which was everywhere. Americans who were there such as Gino Speranza and the ambassador, Thomas Nelson Page, had noted that the gap between people and government was greater in Italy than in the other Allied nations.

So in spite of the friendliness of the people, the Italian government had shown no warmth toward America. On the 4th of July, no American flag had flown from the Quirinale. Plenty of such flags had dangled from the windows of crowded flats in Naples, Sorrento, and Rome itself. But the government held aloof.

This was usually blamed on the Baron Sonnino, the foreign minister. Sonnino, haunted as other Italian statesmen have been by the shades of Metternich and Machiavelli, had been the principal plotter of that devious intrigue of 1915 called the Secret Treaty of London which had resulted in Italy's entry into the war.

Perhaps this was a reason for his contempt of Wilson. To Sonnino, Wilson was a typical Presbyterian schoolteacher—naïve, a hopeless amateur in diplomacy and stubborn in defense of a Puritan idealism which had no relation to practical international politics. America's unreasonable entry into the war with nothing to gain, no territory to acquire, no irredentists to redeem, no strategic defenses to establish, could only be explained, Sonnino thought, by these juvenile perversities of her President.

Sonnino's Treaty of London had been a practical, not an idealistic agreement. Sonnino distrusted idealism. It was a disease peculiar to queasy northern consciences. So he preferred to base his statesmanship on a thing called "sacro egoismo" or "holy egotism."

In 1914 Italy had belonged to the Triple Alliance with Germany and Austria for mutual defense only. Austria's attack on Serbia which had started the war therefore released Italy. So Sonnino was able to dicker with Austria, her former ally. When Austria had been unwilling to offer an adequate bribe in territory to keep Italy neutral, Sonnino turned to the other side. It was a "foregone conclusion," he later said, that the Italian people wanted to fight by the side of England and France against the traditional enemy, Austria. But it would have been bad bargaining to mention this foregone conclusion in London or Paris in 1915. So he approached the Entente Allies with a careless, take-it-or-leave-it attitude and made to them an astonishing offer. If England, France, and Russia would promise Italy the whole of the Austrian Tyrol as far as the Brenner Pass, the Istrian peninsula, a long slice of Dalmatia, a lot of islands in the Adriatic, a slice of Turkey, colonies in Africa, and fifty million lire, Italy would enter the war on their side. No, the Italian people need not be consulted. Their government knew what was best for them. Yes, the treaty must, of course, be strictly secret.

The Russian (Czarist) Foreign Minister had objected that Dalmatia rightly belonged to the Jugoslavs, a subject Slavic people whom Russia was anxious to liberate from Austro-Hungarian rule. Sonnino made a slight concession here but most of Dalmatia remained in the treaty. So the offer, with a few minor changes, was accepted by the Allies, who at the time were forlorn in their hopes and rated the Italian power high. In May, Italy entered the war.

But that was in 1915.

In October, 1917, the Italian armies suffered a terrible defeat. To save Italy from total collapse, eleven British and French divisions had to go to her aid.

So, even after the Italian armies had stood and held on the Piave in November, there was room for doubt as to what the Allies now thought of their bargain. Sonnino knew that they would keep it, though they might ask, with reason, for changes. But what about this Presbyterian schoolteacher in Washington?

America had not signed the treaty. When Trotsky had published it in November, Americans had, indeed, been deeply shocked. Was this, they were asking (just as Russians were asking), the kind of thing men were asked to give their lives for?

And Wilson who had kept priggishly insisting that "we want nothing for ourselves . . ." Wilson, who was forever talking about peoples instead of governments . . . Might he not actually prevent England and France from granting the London Treaty? His power was enormous. Frenchmen believed that France could not win without American armies. Could Italy herself win without them?

So, in December, Sonnino was troubled. He was even more disturbed in January when Wilson's Fourteen Points arrived.

The first point was a slap at the Treaty of London in specific terms. So was the ninth. And the principle of the Fourteen Points Wilson said was the only principle for which Americans could fight. Was he counting, then, on the full vindication of the points at the peace table? Might he insist on guarantees now, before he sent the rest of his armies?

What the Italian people thought of Wilson's speech was not disclosed. The news of it was played down in the press and the Americans in Rome were left, for the most part, to digest it alone.

6

There were no Americans in Berlin—or if there were any, their presence was well hidden. But Americans had been there until April, 1917. During the rest of that year, some of these went to neutral Switzerland.

In Berne the American legation was well equipped to explore enemy information. In Geneva George Herron and, in Berne, Carl Ackerman were often engaged in conversation with Germans. So news came through. It came through slowly and incomplete. In January and February, 1918, after the Fourteen Points had seeped across the Russian border, these Americans were able to construct a picture.

Snow came over Berlin in January. It muffled the sound of the trucks in the streets, it stopped the trams on the curves, it silenced the nervous footfalls of the uncertain walkers. It did not quiet the complaints of the workers in the munitions plants or subdue the voices on the left in the Reichstag. Nor did it muffle the continuous hum of other voices—voices coming in from outside, from beyond the blockade which food and fat and rubber could not pass, from beyond the wall of the guns in the west, from over the frozen eastern marshes.

For weeks the words had come to the factories. A soldier home on leave had brought them to a friend who worked a center drill. Another soldier, invalided back, had died in the house of his workman brother and there, in his tunic, were the words. A truck driver who had been near a front had picked up a handful of words which seemed to have snowed from the sky. All through the hungry "turnip winter" when meat, bread, potatoes, and fruit had failed, when the minds of the men at the benches wandered home and their fingers slid into the machines, the words kept coming.

The words bred other words: mainly questions. Was the war being prolonged to conquer new territory? What about the solemn proclamation of the Reichstag in July that Germany cared nothing for conquest? What did the chancellor, Michaelis, mean when he approved that proclamation, adding, "as I interpret it"? How was the Government interpreting it now? How did "H. L."—the great Hindenburg-Ludendorff combination which seemed to be buttoning up the government in its pocket—interpret it? What was the game that Hoffmann was playing at Brest-Litovsk? When was annexation non-annexation? How could you occupy with troops the enormous areas of Lithuania, Kurland, Estonia and pretend that you were merely "liberating" or "protecting" the peoples who lived in them? What interest would "H. L." have in finding out what the Poles thought about their independence? And, finally—whispered at first, then boldly spoken above the hum of the lathes: *Did we really invade Belgium in self-defense?*

"Belgium, the whole world will agree, must be evacuated and restored." There it was—one of Wilson's Fourteen Points.

The words kept coming to answer the questions. They came from Lenin and from Wilson. Lenin "abolishes secret diplomacy, expressing . . . the firm determination to carry on all negotiations openly and in view of all the people." Wilson calls for "open covenants of peace, openly arrived at, after which . . . diplomacy shall proceed always frankly and in the public view." Lenin asks for a "peace without annexations and indemnities." Wilson says that "the day of conquest and aggrandizement has gone by." Both these men had talked of the exploitation of the masses, making them fight for the profit of the few, but Wilson had pointed direct to the German government speaking of "dynasties" and "little groups of ambitious men who were accustomed to use their fellow men as pawns and tools." Little groups in Germany, living at this moment on rich food—what could it matter to them how long the war went on?

> *"If all got equal food and pay*
> *The war'd be over in a day,"*

sang the men at the machines.

On the 28th of January, the workers in every war production factory in Berlin stopped work.

The sudden strike surprised even some of the Social Democrats in the Reichstag, for it had come without apparent organization or direction. The trade-unions had not even met. It was a spontaneous quitting. But when, finally, the strikers had gathered together, their demands were still more surprising to the puzzled citizens of the capital.

It had happened before, even in war-time Germany, that workers had struck for better food. They had struck for better pay. They had rebelled against army officers in the factory. They had been bitter against labor spies.

But now, on the 29th of January, the readers of *Vorwärts* saw as number one on the workers' list of demands: "The speedy bringing about of peace without annexations or indemnities, on the basis of the self-determination of peoples in accord with the principles formulated by the Russian people's Commissioners in Brest-Litovsk."

In the following week came news of strikes in Hamburg,

Bremen, Leipzig, Kiel, until 300,000 workers were out. From Munich came the echoing demand: "A general peace without open or veiled annexations or indemnities, with recognition of the right of the peoples to self-determination."

Then, in the Reichstag, the deputy Ebert explained the strikes:

"The conquest politicians and with them the entire reactionary army can behave as if enraged; they accuse us of state treason and the prolonging of the war.

"That of course is miserable hypocrisy. This gang has, during the entire war, denounced as treason every political movement which was not in consonance with the annexationist war religion. . . . Its whole propaganda is based on the formula: A peace of understanding is treason to the Fatherland; rather war until we bleed to death than the foregoing of conquest and reparations. . . ."

Respectable tories in the Reichstag forgot their dignity to howl down this upstart tailor's son. Again and again came the cries of treason. And why not? Was not the Fatherland at war, surrounded by enemies, bled white by the British blockade?

The tories need not have worried in February, 1918. The heavy machinery of the military control was already at work. Censorship had come over the Reichstag like a blanket. Martial law had been proclaimed in Berlin. Cordons of police and soldiers besieged the factories. Proclamation after proclamation was issued by General von Kessel, military commander of the city. Bayonets appeared on rifles.

These things were too strong for the instinct of obedience and order which no suffering had as yet burned out of the German soul. The sight of the uniforms and bayonets was final. All over Germany, the workers went back to work. Even Ebert, once he had spoken, saw that the strike had as yet too little power and he urged submission.

The tories breathed again. Strike leaders were arrested, thousands of workers were drafted for the front. Seven great plants in Berlin were placed under military control.

"It is necessary," wrote Ludendorff to the Minister for War, "to be prepared for all eventualities, and it is for this reason that I have consented to leave the desired troops in Germany."

But many Germans in these uncertain January days filed away their copies of the Fourteen Points for future reference. Ludendorff was among them.

3. The Senator and His Friends

HENRY CABOT LODGE of Nahant, Massachusetts, was one of New England's most substantial citizens. He was a scholar and a gentleman. He came of distinguished stock and he knew more or less intimately most of the important men of his day. Old Henry Adams, who had been his teacher, was also his adviser and one of his most cherished friends.

Few men in the United States had educations comparable in scope or distinction, although he had, of course, never studied in Europe. He received his A.B. at Harvard in 1871, at the age of twenty-one. He received an LL.B. in 1875 and became a Doctor of Philosophy (in History) in 1876. He held degrees of Doctor of Law from Williams, Yale, Clark, Harvard, Amherst, Union College, Princeton, Dartmouth, and Brown.

He loved his home at Nahant with passionate devotion. He loved the crags and rocks of the narrow peninsula on which it stood. The howl of the winter winds of New England were music to him and the crashing of the high, wild waves upon the stern granite coast was poetry. He was a true New Englander.

In Washington his home was Number 1765 Massachusetts Avenue, an address which seemed most appropriate to his constituents. Here he could not hear the sea, but it was an extension of Nahant, even so. He was alone now—his wife had died in 1915. Here he could be surrounded by his beloved books which gave him so much deep and abiding satisfaction. He loved to read passages aloud to his friends; he liked to talk with them of literature and life by the firelight.

So it was that a few days after President Wilson's Fourteen Points speech Senator Lodge led his friend Senator Philander Chase Knox of Pennsylvania after dinner to the crackling fire that lit the tastefully furnished, book-lined room.

"What did you think of it?" asked Lodge.

Senator Knox, bald and with a moderate senatorial paunch, sat heavily upon a divan. He was not a handsome man, but as usual he was impeccably dressed. His tendency was to wing collars and striped trousers. One commentator had said of him "he *looks* like a statesman but he wears a derby."

Knox's immobile features registered nothing. He said,

"It was effective."

Lodge poked the fire.

"The only part of it that counted," he said, "was the fourteen points. And yet even some of those are just too silly to be taken seriously. Such as this first one—'open covenants openly arrived at.'"

"Silly?" Knox looked blank.

"Of course. In the first place, the United States can *never* get into any secret agreements—because the Senate has to approve all treaties."

Knox nodded.

"And everyone can see that it's impossible to negotiate any sort of agreement if everything the negotiators say is published in the newspapers the next morning."

Knox smiled.

"And this 'freedom of the seas' point. Our friends the British won't like that a bit. And the third point is nothing but a plea for universal free trade—purely a political item. The fourth point calls for reduction of armaments. All the others except the last deal with boundaries and colonial claims —which certainly can't be settled now."

"The last point was on the Association of Nations," said Knox. "I remember it well. You're for that, aren't you?"

Lodge was silent a moment.

"I used to be," he said, "but now, I'm not sure. . . ."

2

In the spring of 1916 Senator Lodge and President Wilson had spoken from the same platform at a meeting held by the League to Enforce Peace. This organization, headed by the Republican ex-President William Howard Taft, and the corresponding League of Nations Society in England had generally the same aims: insurance of peace by international agreement through arbitration and conciliation; and the use of force to prevent violation of the agreements.

Of course there was nothing new about the idea of a league of nations. The Duc de Sully, the liberal statesman and lawmaker in the court of Henry IV of France, as early as 1638 had a "Grand Design" for an association of Christian "republics," and Henry himself expressed great interest in his protégé's plan, though he never did anything about it. In 1713 the Abbé de Saint-Pierre published his scheme for a league of perpetual peace, which influenced many later students and statesmen, including Russia's Czar Alexander I. This remarkable and unfortunate monarch, under the influence of the Baroness de Krudener, maneuvered Francis I of Austria and Frederick William III of Prussia into the Holy Alliance of 1815, which, badly as it worked out, began as a sincere effort toward a European league for peace.

Even in America there had been a league of nations. The Iroquois Confederacy created by the Seneca Indian Statesman Deganawida, brought five nations into a peace league late in the sixteenth century, and admitted a sixth, the Tuscaroras, in 1722. According to legend the tribesmen uprooted a great pine tree, and buried their hatchets under it, thus generating a familiar American metaphor as well as a long-lived peace. Most of the Iroquois tribes had been good fighters, and the confederacy was remarkable partly because good fighters agreed not to fight and partly because it worked effectively for nearly two centuries.

"I know," Lodge had said at the 1916 meeting, "and no one, I think, can know better than one who has served long in the Senate, which is charged with an important share of the ratification and confirmation of all treaties—no one can, I think, feel more deeply than I do the difficulties which confront us in the work which this League [to Enforce Peace] has undertaken.

"But the difficulties cannot be overcome unless we try to overcome them. I believe much can be done.

"Probably it will be impossible to stop all wars, but it certainly will be possible to stop some wars and to diminish their number.

"The way in which this problem must be worked out must be left to this League and to those who are giving this great question the study which it deserves. I know the obstacles. I know how quickly we shall be met with the statement that this is a dangerous question which you are putting into your agreement, that no nation can submit to the judgment of other nations, and we must be careful at the beginning not to attempt too much. I know the difficulties that arise when we speak of anything which seems to involve an alliance.

"But I do not believe that when Washington warned us against permanent alliances he meant for one moment that we should not join with the other civilized nations of the world if a method could be found to diminish war and encourage peace. . . ."

The President, speaking at the same meeting, urged free

choice of sovereignty by all peoples and the territorial integrity of small nations.

"The world," he said, "has a right to be free from every disturbance of its peace that has its origin in aggression and disregard of the rights of peoples and nations.

"I am sure that I speak the mind and wish of the people of America when I say that the United States is willing to become a partner in any feasible association of nations formed in order to realize these objects and make them secure against violation. . . .

"There is nothing that the United States wants for itself that any other nation has. We are willing, on the contrary, to limit ourselves along with them to a prescribed course of duty and respect for the rights of others which will check any selfish passion of our own, as it will check any aggressive impulse of theirs. . . ."

Was this a pledge that if a League should be formed after the war, a League to conduct the common affairs of nations by conference, conciliation, and arbitration, the United States would take a place in it, and use her wealth and her armed forces, along with other member nations, to enforce the laws and rulings of that League? Most of the President's hearers certainly thought it was such a pledge. President Wilson had not contributed any new ideas for the formation of a society of nations in his speech. But he had contributed one totally new fact which would, if anything would, make such a league possible. He promised that America would come into it.

It did not escape the audience, or many other Europeans and Americans interested in a league, that the Senate might prevent this. The American constitution is a familiar document and a relatively clear one. But league proponents heard no critical blasts at the President. The influential Senator Henry Cabot Lodge was now known to favor some sort of international association; Theodore Roosevelt had been interested in a league for many years.

All this had been before the United States had entered the war. Now in 1918 the nation was in it completely, to the finish. To those who read the President's words, and even to those who had cautiously checked the words of his political adversaries, there seemed no reason to doubt that the United States had cast aside her aloof detachment of more than a hundred years and had chosen to become a member of the world family of nations.

3

Mr. George Harvey, who had helped Messrs. Smith and Nugent make Woodrow Wilson governor of New Jersey, had left the old *Harper's Weekly*, which he had edited for a number of years and which was a dying magazine, and gone over to the *North American Review*, a venerable and erudite monthly.

Mr. Harvey as a patriotic American had been much concerned with the progress of the war, and he had not been editor of the *North American Review* very long before he started a supplement called *The War Weekly*, which was soon detached from the parent publication. In appearance it resembled the *Nation* and the *New Republic*, except that it carried many cartoons and no advertising.

In its early days Harvey supported the President firmly. He wrote about the Fourteen Points address:

Mr. Wilson's declaration was a veritable masterpiece. He has never done, and we doubt if anybody living could have done better. We particularly liked his definiteness. . . . His numerical summary of the fourteen war aims . . . was tremendously effective.

But Mr. Harvey had not founded his new weekly simply to praise Mr. Wilson. As the war proceeded his criticism fell alternately on both parties, but increasingly upon the Democrats and Mr. Wilson. This may have been because one of Harvey's closest friends was Theodore Roosevelt, who was said to have more than a literary interest in *The War Weekly*.

Not only Mr. Lodge and Mr. Harvey had been thinking over Mr. Wilson's fourteen points. In the offices of the *New Republic*, fresh-sprouted liberal weekly, Herbert Croly raced against his deadline. His friend Colonel House had told him the speech would be a great one; he was full of hope but prepared for disappointment. Croly, who six years before had written one of the most hopeful books about America and her future to be published by a liberal in many years, was not disappointed. To him the speech was a part of the thing he had written about—The Promise of American Life. And after he read it the words came fast on his typewriter and appeared in the magazine two days later:

Once again [he wrote] the civilized world and particularly that portion of it in armed alliance against the Central Powers, have reason to be thankful for the superb leadership of the President of the United States. Mr. Wilson has seized the opportunity offered by the Russian peace negotiations with the Central Powers and the essentially equivocal and treacherous answers returned to the Russians by the German and Austrian governments to publish the frankest, the most uncompromising and the most inspiring statement of war aims which has yet issued from any belligerent. In the President's latest statement, the ambiguities and the inadequacies of Lloyd George's recent speech vanish and are replaced with a program for a settlement of the fundamental issues of the war, which is based on a correct diagnosis of our international maladies and which is infused with the red blood of a binding, a healing and a leavening faith. . . . Rarely in the history of the world have words been used with such startling effect to cleanse the nations of obstructive and sinister obstacles to the fulfillment of its better purposes and to charge the hearts of men with a victorious hope and a living faith. . . .

But in the same issue of the *New Republic* William Hard talked of the "breakdown" of the war program, and accused the author of the words of victorious hope and living faith with being utterly un-co-ordinated, with failing to keep in touch with what was going on, with failing to meet often enough with his lieutenants—Hoover, Garfield, and the rest —to know the truth about his war organization. . . .

In Washington busy reporters called senators and representatives. Their views on the speech, if pithy or startling, would rate separate stories or maybe a box on the front page; if undistinguished, they would be lumped together under a headline, CONGRESSMEN DIVIDED ON PRESIDENT'S MESSAGE.

Senator Borah found praiseworthy "that part of the message which related to Russia." Said he, "I have thought from the beginning of the Russian revolution that we should give more consideration and greater encouragement and sympathy to the people of Russia." Not a word about the fourteenth point which called for a League of Nations.

Acting Republican Floor Leader of the House, Representative Gillett, said, "I am in hearty accord with the President's address, unless he meant universal free trade . . ." Part-Indian Charles Curtis, of Kansas, was stronger: "The United States will not have economic free trade fastened upon it at any peace conference!" Senator Smoot asked: "What can it mean other than an elimination of all tariffs? If that is what the President means, this country will never be committed to such a policy in any treaty of peace."

The Democrat of Oregon, Senator George Earle Chamberlain, was unrestrained in praise: "It is one of the greatest state papers that the President has ever delivered. Our own people as well as the people of the world will understand this statement of the terms and conditions of peace."

Less than a week later, this same senator, without consulting his close friend Woodrow Wilson, introduced a bill to create a new Munitions Department, a measure he well knew both Secretary Baker and President Wilson thought would be merely an additional source of friction; and two weeks later at a National Security League luncheon in New York he stated flatly, "The military establishment of America has fallen down because of inefficiency in every bureau and department of the Government of the United States." And having thus spoken, the Democratic Senator hustled over to a meeting of the Republican Club and said the same thing. Here Colonel Theodore Roosevelt leaped to his feet and led the applause, and the ovation given Senator Chamberlain lasted a full minute.

Out in the Senator's own Northwest, things were happening to support his contention.

The Emergency Fleet Corporation, having got disquieting rumors about a contractor in Olympia, Washington, who was supposed to be building a great many ships, sent accountants and officials to look things over. They saw the lush green forests of the Olympic peninsula, yielding countless board-feet of Sitka spruce and Ponderosa pine and Douglas fir; they saw the fabled waters of Puget Sound shimmering in the sunset; they ate the tiny, sweet Olympic oysters; but they found no ships. Outside the shipyard all was beautiful and fragrant; in it all was otherwise. The government men knew it at once—anyone could see that ships were not really being built here, though keels had been laid down, materials were piled about the yard, and workmen plodded to and fro looking as though they had something to do.

The Emergency Fleet Corporation had no authority to

go over the company's books, but the accountants found that the government had paid the company $1,724,000, of which $400,000 had gone for brokerage fees to a New York firm for landing the contract, and more than half a million more for purposes having little or nothing to do with building ships. Far more than a trifle had gone to subsidiary companies for materials—at high prices.

A Senate committee some weeks later asked Admiral Bowles what the EFC had done about it.

"We took over complete control of the company," he told the senators, "prevented the brokerage firm from collecting any more money, took a $750,000 mortgage on the plant and took over bonds of the subsidiary concerns. The president of the corporation was drawing $25,000 a year. We cut him to $10,000."

One of the senators asked what he did to earn even that.

"He gets that for keeping quiet and helping us keep things moving," said Admiral Bowles. "I admit that it looks like a good bit of money, but we did the best we could under the circumstances."

"We have spent nearly two million dollars with this firm," said Senator Nelson. "How many ships have they built?"

"None. The most progress on any of them is but 3 per cent."

In another capital committee room the vice-chairman of the Supply Committee of the Council of National Defense was being grilled by unfriendly senators who looked down upon him from their horseshoe-shaped rostrum, of which he was the focal point.

Charles Eisenman, his collar wilting though it was January, refused to be intimidated, and took his verbal beating standing up. He put the blame for the shortage of uniforms and blankets which had developed in the camps of the nation, upon the Army Quartermaster. At any rate, he wasn't admitting it was *his* fault. But this was only the beginning. Senator McKellar wanted to know whether Mr. Eisenman was financially interested in any contract for army supplies.

"I'm a stockholder in the Cleveland Worsted Mills," replied Eisenman. "They have two contracts totalling $570,-000, for wool. But I never advised the purchase of the wool from that company and had no part in making the contracts."

"But the contracts were let by the Supply Committee to your firm?"

"Yes, that's right."

"You assume responsibility for these contracts?"

"Yes, but the Depot Quartermaster's department at Cleveland had placed the orders with the firm before I knew anything about it. I had nothing to do with getting the contract."

"Now," persisted Senator McKellar, "did you know that Congress passed a law at the last session, prohibiting any agent of the government dealing with himself in government contract work?"

"I knew that very well," replied the witness, with some heat.

"With the full knowledge of that you permitted that contract to be made between your firm and the government?"

"The contracts were made by the Supply Committee. I have already explained that I took no part in them whatever."

"Well, how did you get around the law?"

"There was no 'getting around' it. We let contracts of that character every day."

Senator McKellar looked shocked.

"You do?"

"Oh, yes."

"Well, that's what this committee wants to know about; it's quite important."

But important as it was, Senator McKellar did not seem to care to pursue the point.

So the inquiry faded into history. Like so many investigations, it made the front pages of the newspapers and died there. The labored efforts of the senators to prove Mr. Eisenman dishonest came to nought. Perhaps that did not matter; perhaps that was not the purpose. All over America men read their papers, clucked their tongues, and shook their heads despairingly. With Washington in such a muddle, how could we ever win a war? Well, the Senate was doing a mighty good job in burrowing down into the muck and uncovering the myriads of little creatures called bureaucrats who were, perhaps, responsible for all the corruption and inefficiency. And letters clogged the mails to Washington, urging the solons to keep up the good work.

4

It was on January 22nd that Colonel Theodore Roosevelt journeyed to Washington to spend four days with his son-in-law and his daughter, Representative and Mrs. Nicholas Longworth. He seemed in excellent health as he bustled from the train and faced the reporters.

"I am here," he said, "to help every man who sincerely desires to speed up and make effective our preparation in this war. I shall stand by the efficient and against the inefficient man. No man is really and intelligently loyal to his country who does not take this attitude."

"Did your recent talks with Senator Smoot and Senator Madden in New York decide you to make the trip?" asked one reporter.

"My motives are strictly nonpolitical, if that is what you mean, sir. I have explained them to you."

The Longworths' house at 1736 M Street was a sort of

headquarters for all Republicans (and Democrats) who didn't like the way President Wilson was conducting the war. While the Colonel was there it was a very busy headquarters. T.R. established himself on the first floor immediately upon arrival. The family entertained upstairs, where there was a convenient library. A nearly continuous stream of people came to see the Colonel in his temporary offices. At one point his daughter and hostess leaned over the banisters and counted thirty-three newspaper men. They were "fairly stacked in the small hall," she remarked.

That night Alice Longworth and her mother were packed off for dinner and the Congressman gave a men's dinner for his father-in-law. About twenty prominent Republicans attended, and party strategy was the most important topic of conversation. Several of the guests thought the Republicans should immediately demand a coalition cabinet.

"I disagree!" snapped the guest of honor. "Any such program should be followed only after a caucus of Republican senators."

"But don't you think Republicans should take a larger part in running the war, Colonel?" someone asked.

"Emphatically, sir. But it is a complicated problem. To begin with, there are more Republicans in the war administration right now than most people realize. There is Pershing, for instance—not a politician primarily, but still a Republican. There is Admiral Sims. That means that the command of the armed forces is directly under Republicans."

"Oh, but, Colonel, they don't count."

"Perhaps not. But right here in Washington— Well, the Aircraft Board is under Howard Coffin and Colonel Deeds— both Republicans." The ex-President chuckled. "When corruption was charged against the board, whom did the President set to investigate it? Charles Evans Hughes! Set a Republican to catch a Republican!"

The guests politely roared with laughter. The Colonel went on with his list.

"There's Benedict Crowell, assistant secretary to Baker in the War Department. There's Stettinius from J. P. Morgan's. McRoberts of the National City Bank is chief of ordnance procurement. Charley Schwab, I have it on good authority, will soon be put in charge of the Emergency Fleet Corporation. Vance McCormick is a Democrat, but his War Trade Board has five Republicans out of eight members. Harry Garfield is a Republican—at least I've always thought so."

"That's the point, Colonel. Republicans are doing most of the real work and aren't getting the credit. Under a coalition cabinet Wilson couldn't take all the credit."

There was a twinkle in the Colonel's eye.

"Wilson can have all the credit he's getting," he said. "I wouldn't want to share it with him."

Another appreciative general laugh from the guests. It was a good point, they thought.

"No," continued the Colonel, "if we demand a coalition cabinet, Wilson's men will see to it that it doesn't work—and they can blame us. We would have made the suggestion."

The Colonel's logic seemed unassailable to the gentlemen present, none of whom was anxious to be blamed for the failure of a war cabinet. Nothing more was heard of the coalition cabinet scheme.

When the dinner broke up, there was general agreement that the Republican party had had a new birth. From now on perhaps its fortunes would look upward. As the New York *Times* put it the next morning:

No doubt seems to remain that Theodore Roosevelt has become leader of the Republican Party. His leadership was amply attested at a dinner given last night in his honor, by his son-in-law, Congressman Nicholas Longworth, at the latter's home where the Colonel is stopping. The whole war situation was discussed with especial reference to the part that should be taken by Republican members of the Senate and House, and there was a remarkable agreement with the views as to policy that Colonel Roosevelt expressed.

A week later the Colonel went to the hospital with painful abscesses, aftermath of his trip through the jungles of Brazil. Periodic illnesses had plagued him since the anxious day his son Kermit had brought him, with an injured leg and wracked with fever, down the green and turbulent River of Doubt to civilization and medical care. Now four years later one of the operations left him deaf in one ear.

But there were many who sought T.R.'s advice even as he lay in the Roosevelt Hospital. There were others to carry on, and one of them was Nicholas Longworth, of Cincinnati and M Street. In Congress Longworth deplored certain pro- visions of the War Finance Corporation Bill. The son-in-law of the man who had for three years criticized Wilson for fail- ing to take a bold enough stand, for hesitating too long to use the powers invested in him, now accused him of danger- ous disregard of democratic procedure. He charged him, in- deed, with taking over the war.

"This," said Longworth angrily, "is not the President's war. It is not the war of the Democrats or any other party. It is the war of the American people. We stand behind the President not as an individual, not as a party leader, but be- cause he, for the time being, represents the American people. Our loyalty is pledged not to a person, but to the country and the cause. True patriotism in times like these should be evidenced not in mere empty professions of loyalty but in making that loyalty count in the actual winning of the war. Can that be done best by an attitude of fawning servility to those in the seats of the mighty or by constructive criticism of our shortcomings and suggestions of improvements? That is the question and there ought to be but one answer. If the President, in his magnificent isolation from the common people—an isolation among rulers comparable only to that of the Mikados of ancient Japan—is to be immune from any criticism of his acts or those of his subordinates, then this war must be fought as no war in history was ever fought."

Possibly the most unpopular bureaucrat, to the Congress, was George Creel. And after a quixotic member of a lecture audience had asked him the strange question, "What do you think of the heart of Congress?" and received the monstrously indiscreet reply, "I haven't been slumming in years," even more congressmen were out after his scalp. They said members of the A. E. F. in France couldn't get their mail because Creel took up all the shipping space for his tons of pamphlets. The congressmen said he spent government money spreading the doctrine of free trade and other Democratic party propaganda. They said he was Wilson's personal press agent at the taxpayer's expense. Senator Lodge was indignant about the "useless" activities of the publicist. "Mr. Creel," he said, "is a man to whom Congress refused to give power. . . . The office he holds is created under the $100,-000,000 fund given to the President for the general defense of the country. Mr. Creel, apparently, is part of the general defense of the country, and the little government publications which he is publishing, and the scores of people whom I am told he has employed to do what might be done by a stenographer and a couple of clerks, are being paid out of that fund."

Here it was the end of March, Senator Lodge pointed out, turning his attention from Creel. America had been in the war almost a full year, and not one American airplane had reached American forces in France. Senator Poindexter, of Washington, wrung his hands over the long delay of the

Shipping Board in supplying ships, telling the Senate that the Board had declined offers from shipbuilders on the Pacific slope that would have put many vessels on the ways months before. Although spruce is needed in the making of airplanes, the Senator added, the Aircraft Production Board brushed aside offers of the growers in the West to supply all the spruce the Government wanted and at its own figure.

Senator Hiram Johnson, of California, urged "pitiless publicity" in the conduct of the war. He called the War Department's failure to equip the American Army with airplanes "an outrage upon the American youth on the battle lines."

"There is no use holding back the truth from the people," said Democratic Senator Thomas, of Colorado. "They must know what is going on. I would rather see my party perish than fail to tell the people the truth about this war." For which Senator Lodge commended him for his courage and devotion to country above party.

"The fate of the war is trembling in the balance," added the Massachusetts senator. "Our gallant allies are holding back the German advance at enormous sacrifice and with a courage that goes beyond the range of eulogy. In this dark hour it is a crime to keep from the American people facts well known to our enemies, but about which our own citizens are misinformed.

"We have granted powers and we have given money without stint; but appropriating money and granting powers will lead to nothing unless the money is wisely expended and the powers are efficiently exercised.

"The world looked to us a year ago and said we had come to the rescue of the situation. . . . What have we got to show in accomplishment? A wasted year!"

4. Brotherhood or Empire

BY the middle of February few Americans were left in Petrograd. The ambassador, David Francis, was packing up his embassy to move it to a safer place. Edgar Sisson and Arthur Bullard of the C.P.I. had stayed on. They had come to suspect Lenin's motives. Sisson even believed that he was in cahoots with the Germans. It was a time when every sort of conjecture was possible, a confused, disordered, angry, divided, disillusioned and sorrowful time. So it is impossible to report it from the point of view of the distressed onlookers. The truth appears only in the documents and records of circumstantial evidence which were later assembled.

It was on the 17th of February that the blow fell which stunned all conscious Russia. For the next two weeks there was chaos such as Petrograd and Moscow had not seen even in the November revolution. Then, on March 3, the curtain came down in silence while the tragic music of the last scene resounded and echoed in the far corners of the world.

The tragedy took place at the headquarters of the German Eastern Command at Brest-Litovsk where the armistice with Soviet Russia had been signed December 15th. The drama had lasted a little more than two months. Looking back, some of the spectators—those who, to the end, believed in German justice—thought it strange that it could not have been prolonged. But those who were convinced that every lamp of civilization in Germany had long been extinguished by the German Supreme Command were surprised that it had lasted so long.

On December 20th peace negotiations, following the armistice between Soviet Russia and the Central Powers, began at Brest-Litovsk. The delegates met to discuss the general basis of peace. After that there would be ten days' intermission to give the world a chance to hear what the basis was. Trotsky and his romantic followers were still convinced that when the world got this beautiful news of brotherhood and good will, revolutions would spring up in the nations of the Allies and the workers would force their governments to make peace on the same basis. Then this horrible war—all of it—would end.

"It didn't work before," said Lenin, his hard, calculating eyes watching the round, fiery face of Leon Trotsky.

"There wasn't time," said Trotsky. "The revolution has been rising since then—especially in Germany."

"Has it?" said Lenin, turning away. He spread out his hands as if, like a father to a teasing child, he said: "Try it. The fall may do you good."

The play at Brest-Litovsk had opened with a comic scene. About a hundred of the dramatis personae were assembled there. There was the big aristocratic Field Marshal of the German Eastern Command, His Royal Highness Prince Leopold of Bavaria. There was little Joffe, the scragglybearded, soft-eyed, pince-nezed Soviet delegate—a Jewish intellectual just out of prison in Siberia. There was the reasonable, often gentle Baron von Kühlmann, German foreign minister, whose liberality had already angered the High Command. There was Anastasia Bitsenko, a stalwart woman Bolshevik, an assassin who had spent years in Siberia for her crime. There was Count Ottokar Czernin, the handsome Austro-Hungarian foreign minister, a person of gentle breeding and what Vienna thought were liberal views, now disheartened and on the verge of a breakdown because of starving conditions in his homeland. Most picturesque was the

Russian window-dressing: big, bearded, ungroomed, inarticulate Stashkov, representing the Russian peasant, and Obukhov, the worker who knew the revolutionary slogans by heart but had never encountered polite society. There was General Max Hoffmann, German chief of staff in the east whose cupid-bow mouth faintly disguised his trained brutality and whose occasional mental wanderings from the military had won for him the suspicion of brilliance in Berlin. And there were Turkish and Bulgarian officers and government officials.

The first act opened with a dinner party at which the Germans made the immense concession to democracy of mixing all these people up together. No one blushed when Obukhov shoveled in his food with a knife and used his fork for a toothpick or when Stashkov asked the decorous German orderly whether red or white wine was stronger and then got drunk on both. It was an astonishing show and gave the soviet delegates the sense that things were starting right.

A few days later, on Christmas Day, they were convinced of it. For on that day the Germans and Austrians accepted five of the six soviet tenets including one which provided for "no forcible appropriation of any territories taken in the course of the war" and the withdrawal of all occupying armies from these territories. Little Joffe almost danced with joy and rushed to the telegraph to send the news to Petrograd. No annexations! But it was a triumph!

Lenin, back in Petrograd, read the telegram.

"Let them try," he said, and went back to his own deep thoughts.

Three days later the Germans, overhearing Joffe's shouts of joy in which he mentioned Kurland, Russian Poland, and Lithuania as territories to be evacuated by the Germans, hastily called him into conference. They had not meant Kurland, Russian Poland, and Lithuania, they explained. These countries, they said, had decided of their own free will that they wanted to separate from Russia. Had not the soviets declared that there should be self-determination of all peoples? It did no good for Joffe to protest that the peoples of these lands had certainly not announced their wish to be annexed to Germany. No, no, Herr Joffe, you must not be unreasonable. And, still politely, lest Joffe had overlooked it, the Germans pointed to the tag on their acceptance which said, "If the Entente would also agree to negotiate a Peace on similar terms." It was the end of Joffe. He left that night for Petrograd.

The curtain went down then on the first act and the principals went home to talk to their governments and wait ten days for England, France, and Italy to "agree to negotiate a Peace on similar terms."

There began then in Germany a fight which ended official recognition of the liberal elements and drove the Social Democrats, the rebellious workers, and every advocate of justice and decency underground. In the midwinter recess of the Brest-Litovsk conference only the first round of this fight took place, but it sent the German delegates back to the conference trembling with the shock.

Hindenburg and Ludendorff went into a black rage over the Christmas agreement. Even with its tags it was a "renunciation" of everything they stood for and had fought for. "It was frank surrender," wrote Hindenburg to the Kaiser. Both he and Ludendorff threatened to resign. The militaristic press supported their anger. "Never before," wrote the *Tägliche Rundschau*, "have we so completely given up diplomatically everything which has been so dearly bought with the blood and lives of hundreds of thousands, with the sweat of millions, with the deprivation of our children, and with our own hunger."

Yet at this stage—it was before the strikes in Germany—the liberals were still able to speak. The leftists in the Reich-

stag were still strong, the leftist press was still allowed to
put its opposition to the militarists in bitter terms. The German people, they said, have not given their blood and sweat
and lives for the annexation of territory. If the people find
out that this is the object of the war, they will stop fighting.
"The overwhelming majority of the German people," said
a socialist deputy referring to the threats of Hindenburg and
Ludendorff, "will not shed a single tear over the General,
whoever he may be, who opposes a peace by understanding
or who would rather resign than continue to fight for such
a peace."

In Austria-Hungary, the liberals or antimilitarists were
still more powerful and more vocal. For the Hapsburg
monarchy the war had gone badly. The men of the rebellious peoples who formed an unwilling part of the monarchy
—Czechs, Slovaks, Poles, Jugoslavs—had deserted in droves
from the Austro-Hungarian armies. Now there was a food
shortage and the wolves of hunger were howling in the
Vienna streets. So Count Czernin was instructed to get a
peace with Russia at any price at Brest-Litovsk. A "bread
peace," they called it. Food, food, food! At the cost of honor
if need be. But food, and no more fighting, no more armies
in the east.

By the end of the recess, no word had come from the Allies
about making peace with Germany.

So on the 9th of January, the delegates went back to the
cold citadel on the Polish plain. The headquarters at Brest-
Litovsk was only a collection of makeshift buildings amid
the ruins of the town. Yet even in the shambles the German
officers saw to it that the comforts were not missing. Shivering German soldiers stoked the stoves. There was a working
railroad and trains brought good rich food made possible
by civilian sacrifices. However the people at home might

starve themselves on turnips, there was fresh meat and the best Moselle and Rhine wines for the generals.

In Joffe's place came Trotsky. In contrast to the pleading, gentle Joffe, Trotsky was straight dynamite. His explosive energy was inexhaustible. He could argue, orate, spit his contempt, roar his unanswerable logic for days at a time. Yet he could drop his voice to a whisper to wheedle and persuade. He was a master of sarcasm, dialectics, and filibuster. He was educated, in the narrower sense, probably beyond anyone at the conference. Yet, though he could command an encyclopedia of facts and use them with precise expediency, he was a romantic at heart and his bright dream always stood between him and the moment's reality.

Trotsky's power at Brest-Litovsk lay in his tirelessness. Men drooped with fatigue when he entered the room. Generals chafed, fidgeted, and sweated. Ministers got chronic headaches. Technical experts lost their grip on their slide rules and the lines of maps danced before their eyes.

These were Trotsky's weapons and, for the first week, he used them with full effect. One effect was on German pride. Men like Kühlmann, who was chairman of the conference, and, at times, even Hoffmann, hated to be beaten in argument by this proletarian. Also they wanted the record to look reasonably clean, for the Russians had insisted on full publicity and however the Germans might control their newspapers, the Russians would see to it that the news got into Germany. Indeed, under the very noses of the Germans at Brest-Litovsk, the Soviet's propaganda was being distributed in German to the German headquarters troops. So the Germans wanted, in these uncertain days when the fight was still going on at home between liberals and jingoes, to dress things up: to call "annexation" by some sweeter name and keep the fairy tale going that the German martyrs were still fighting in self-defense against the aggression of the world. So Trotsky was given his day.

But while Trotsky worked, as he thought, for the fulfillment of his dream, a realist back in Petrograd sat in his office through a sequence of lonely midnights and pondered the facts. Lenin was never deceived by phrases or oratory. His vision pierced the fog of words and dreams. Behind Brest-Litovsk he saw the German army, strong, equipped, disciplined. Behind the army he saw a people still docile, still scared of the whip which the generals held. These things would break down in time but it would take months, perhaps years, of military defeat, starvation, and propaganda.

On the Russian side of Brest-Litovsk he saw no Russian army. Instead he saw only a disorganized rabble, ill-armed, ill-fed, suffering from its own propaganda, craving only peace and bread. Most of the soldiers had actually gone home after the armistice. The fine, new, revolutionary Red Army already existed, to be sure, but most of it was on paper. To mobilize a new fighting force in Russia would be the work of at least a year. It would require equipment and transport which just weren't there.

So at Brest-Litovsk itself Lenin saw only a game. Trotsky was a ferocious mouse, to be sure, but when the cat chose to pounce he would be only a mouse. And the cat was not the mild Kühlmann, but Erich von Ludendorff.

All these realities had crystallized in Lenin's mind since November. The German revolution had been only a will-o'-the-wisp. It had been a useful fancy because it had helped consolidate the Russian revolution. It had made a nice talking point for his speech at Smolny.

Now there were two possibilities. Either Trotsky would refuse the terms the Germans offered and the German army would march into Petrograd and destroy the Bolshevik revolution, or Trotsky would accept the terms, however harsh, and though huge pieces of Russia would be torn away, the revolution would go on. It would simply operate in a smaller Russia. What was Russia? It was the revolution that counted. If that could be kept intact and the Bolsheviki kept solid behind it, it could eventually move out even from a small center and spread over the world.

But would the Russian people agree to that? Would they be willing to see enormous Russian provinces pass into German hands? Suppose they insisted on fighting? Then he must convince them.

Through January Lenin watched events move toward his prophecy. He learned of the separate delegation which went to Brest-Litovsk from the Ukraine. The Ukraine, under the influence of rich landowners, had declared its independence of Soviet Russia. It had only been a declaration, as Lenin knew. The population was overwhelmingly pro-Bolshevik. He had discovered this when he had sent a detachment of the new Red Guards to Kiev. The Ukrainian capital had fallen into their hands amid cheering crowds. Yet the delegation of the small Ukrainian independence party had gone separately to Brest-Litovsk. There they had invited the Germans to send a German army into the Ukraine to support them, to drive out the Bolsheviki and oppress the people! Treason? Call it that if you like. Landowners, capitalists, bourgeois were all traitors at heart. But they would learn. When the Germans got into the Ukraine they would stay there. It was the bread basket of Russia. It would give thousands of tons of grain to hungry Germany and hungrier Austria. Wasn't Czernin too, for all his high ideals, dickering with the Ukrainian delegation for peace and wheat?

Meanwhile letters kept coming from Trotsky full of anger, suspicion, and the old dream. He reported rumors. First there was the horrible rumor that many Englishmen, Americans, Russians, and even Germans were saying that Lenin and he had been bought by German gold. To scotch that, the Russian delegation at Brest-Litovsk must fight like tigers against the German terms. Then, after Wilson's Fourteen Points speech had been digested in Germany, came the rumor that the German staff was on the point of accusing Lenin and Trotsky of being Wilson's agents. Lenin filed the letters away. Then came one which he could not file.

He could not ignore it because it was all based on Trotsky's most romantic picture. It was so rosy-colored that Lenin knew it would rouse the other romantic Bolsheviki. Also it asked for an immediate decision—a decision which Lenin dared not give without consulting his colleagues at Smolny. Trotsky wrote:

It is impossible to sign their peace, Vladimir Ilyich. They have already agreed with fictitious governments in Poland, Lithuania, Kurland, and others concerning territorial concessions and military and customs treaties. . . . We cannot sign their peace.

Then came the dream. To Lenin it was pure fantasy.

My plan is this:
We announce the termination of the war and demobilization without signing any peace. We declare we cannot participate in the brigand's peace of the central powers. . . .
The Germans will be unable to attack us after we declare the war ended. At any rate, it would be very difficult for Germany to attack us, because of her internal condition. . . . The internal strife is demoralizing the Government. . . .
We declare we end the war but do not sign the peace. . . .
We must have your decision. . . . We can still drag on negotiations for one or two or three or four days. Afterward they must be broken off. . . . I clasp your hand. Yours,

TROTSKY.

A postscript asked Lenin to telegraph yes or no.
Lenin consulted the leaders of the Bolshevik party. As he

feared, Trotsky's heroic idealism captured their hearts. So he wired Trotsky to come to Petrograd. Trotsky came and made an eloquent speech to the party bosses. "No war—no peace!" To the slogan-loving revolutionaries, the words were irresistible.

"But the Germans don't understand such phrases," said Lenin. "They will attack."

"Then we will fight!" shouted the aroused revolutionaries. They went wild with military fervor—these men who had talked so hard for peace two months back.

"What shall we fight with?" asked Lenin.

Courage. Rage. Righteous wrath. An aroused populace.

Quietly Lenin explained that fighting was done with shells and bombs and bullets. His realism won some supporters. But those he did not win threatened to imprison him as a traitor. And when it came to a vote, Trotsky carried the party.

But by the time Trotsky got back to Brest-Litovsk, the fight between the liberals and the army in Germany was over. With the end of the January strikes, Hindenburg held the German government in the hollow of his hand. Everything but himself and Ludendorff had vanished from the surface of the German earth. With the suppression of newspapers, the power of the Reichstag leftists had almost disappeared. That an enormous army of discontented folk continued to work beneath the surface did not matter to the German delegates at Brest-Litovsk. Underground rebels work slowly. By the time they got under way, Germany would have won the war.

So Trotsky's dream, beautifully told as it was, only bored the Germans. When, with a magnificent gesture, he turned his back on the document presented for his signature, Kühlmann declared the conference at an end and General Hoffmann went to the telephone.

This was on the 11th of February. On the 13th Trotsky
addressed an enthusiastic throng at Petrograd. On the 16th
the news came through that Germany had declared the armistice at an end. On the 17th a proclamation went out from
the Germans to the Russian people which said that the Germans were on their way to "liberate" the unhappy victims of
Bolshevik tyranny. On the 18th the German army advanced,
capturing Dvinsk and Luck and in the next few days marched
150 miles, taking 2,000 guns, quantities of equipment, and
countless thousands of prisoners. There was virtually no resistance. On the 19th Lenin and Trotsky sent a telegram
accepting the peace terms, but Hoffmann did not stop his
armies until the 26th. By this time German forces had arrived at Narva, less than a hundred miles from Petrograd.
Meanwhile the Germans delayed their reply and, when on
the 23rd it arrived in Smolny, it contained, not the terms
Trotsky had refused but another set of terms, far more severe. They were accepted on the 24th.

So the realism of Lenin won. Yet even after the German
advance started there was a hard fight in the councils of the
Soviet government. Petrograd was in turmoil. The patriotic
fever ran high. Thousands of workers who had fought so
hard for peace were willing to go out to fight the advancing
Germans with their bare hands. Again Lenin was called
traitor and coward. There were rioting and destruction in the
streets. But Lenin's persuasion won at last and the motion
to accept the German terms was carried in the Central Executive Committee of the Soviet Congress by a small majority.
On the 3rd of March, the Treaty of Brest-Litovsk was
signed and the curtain came down between Soviet Russia and
western civilization.

Yet western civilization was rocked to its foundations by
the ending of the remote drama. In all the Allied nations,
statesmen and orators and politicians made hasty guesses

about the debacle and leapt to their feet to shout that it
served the treasonable Bolsheviki right. If their revolution
and their disgraceful armistice had not cut them off from
their allies they would have been saved this humiliation. But
no, they preferred the lies of their leaders, the sneaking
double-dealing Lenin, a cynical atheist, to the patriotism of
the great Kerensky. Their whole philosophy was anarchy,
nihilism; their aim the destruction of the human race. They
were unwashed, unenlightened, and unredeemed.

But here and there, even in the bourgeois press of the
world, even in occasional spaces in the world's Park Avenues
and West Ends, and among slower thinkers in the world's
parliaments, there were words of sympathy, candid or disguised. For however it might serve the Bolsheviki right,
there was no blinking the naked brutality of the German
dictate. However you might dislike a man, it was unpleasant
to see him kicked in the face by your own enemy. What
might that same boot—still smelling of his blood—one day
do to you?

The Treaty of Brest-Litovsk deprived Russia of Finland,
Kurland, Livonia, Lithuania, Russian Poland, the Ukraine,
Ardahan, Kars, Batum, and eastern Anatolia. (The last four
went to Turkey.) The loss of these provinces cost Russia
34 per cent of her population, 32 per cent of her agricultural
land, 54 per cent of her industrial enterprises, and 89 per
cent of her coal mines.

Article II forbade all propaganda against the Governments of the Central Powers—Germany, Austria-Hungary,
Turkey, and Bulgaria. (Article II was never, for an instant,
obeyed.)

So the more sober thinkers came to dwell more and more
on Germany's capacity for dictating peace, and, as time went
on, the resolve grew among the people of the Allies never
to yield until their monstrous enemy was beaten.

In the spring of 1918 it was a hard resolve to keep. Already, by the 3rd of March, enormous bodies of German troops had been transferred to the western front. There, as allied army reconnaissance discovered too late, Ludendorff was putting them through a new kind of training—training for attack, for open warfare independent of trenches and for fast movement.

Less than three weeks after the defeat of Russia, the blow fell in France.

2

As dawn came on March 21st, fog hung so low and thick that the British soldiers along the Oise could not see fifty feet into no man's land.

The men of General Gough's Fifth British Army had been there a long time. There had been sharp German raids for a month—sporadic attacks here and there—and the British had thrown them back. Many a time when the nights had been white with star shells and the furious big guns had talked an hour or so, these men had said to one another, "Here it comes." But it had not come. Probably, the private soldiers thought, it had not come because we had stopped each start. They began at last to wonder if it would come, though warning orders passed daily down the trenches. The men were alert; they expected and handled the raids but they had almost given up expecting "it."

They had long been inured to trenches. When no Germans came they fought the rats. When the Germans came they fell back, if they had to, to another trench. If they advanced they advanced to another trench, a few yards forward. There was always a trench. Trenches were home and office, places of work and play, the reality of life. When "it" came, it would be only a longer march forward or back from trench to trench.

" 'Twould be a fine morning for the show," said a boy looking at the fog.

"The show your grandmother."

"It'll come sure enough."

"It might not—never."

Then the guns began. The boys could not see the rockets that had started them. They could only hear the shells moving above on their different levels with their different whines. The men in Gough's lines could not know that on fifty miles of front from Arras to La Fère, seven thousand German guns had spoken at once. They only knew that there was shelter for the instant in the trench and that, from all past knowledge, it was only another raid.

Then the bombardment covered everything. Suddenly—too quickly—the barrage lifted to a line farther back. The soldiers in the trenches could feel, then, that imminence of enemy flesh and steel, and they felt through the opaque fog, the charge of men coming. It was too soon—it was wrong—it wasn't cricket—the blasted fog had hidden the German infantry charge. Then came the grenades, the scorch of the flame-throwers, the cold steel. No one knew what had happened. Men only knew that there was not time to take cover in another trench. You must jump the trenches now to get back fast enough. And then, after hours of retreat, there were no more trenches.

That was when the panic came. Where there was a trench there was hope. There your back was to the wall. There was a parapet against the little bullets of machine guns. But in the evening of the 21st, there were no more trenches for the soldiers of General Gough's army.

So from the vast open plain of this running rout, the news went round the world. The news did not say that men were lost from their units, their friends, their officers, mingled with the enemy, overrun by wave on wave of field gray. But staff officers in the rear moving the pins in their maps could see in their trained fancies the details of the tragedy.

Behind the staff officers sat the great generals whose word could alter the direction of a hundred freight trains, start lines of camions between the fronts, to whom troops were solid blocks to be thrown in here and there like stoppers in the sluiceways. And behind the generals were politicians jealous of one another's power, men who still could not conceive of orders being given Englishmen in the French tongue. And behind the politicians sat editors and strategists in armchairs who saw precisely what the Germans were doing—there it was on the flat map before them which showed no hills or canals or streams or cover or pitfalls or poisoned water or hunger or intestinal weakness—the Germans were splitting the British from the French and winning the war.

On the 26th in the village of Doullens where spring was evident in the new, pungent fragrance of the dunghills, a group of dignitaries met to decide what next. The benumbed populace, dreaming as they prodded their thin cattle through the streets, of sugar and coffee and missing men, looked up startled into the suddenly tender eyes of Foch, marveled a moment at the broad back of Haig, the striped trousers of Lord Milner, or the incredible likeness of Clemenceau to all his pictures.

These men and Pétain and the British generals, Wilson, Lawrence, and Montgomery, and Poincaré and Loucheur went to the town hall and talked. It was a strange meeting. Men were always taking one another aside and whispering in corners. Pétain, as if it were needed, spoke solemnly of the desperate situation and Haig agreed but no one listened. Foch stood apart and chafed silently at this ceremony over a foregone conclusion, a word years overdue that must be uttered, written, accepted.

"It will be better for you to name him," whispered Clemenceau to Lord Milner.

"Foch," said Milner who had crossed the Channel to say it.

So Clemenceau sat at the table and wrote:

"General Foch is charged by the British and French Governments to co-ordinate the action of the Allied armies on the Western Front."

The word "generalissimo" was not used. The written message must be restrained, obscured for home consumption in proud, aloof England.

The American Government was not mentioned. It was scarcely necessary. Clemenceau and Milner had both seen the insistent messages from the American President asking for unity of command.

So the meeting ended. And everyone knew that if human ingenuity could turn the tide, the tide would be turned.

Two days later an olive-drab car with a four-starred blue flag on its hood drove down the road to Clermont-sur-Oise. As it came near the town it met the stream of camions moving to the front. The drivers smiled as the car passed.

"Ils viendront, alors."

"But only one. The general?"

"Yes. They say he is a brave, serious man."

"They will need a brave man. And the others?"

"They say there will be a million by May."

The car moved slowly into the town. Captain Marenches, the general's French aide, leaned out of the car, spoke to a soldier.

"But he must be here," the aide insisted. "I know he is here."

Soldiers gathered respectfully about the car. Then an officer came and Marenches called him by his first name.

"How goes it?"

"Badly but it will be better now."

"My general must see him."

"Say nothing then. But I will put a man in the car to guide you."

The man, speaking little, waved them out of the town to a lane of poplars leading to a farmhouse. The house was hidden in flowering shrubs. A great cherry stood in front in full blossom.

"It is beautiful," said the general.

"It is quiet at least," said Marenches, "with the Boche so near."

The stiff, straight general went into the house. He recognized the backs of four men bent over the map. They were Clemenceau, Pétain, Loucheur, and the man he had come to see.

Clemenceau looked up, drew the others outside, leaving the general and Foch.

"My friend, you have come! You have found me hidden here."

The general spoke a moment and Foch seized his arm.

"But you must tell *them!* You must tell them all!"

He pulled the general to the door, across the lawn to where the others stood. They wondered at the emotion in their supreme commander's eyes.

"My general has come, gentlemen, with a message from his people."

Clemenceau glanced up at the tight, immaculate uniform and asked himself if, even in bed, this formidable man would know how to relax. Then he saw the faint smile as the general spoke.

"Je viens pour vous dire que le peuple américain tiendrait à grand honneur . . .

"They would be honored if our troops were engaged in the present battle.

"I ask it in my name and theirs.

"In this moment there is no question but of fighting.

"Infantry, artillery, aviation, all that we have is yours.

"Use them as you will.

"Others will come, as many as are needed.

"I have come expressly to tell you that the American people would be proud to take part in the greatest battle of history."

The general turned then and walked away. At the car, his aide said,

"My general, I would not have believed it!"

Pershing turned on him sharply.

"That I would offer our men . . . ?"

"No—that your French could be so perfect!"

3

With cool indifference to the indignities of man, spring moved over Europe, precise and businesslike, putting on an excellent show for anyone who cared to look. In France, blooming orchards, sprouting grain, and reviving farmyards produced sights, smells, and sounds which were highly nostalgic to tired fighting men.

As the gigantic German attack pushed on into new areas, spreading out south and west over northern France, these things had different effects on German and Allied soldiers. To the Frenchman, the sights and smells meant the home which he was immediately losing, the home from which, yard by yard, he was being driven. If he lost it, all the hope of the spring and the next spring would be gone with it. The Briton was fighting with his back to the homeland as the enemy pushed him toward the Channel. Every lost French farm was his loss too and a threat to his country. But to the German the spring was a reminder of a home far away from which he was forever moving farther. For what?

It was not only the spring which made him ask the question. As each batch of replacements came in, there was fresh news from the home front. It was news of hunger, of shortages of clothing, of longer hours of work, of constant questions. What are our conquests gaining for us, the common folk, the ones who are dying, bearing the full weight of the war's cost? What had they gained for us in Russia where our Supreme Command had annexed such vast territory at the expense of the Russian workers? Had the men at the front heard of Brest-Litovsk? The Brest-Litovsk treaty had proved beyond all argument that this was a war for conquest! What price now this *Unsinn* about self-defense, fighting for our homes!

In the farms of the Lys valley which the direct blows of the war had not yet struck, the Germans found quantities of cows, hogs, geese, and chickens. For years they had not dreamed of such luxury. Thousands turned from the war to barnyard hunting. For days they gorged themselves while the thinned lines moved on. Officers kicked and prodded them, but the hungry *gemeinen Soldaten* laughed and went on eating.

The Allied generals behind the lines took note of these things. They got considerable material for thought from German prisoners and relayed it back to the staffs. Some of the staff officers, poring over the printed matter found in the pockets of German soldiers, asked themselves if, even after she had stopped fighting, Russia, perhaps, was winning the war? Other officers shook their heads. The stuff, they said, was dynamite. But it could be as damaging to French soldiers as to German. The Russians did not care who was corrupted by their revolution. For us Allies it was simply a race as to which side was first corrupted. And if we beat the Germans we should probably have to fight the Russians afterward.

But the Allied generals who handled grand strategy—who stuck pins all over the map of the world—had other concerns. In April, when the skies over France were darkest, these generals and the war ministers behind them saw a streak of light on the eastern horizon. It was a curious place to find it. With Brest-Litovsk every star of hope in the east had seemed to fade. Yet now—southwest of Brest-Litovsk but still in the east—the hopeful dawn was becoming very definite.

Austria-Hungary was cracking up.

4

Through centuries this great, sprawling empire had grown into grandeur and arrogance, reaching out to conquer the weaker peoples round its fringe and subduing them under the despotic rule of a single family. By 1914 it had become one of the shining symbols of the old order. It was a fortress against democracy. Vienna flashed with bright uniforms, the smart horses of the aristocracy pranced and trotted in the Ring, and a gay, lazy, and generally charming leisure class trusted in the mysterious intrigues of the Hapsburgs for its protection.

But below this glittering surface, the Dual Monarchy of Austria-Hungary was a strange phenomenon. It was a melting pot which never melted. At least five separate nations, speaking different languages, were held together by the adroitness of the ministers at Vienna and Budapest who played their games not only with internal jealousies but with a watchful eye on the bigger game outside—the game of the balance of power in Europe. The Emperor, acting with absolute authority, used his armies, his police, and his secret agents to carry out the moves decided upon by his ministers. Successive postponement, violence, suppression, economic and political threat and bribe, constant reliance on the support of Germany—this was the Hapsburg way in 1914 and it worked well enough in time of peace.

Austrian Germans and Hungarian Magyars had patched up a partnership which kept their mutual suspicion underground as long as the people had no say. So the center was stable enough. But round the fringe stood the insurgent Slavic peoples: the Czechs and Slovaks to the north, with their old, proud traditions of independence; the Poles, with their passionate longing for reunion with their brothers under Russian and German rule in a new Poland; and the fierce Jugoslavs to the south, whose growing bitterness came to a climax with the murder of the Hapsburg heir at Sarajevo in June, 1914.

A few wise men in Vienna and Budapest knew that such a country had no business to go to war with an outsider. The instant such a diversion occurred, taking the attention of the master cooks off their great seething pot of unmixable ingredients, the pot was certain to boil over. But the arrogant Hapsburg cooks were deluded about their skill. They had done such things before, working fast.

Serbia was an intolerable threat with her sympathy for the Jugoslavs and her Adriatic ambitions. The assassination of the beloved Archduke was an excuse—whether or not the Serbs had actually done the job. So why not reach out now—with powerful German help—grab Serbia, throw her in the pot, and get back to their stirring before the boil began?

So the ministers had concocted their ultimatum to Serbia and almost immediately war had broken out all over Europe.

The dissolution of Austria-Hungary began at once. It began slowly and was not at first visible. The Austrian shock troops were good soldiers. But even in the early battles the rebellious men of the separate nations, drafted against their will into the armies of their hated bosses, saw their chance.

Jugoslavs deserted across the lines into Serbia. In the battles of the wild Carpathian mountains, Czechs and Slovaks kept disappearing from the ranks. Later, when they grew bolder, they would advance toward the Russian lines singing their patriot's song, *Hej Slované,* and whole regiments would be absorbed by the Russian "enemy." Still later, some of these men formed units of the Russian army and fought the Austrians. In those days, when they heard the song rising from the troops opposing them, they would cease firing and Czech met Czech in a happy embrace.

The Poles bided their time. Their problem was more complex, for Russians as well as Austrians and Germans were their enemies. But secretly they cherished their plan and they became of little use to the Dual Monarchy.

The situation was hard for the single-track generals of the old army to figure. Nothing was clean-cut or even military. You could no longer guess the outcome of a battle by an estimate of soldiers, guns, ammunition, or skill. You stuck your pins in the map for the next day's operations and, in the night, it seemed as if some mischievous, unseen hand changed them. A strong, apparently disciplined division was ordered to attack a manifestly inferior force; the men moved into the offensive and suddenly they were gone. Instead of the definite diapason and staccato of the barrage, shouts of "Kamerad!", "Tovarish!" rang on the dead air.

In 1916 food shortages began on the home fronts. Hungary, the granary of the Dual Monarchy, decided it needed its own food and it stopped food shipments to its partner. So there came a split in the central structure of the Hapsburg building. As starvation began to stalk through Vienna, the old emperor, Francis Joseph, died and his frightened successor Karl sent out peace feelers which antagonized Germany.

In 1917 came the revolution in Russia and the disgruntled

troops in Austria-Hungary's armies reached eagerly for the propaganda which poured across the lines. Revolutionary gossip and desire spread like a plague over the shattered country. Workers struck, transportation was paralyzed. Except on the Italian front under strong German leadership the armies were breaking down.

In January, 1918, Wilson's speech of the Fourteen Points so roused the favor of the Hungarians that they rebelled further against their German partners. Even Count Czernin, the Hapsburg Emperor's foreign minister, admitted the power of the President's words. "A new star had risen," he said, "on the other side of the ocean, and all eyes were turned in that direction."

In January too prolonged strikes for peace and bread paralyzed the whole of Austrian industry. Are wars still won with guns, the old guard asked itself, or only with words?

In March Count Czernin returned from Brest-Litovsk where he had been forced to concur in the brutal dictate to Soviet Russia. He returned to meet masses turned pro-Bolshevik, burning with shame and rage at the terms of the treaty. Was Russia, after laying down her arms in such humility, winning the war against the Hapsburgs too?

So, in France and England, the grand strategists who could see far enough watched the streak of light in the east widen with the growing spring.

5

In May the more philosophical watchers of the war—in the quieter reaches of the world where discussion was practical—began to ask themselves if the war must end in either autocracy or bolshevism. Was there no middle ground? Was true democracy—the democracy Wilson wanted to make the world safe for—impossible in Europe? In America, no; but

America, which had evolved through democracy, was far away. Its culture was not Europe's culture. In Europe did the future hold only a choice of dictatorships—the absolutism of kings or the absolutism of a proletariat?

Suddenly, as these people watched, there rose from the very ruins of the Hapsburg domain a phantom almost too beautiful to be believed. If it were a reality it would answer many questions at once. It would be the first fulfillment of the ideal of self-determination. It would be a symbol of the security of small nations. And it was, if the watchers were not mistaken, an embodiment of undefiled democracy in the very heart of Europe!

A quiet, scholarly man with a gentle, bearded face and searching eyes had long been moving through western Europe trying to draw the watchers' attention to this growing phenomenon. It had a difficult name—that was one of his handicaps—especially for English tongues. It was hard to spell, harder to pronounce. When he called it "Bohemia," Englishmen and Frenchmen alike jumped at the sound. They all remembered Good King Wenceslas, of whom respectable Englishmen sing on Christmas Eve. Most of them remembered John Hus. And they had seen the beautiful products of the Bohemian glassmakers. But Czechoslovakia—?

"What does it mean, Dr. Masaryk?"

"It means the union of Czechs and Slovaks in a new state after centuries of oppression. We cannot call it Bohemia . . . that is only the Czech country. I myself was born a Slovak."

"But does it exist . . . as an independent state?"

"It exists. Its National Council has branches in France, Russia, Italy, America. It is a government in exile. On the day Austria-Hungary falls, it will function from Prague."

So Thomas Masaryk explained a living faith which would become a government on a certain day. He talked and wrote constantly of democracy. It was easy for him to talk so. He had been born a serf, the son of a coachman. His first job had been in a blacksmith shop. He had educated himself and become a teacher. At the universities of Vienna and Prague he had explored the depths of philosophy, literature, world history, political science, but most widely the evolution, doctrine, and mechanics of the free government of free peoples. When war broke, he left Prague knowing that the time for his supreme mission had come and, working underground from Geneva, Paris, and London, he had organized the liberation of his people. Wherever there was an exiled Czech or Slovak, he drew him into the fold, started him to work. To others—to ministers and statesmen of France and England—he explained the coming republic, won their support.

"Use our men in your armies," he said. "I will organize them for you into legions. They will fight like demons against your enemies and ours."

In May, 1918, the echo of Masaryk's cry resounded through the world. In May the news came through of the Czech legions in Russia—the "Česka Družina"—and their heroic story was told from London to San Francisco. So, in May, the phantom became reality and Masaryk's way became easier.

Czechs and Slovaks, deserters from the Austrian armies, had joined with pre-war Czech and Slovak exiles in Russia to form a solid band. From it had developed a fighting force of 70,000 men. They were equipped, trained soldiers. In the summer of 1917 Masaryk had assembled them at Kiev in the Russian Ukraine. Many of these soldiers had belonged to fighting units in the Russian armies. When the Bolsheviki had made peace and demobilized the Russian armies there was nothing left for the Czechoslovak Družina to do. So Masaryk had got from France an invitation to them to join the French army.

There was only one way for them to go. They must move east across Siberia, east across the Pacific, east across America, and across the Atlantic. In other words, they must circle the world.

"It will be a long trek," Masaryk told them, "but it is a long war."

They started in March. In May the news came of how the Germans had pursued them in the Ukraine after Brest-Litovsk, of how they had fought a brilliant rear-guard action while they entrained, of how the Bolsheviki had turned against them at Cheliabinsk, and of how they had captured the town. In June the news came that they were capturing the whole of the Trans-Siberian railroad and stringing their outposts along it to Vladivostok on the Pacific. The news was complex, hard to understand, but it was an adventure story that was refreshing after the deadly years of trench war. The rights and wrongs of it were not analyzed. The gist of the story was that these men were fighting for liberty and independence against all comers. They had no bitterness against the Bolsheviki. They had great bitterness against the hordes of German and Austrian prisoners released under the treaty of Brest-Litovsk who were returning home. These they fought openly. If Bolsheviki took the part of the Germans they fought the Bolsheviki. That these heroes could capture, hold, and operate 4,500 miles of railroad and control the towns along it in order to make possible a trip around the world to meet an old enemy was enough to entrance romantic hearts everywhere in the tired world.

Masaryk was not with the Družina on its long journey. He had gone ahead over the same road. His mission for the summer was in America. There he would rally the million emigrant Czechs and Slovaks to his cause and rally the American people behind them.

He had been disturbed by Wilson's Fourteen Points speech.

Most of it was in tune with all his convictions. But the tenth point left him in doubt.

"The peoples of Austria-Hungary, whose place among the nations we wish to see safeguarded and assured, should be accorded the freest opportunity of autonomous development."

Did this mean that Wilson wanted the Dual Monarchy left intact and some mere formula of home rule given to the subject peoples? To Masaryk "autonomous" was an ugly word. The Hapsburgs had used it toward the Czechs and it had meant nothing. And Wilson had delayed eight months before declaring war on Austria-Hungary.

So when Masaryk left Russia in March he knew that he must clear all doubts in Wilson's mind. If the tenth point meant what it seemed to mean it must not be applied in any peace dealings with Austria. If it were, it would kill the new republic. So first of all he must show the Americans and their President the immediate need of dissolving the Hapsburg world.

In May when, in America, the news came to him of the Družina's adventures, he knew that his work was half done. To Americans the story would be irresistible. If it inspired them to join hands across Europe with this little sister republic, the safety of democracy in the postwar world would be assured.

6

In June the Imperial German Government—now the servant of the High Command—read the communiqués with satisfaction. The hero, Hindenburg, whose mind was slowing down with age, sat in headquarters and passed the good news along to the Kaiser and the Chancellor. Neither he nor the Kaiser nor the Chancellor suspected that there was a filter between Hindenburg and the field. When the staff generals clicked their heels before the chief and told him of the new advances, the new conquests, the new crackings of the enemy, the old man took their words in good faith and never troubled to rummage in the files of the staff offices. If he had, he would have been surprised at the muck which had been filtered off the news before it had been served to him.

The hero Ludendorff was more familiar with these files. But Ludendorff was swayed by a powerful faith. His faith was first in himself and his infallible strategic mind. Secondly it was in the discipline of the German soldier and the power of the German officer to maintain it. This discipline, indeed, ran through the entire Prussian system; it included the relations between the Junkers and the peasants. One commanded, the other obeyed. There were no questions, no afterthoughts, no private reasoning. The private soldier did not think. If he showed symptoms of thinking, he was slapped across the face with a whip. That, at least, was the theory, though the practice had been modified when the psychologists had come in to meddle with the army.

So when Ludendorff learned that men had stopped, during an advance, to eat the rich loot, it was the fault of the junior officers. These officers must be disciplined. If discipline did not work, they must be replaced. So, for a time, Erich von Ludendorff ignored the files and worked out his offensives on the map.

But the lesser officers at the Avesnes headquarters—men like General von Kuhl—were more concerned over the reports they concealed from the old man. They had long been concerned over the masses of Russian stuff found in the bulging pockets of private soldiers. Copy after copy of the Russian propaganda newspaper, *Die Fackel*, printed in the most seductive German, had been found under the shirts of the boys.

Then had come the poison dropped from the little free balloons that kept drifting from the west. There were cartoons showing the Kaiser and his six sons goose-stepping between crowds of starving German women and children. There were cold columns of figures showing the contingents of Americans arriving month by month in France. There were figures showing (in grams) the immense rations given American soldiers with the significant postscript that the American general had ordered these same rations for German prisoners in American hands. Worse still was the succession of Wilson speeches with their incisive line between German government and German people, their cold fury against the German military caste, their promise of lasting peace in a people's world, their insistence upon "mankind" without distinction of race or nation. Enough of this poison was found to show what quantities of it must be still unfound, still eating its way into the hearts of the weary fighters.

Then there were the half-finished letters home: "How can we be right if the whole world is against us?" "They say our leaders have lied to us—write me if this is true." "The officers have everything while we starve on ersatz bread." "The enemy allows 75 grams of fat a day as the least a civilian can live on, yet you must live 12 to 14 days on that amount." And the letters from home to the soldiers: "They have taken our cows for the army. . . . Are these for you or for the officers?"

But finally, most alarming of all, were the leaflets found on soldiers returning from leave—poison circulated inside Germany itself, by the revolutionary Independent Socialists. Here was naked treason—orders to the soldiers from an organized, powerful underground force—orders to desert to the enemy:

Take heed where your government and your Kaiser are leading you. Unite yourselves with the main conditions which are declared by the Allies and force your government to do likewise. Then we can end this war without trouble and conclude an honorable peace for all.

Many army officers were aware of the steady work of this political party. It had begun with the navy as far back as July, 1917, when it had engineered a mutiny at Kiel. But since January when the great strikes were suppressed it had developed an even more efficient propaganda service than that of the enemy. Secret police, counterpropaganda had little effect. You never could reach it. You rounded up little groups of men in one place and sent them to prison, but overnight another group would spring up somewhere else. The leaflets were hidden between the folds of newspapers on the news-stands; they were thrust into the pockets of innocent citizens on crowded tramcars. "Pass this on. Give it to a soldier. It may save many lives."

Ludendorff concentrated on his maps. He looked back over his past offensives and planned a new one. The great March show of which he had written to his Kaiser, "It will be a mighty struggle . . . it will be difficult; but it will be victorious," had gained 1,500 square miles. It had cost the enemy 160,000 casualties. Yet somehow the bent Allied lines had held in the end. There had been no breach. In the April attack on the Lys river, he had pushed the British back thirty miles at one point, yet here again the elastic front had stiffened. In May his forces had swarmed over the Chemin des Dames, but it seemed as if this advance had moved almost too fast; he could not follow it up without a rest. While he rested the French lines re-formed. Behind them his air observers told him many Americans were waiting. Nonsense, said Ludendorff, they are green soldiers, they cannot fight. But they were helping French morale, his officers told him. But Ludendorff was not concerned, like the mighty Bismarck before him, with such "imponderables." In June he went again at the French on the Matz. Was Foch withdrawing deliberately? There was a coolness about this "generalissimo" which was disturbing.

In July Ludendorff was asked by a government official who had watched these enormous but indecisive offensives, if he was still sure of victory. "Decidedly yes," he replied. But in July, close to Paris, the army operating on the Marne met two regiments of United States Marines. It was not a serious setback but it was an omen. Air observers and other intelligence services multiplied the reports. There were a million and a half Americans behind the Marines. And French soldiers after Château-Thierry had been seen everywhere with tiny American flags stuck in their rifles.

Yet at the beginning of August Ludendorff said: "Five times in this war have I had to withdraw my troops that I might defeat the enemy in the end. The sixth time, why should I not succeed?"

Then, on the 8th of August, he saw the final lie of the loaded dice. On that day he saw his armies not withdrawing in good order to prepare the next attack, but in full rout. He saw whole bodies of German soldiers surrendering *en masse* to a few enemy sergeants. It was then that his suppressed memory of the headquarters files swept over him. He had been stabbed in the back! It was not the enemy army which had beaten him. It was the rotting home front, corrupted by traitors. It was the "poison raining down from God's clear sky."

It had all been incredible because it was so un-German. It was not German for soldiers to speak of a military attack as if it were strike-breaking in a factory. It was not German for men being relieved at the front to call the men of their relief "black legs" and to accuse them of "prolonging the war" because they obeyed orders. It was certainly not German for men to sit down to supper when they were commanded to advance. Civilian agitators said that such things were human when men were exhausted and starving. But it would have been German to stay hungry for the sake of the Fatherland.

So Ludendorff on the 14th abruptly informed his government that under these circumstances leadership had assumed "the character of an irresponsible game of chance" and that "the war must be ended."

The conference of the Emperor, the imperial chancellor Hertling, the foreign minister von Hintze, and the field marshal von Hindenburg, to which he addressed this ultimatum was surprised by his statement. A month before, von Hintze reminded him, he had said at the Avesnes field headquarters that he was "certain of finally and decisively beating the enemy in the offensive then going on." The sudden change made these people believe that Ludendorff was suffering from a nervous breakdown. Hindenburg said it would still be "possible to remain fixed on French territory"; the Kaiser said, "We must prepare to seek the opportune moment for coming to an understanding with the enemy," but no one thought the moment had come.

There were other things afoot. A new government was to be constituted. The popular franchise in Prussia was to be put through so that the people would have a voice in national action. These things would make the German government appear more democratic to the enemy—more reliable for negotiation.

But Ludendorff knew that delay at this point was dangerous. He had seen the effect of British tanks. He knew how fast events were moving. Later might be too late. Later, Germany might be forced to accept a victor's terms.

The General's thinking was simple. The war had been forced upon Germany. What the enemy called the "rape" of Belgium, the theft from Russia, had been military necessities. Submarines had sunk civilian ships but this was self-defense. This and the bombing of civilians from the air did not compare in deliberate brutality with the slow starvation of German civilians by the British blockade. Now Germany was ready for an honorable peace. She was ready to make concessions in view of the enemy's apparent military advantage. But there was no reason for unconditional surrender.

Through August and most of September the government made no move for peace. On September 10th Hindenburg came over to Ludendorff's side and asked for a parley with the enemy through a neutral power "without delay." On the 17th came a smashing Allied attack in Macedonia and in the next ten days the entire Bulgarian front collapsed. On the 28th Bulgaria surrendered on terms which brought the Allies to the Danube. Before the end of September British successes in Palestine and Syria completed the iron ring round the Central Powers on the west, south, and east.

From the 1st of October the appeals to the government from the army took on the color of panic, Ludendorff saying, among other things, that the army "could not wait forty-eight hours." But the ministers persisted in their delay. Prince Max von Baden who headed the new "popular" government still wanted to "wait a week and not give the idea that military collapse had forced the change toward democracy."

So, in these desperate weeks there piled up on the record a mass of alibis for all the parties to the German dispute. Ludendorff could say that he had warned the government in time to salvage German honor. The successive chancellors, Hertling and Max, could say that Ludendorff, broken in nerves, exaggerating the military weakness, had forced the government to capitulate.

But Ludendorff's "breakdown" did not prevent considerable concentrated thinking on the approach to peace. The enemy must be made to speak. "Would he talk of conciliation or violence?" Ludendorff balanced the question. Looking toward Lloyd George and Clemenceau, he saw only violence.

Having shied away, therefore, from Britain and France, the general took an old paper from his files. Here were terms of peace stated "in the most solemn form imaginable." Their author "and the great country he represented, must feel themselves bound in honor by these declarations."

Ludendorff brought the old paper to the attention of the responsible men in the government and told them they must go to its author to ask for peace. In the first week in October his argument prevailed. The government leaders, reading words which, in January, 1918, had provoked laughter and scorn throughout Germany as "no terms at all," based a solemn peace note upon these Fourteen Points and sent it, via Switzerland, across the Atlantic to the President of the United States.

5. Vote for What?

THE Blackstone Hotel on the edge of the Loop is one of Chicago's finest, and the well-dressed diners-out on a May evening in 1918 indulged in no more than a polite and casual glance as a much cartooned figure strode into the great dining room, accepted the excited attentions of the head waiter, and was led, alone, to a little table on the far side of the room. It was natural that Colonel Roosevelt should stay at the Blackstone, though it may have occurred to a few that it was odd to find him dining alone.

But a few minutes later the calm acceptance of the Colonel in their midst, which had hardly caused a ripple in the quiet hum of conversation and the tinkle of thin glassware and brittle laughter, changed to dumb, open-mouthed wonder. Here was something frankly to be stared at!

Colonel Roosevelt, although deaf in one ear, heard the crashing silence which had suddenly settled on the electrified room. He stuffed into his mouth the generous bite of T-bone poised on his fork, and turned.

He stiffened in momentary surprise, then flung down his napkin and rose. The only other living ex-President was descending upon him.

No caricaturist had ever shown more teeth in Colonel Roosevelt's mouth; none had ever shown William Howard Taft with a more genial grin! The handshake was one to shake the foundations of the building. Mr. Taft's left hand flew to Mr. Roosevelt's right shoulder; Mr. Roosevelt pounded Mr. Taft on the back.

The stillness of the room gave way to a resounding burst of cheers and applause. The two men, startled, looked at each other and smiled and bowed to the other Republicans in the room. Then the Colonel, with elaborate pantomime, indicated the vacant chair opposite him, and both men sat 'neath hovering waiters and were watched by frankly fascinated eyes. Out of nowhere reporters unaccountably appeared, and men with cameras and flash powder. But Taft and Roosevelt waved them away and continued an animated conversation.

It did not last very long—Colonel Roosevelt soon rushed off to take a nine o'clock train for Des Moines, for he was on a speaking tour. Taft received reporters later in his room but gave them little satisfaction. He told them the Colonel looked fit after his illness; on the way to the train T.R. was close-mouthed too, but "Taft looked bully!"

For six long years the two foremost Republicans had not been on speaking terms, and the party certainly had not prospered by their coolness.

The reasons were long dead. What need to remember that Teddy Roosevelt virtually single-handed made William Howard Taft his successor in the White House and then proceeded to disagree with most of what he did there? Best forgotten now was the Colonel's decision to split the party by running independently in 1912. Why recall the victory of Wilson or the fact that T.R. drew more votes as a Progressive than Taft as a regular Republican? And the words, the biting, ugly, sour words of the campaign, friend against friend—these are lost as soon as the votes are counted.

Yet these two round and jolly men had refused to forget, and Republicans could be Taft men or Roosevelt men, or, if they would, be so unimaginative as to be Hughes men. The split which had knocked the party out had lasted far too long. Now the party was pulling itself together. Suddenly awake after the count of nine, there was realization, fear of the tenth count, determination to get up and slug.

The meeting in the Blackstone had, needless to say, not been wholly accidental. Taft had opened negotiations. He had done it in the smoothest, most gentlemanly way possible. Roosevelt lay ill with the abscesses that had given him so much trouble. Taft sent him a telegram, wishing him speedy and complete recovery. You could do that much in sportsmanship even for an implacable foe.

T.R. was delighted. He wired thanks for the good wishes, and as soon as he was on his feet again he wrote Mr. Taft a letter, with more thanks, enclosing a speech he was going to make.

The mend made in the Blackstone dining room was a strong one. Only a few weeks later at an unofficial Republican state convention at Saratoga, New York, the reunited friends sounded the Republican keynote for the year. Taft was willing to grant Wilson's ability to make a fine speech and to state lofty aims, but gave him little credit for administrative ability, which he, Mr. Taft, regarded as extremely important. Roosevelt gave the President even less.

The gist of the message of the two ex-Presidents was clear: Elect a Republican Congress this year. And during the next six months the attention of the country was divided, shifting back and forth between President Wilson's diplomatic duel with the leaders of the Central Powers and his political duel with his opponents at home.

2

During the summer Dr. Thomas Garrigue Masaryk, of Prague, obtained in Washington what he needed above all things. He had traveled all over America, held meetings in Chicago, Pittsburgh, Cleveland, and other cities. And everywhere, among the American people, those of Czech or Slovak origin and those of other origins, he had found friends and helpers.

Finally he won the support of Woodrow Wilson for the Republic he proposed to set up as soon as the war was over. He had convinced the American president that the "autonomy" mentioned in the tenth of the Fourteen Points was not enough for the needs of the Czechs and Slovaks, and that a new nation must be formed. In September Wilson recognized the independence of Czechoslovakia, and in October he wrote the Austrian government that, in view of this recognition, the Fourteen Points were no longer entirely applicable as a basis for peace between the United States and Austria.

So Czechoslovakia was born in Washington.

But Masaryk was under no illusion that his task was over. Nor was his responsibility limited to making arrangements for a new government at the sad and ancient city of Prague, and the necessary diplomatic negotiations in connection with his homesick countrymen along the Trans-Siberian railway. For Czechoslovakia, which could never be a major world power, must depend upon statesmanship and understandings with its neighbors to succeed in intrigue-laden Europe. The welfare of all was essential to the welfare of each.

That is why, on October 22nd, Masaryk sat in Independence Hall in Philadelphia. The occasion was a meeting of a minor league of nations he himself had fathered—the "Democratic Mid-European Union." Before him were representatives of all the neighbors of Czechoslovakia—men from Lithuania, the Ukraine, Rumania, Albania, Estonia, Finland, even from Syria. There were Ugro-Russians, Carpatho-Russians, Letts, Italian Irredentists, unredeemed Greeks and Poles.

There were some differences to be resolved. The Italian

delegate denounced the Pact of Rome, which had been an effort to patch up Italian-Jugoslav disputes, and seemed to feel that nothing else was important. The Jugoslavs wanted only a repudiation of the Treaty of London of April, 1915.

But in the end, all signed the joint declaration—a Declaration of Independence for the peoples of Central Europe. And a new Liberty Bell, cast for the occasion, rang out in Independence Hall. Masaryk in America had built another bastion, a diplomatic one, for his country. The United States had been host to the refugee founders of the little league of nations.

3

Early in March the state of Wisconsin was engaged in a bitter row over its own Senator and his opposition to the war. There was a seventeen-hour debate in the Assembly over a resolution previously passed in the upper house. Finally passed by a vote of 53 to 32, the resolution read in part:

The people of the State of Wisconsin always have stood and always will stand squarely behind the national Government in all things which are essential to bring the present war to a successful end, and we condemn Senator Robert La Follette and all others who have failed to support our government in matters vital to the winning of the war, and we denounce any attitude or utterances of theirs which have tended to incite sedition among the people of our country and to injure Wisconsin's fair name before the free people of the world.

As everyone knew, Wisconsin had a large German-American population. As everyone knew, the state also had a great many Socialists. And both these overlapping groups were opposed to war and behind Senator La Follette. The resolution was a slap at Germans, Socialists, and La Follette. But it was more than this. Politically it cleared the way for the

nomination of Irvine R. Lenroot, straight Republican, to fill
the vacant seat of the late Senator Paul Oscar Husting. Lenroot was elected on April 2, 1918. His democratic opponent
was a prominent lawyer named Joseph E. Davies,* a good
party worker and a staunch supporter of the administration.
In fact, Mr. Wilson had written him publicly expressing the
hope that he would be elected, for the President had no
liking for and no faith in Irvine Lenroot. And he wanted
men in the Senate who would support him. It seemed important.

Lenroot's election was not entirely unexpected. He had
demonstrated his political strength in the state, and Mr.
Davies had not. Nevertheless to many Wilson supporters it
was a bad omen; a measure of the President's dwindling
influence in the Middle West.

The Chicago *Tribune* led the anti-Wilson, anti-English,
anti-League forces in the Middle West, and it was a power
to be reckoned with. Its former publisher, Medill McCormick, was tired of the House of Representatives. Perhaps
encouraged by Lenroot's victory, he decided to try for the
Senate seat held by a much more decorative gentleman, James
Hamilton Lewis. In this he was ably aided by his wife, old
Marc Hanna's daughter Ruth. He counted on the influence
of the *Tribune* and on the increasing isolationist feeling in
Illinois to elect him. Other factors entered during the summer. Booming war industry had brought thousands of
Negroes from the cotton fields of the South to the war
plants of the northern cities. There had been race riots in
half a dozen cities, but the most violent had been in Mc-
Cormick's own state. The Chicago riots were serious; but the
carnage in East St. Louis, Illinois, was even more frightful.
Both were politically significant.

* Later United States Ambassador to Russia.

White industrial workers who feared the influx of Negroes in many cases blamed the administration and the war for bringing them north. On the other side, the Negroes were traditionally Republican if they voted at all. So both opposing groups could be counted on to vote for a Republican, not a Democratic, candidate. And the anti-administration press of Illinois did little to smooth out the troubled race relations of the state.

Racial antagonism was hot and furious in other places as well—Philadelphia and Washington had race riots during the war, and so did several smaller cities. But in Illinois it affected directly the national political picture. . . .

Not local and nowhere decisive, but not negligible either, was another political development of March, 1918. Many months earlier, the Socialist party of the United States, meeting in the German-American stronghold (and to some extent the Socialist stronghold) of St. Louis, had issued a manifesto declaring the war against Germany "the most unjust in history." The party had opposed Wilson's foreign policy bitterly and openly. It wanted no part of this imperialist war, neither side of which was fighting for what it regarded as the good of humanity.

Since then two things had happened. One was the Treaty of Brest-Litovsk, which put the Bolshevik revolution in Russia at the mercy of Germany; the other, President Wilson's Fourteen Points speech, which took imperialism out of the war.

Twelve hundred Socialists and other radicals gathered in Aeolian Hall in New York on March 2nd to cheer the name of Woodrow Wilson and to adopt, almost unanimously, a new resolution: a demand that all Socialists in America unite behind the President and the war as the only means of saving democracy from the German autocrats. Now radicals of all shades must unite in a solid front, must let bygones be bygones, must support the war. "Socialists everywhere," said the resolution, "conscious of their full duty toward their brothers in Russia, must place themselves now in the vanguard of a holy crusade against the mad dogs of Europe."

Officially the Socialist party never adopted this resolution. It split instead, and only part of it backed the war. But its partial support of President Wilson gave new ammunition to his critics, who could and thereafter did call him "radical, socialist"—and worse. He had not sought Socialist support, and the Russian Soviets themselves had been notably cool toward him. It hurt nevertheless. And in New York it forced both major parties into an agreement on coalition candidates, who managed to defeat the two Socialist Representatives in Congress: Meyer London and Morris Hillquit.

4

In still torrid Washington shirt-sleeved members of the House Ways and Means Committee sweated over a new revenue bill to help pay the costs of the war. It had to be a big one, that they knew. Chairman Kitchin and the rest of the committee had very nearly come to an agreement, after weeks of tempestuous hearings, on a flat normal income tax rate of 12 per cent after exemptions. Surtaxes too would be stiff, and there were plenty of other new levies, many of which, as politicians, the committee members could regard only with trepidation. Yet more taxes there must be, and none was likely to be popular.

Now a big revenue bill just before election is a painful thing and not one to make for harmony. Republicans, wanting the public to see the actual terms of the bill and to know how much they would have to pay for the war, were in a hurry to get it through. So when the Treasury Department, on the eve of the bill's completion in committee, sent over a list of sixty administrative recommendations, all new and most of them complicated, there were immediate and indignant howls. The administration was charged with delaying the bill, trying to stall until after the election, playing politics. For all these suggestions would have to be considered carefully, and some of them at least would be written into the bill. In fact, the longer the committee studied them, the clearer it became that many, perhaps most of them, were reasonable suggestions which could not be brushed aside. And the more reasonable they proved, the more indignant the opposition became; the more time it took to make the bill foolproof, the more bitter the charges of "politics."

The debate on the tax bill seemed to take the lid off politics. Democrats, exasperated, felt that there was no legitimate function of the government which could be carried on without bringing blasts from Republicans. They were damned if they delayed putting through a tax bill; they would be damned if they rushed it through without adequate study. In October came the tremendous impact of the fourth Liberty Loan drive, and Will Hays and other Republican leaders issued patriotic statements calling on all Republicans to forget politics and work for the drive. They all did, and the drive was an enormous success, but there were whispers. Why had the Treasury Department chosen this particular period for the drive? Was it because the election was coming? Was this why Woodrow Wilson, with Rear Admiral Grayson, Brigadier General George R. Dyer, and the faithful Tumulty, had walked at the head of New York's "Liberty Day" parade, three and a half miles from 72nd Street to Washington Square? In rare good humor and with springy step the whole way, the President had got a terrific ovation. His hike sold bonds; did it perhaps do more than this, and if so, could it be called a political act?

Later there was something else which, for the Republicans

at least, complicated the campaign in New York and many other eastern cities. This was the epidemic of influenza. Two hundred thousand coolies from North China were supposed to have brought it to France when they came to do war work; a few hundred returning soldiers and travelers had brought it across the Atlantic. Within three months nearly one-quarter of the entire population had caught the disease; over 400,000 died of it. No one knew how to prevent it or how to cure it. But one of the methods used in efforts to control it was prohibition of public gatherings. Theaters were closed, and schools, and even factories and stores and business offices. Naturally there could be no political rallies in the cities worst affected; though there were meetings where the plague had not struck so hard. This meant that campaign methods had to be changed. There were more political billboards and newspaper advertisements; more activity than usual by magazine and newspaper writers working for the national committees.

In France the German hordes step by step were moving back, hotly pursued, though at a distance, by Colonel Theodore Roosevelt, who proposed to drive them clear back to Berlin, no matter what the cost, and who feared that Woodrow Wilson would not drive so far. Indefatigable in his prosecution of the war, though in delicate health, the Colonel went to Springfield, Illinois, there to make a fighting speech at the Illinois Centennial Exposition. (In Illinois, it will be recalled, there was a crucial fight for a Senate seat: Medill McCormick and the Chicago *Tribune* against James Hamilton Lewis, the pleasant Democrat with the fine haberdashery and the bifurcated beard.) The band played and the people cheered.

"We are not internationalists," the Colonel shouted to an enthusiastic crowd. "We are American nationalists! . . . Let us remember this when the peace comes. Don't trust the pacifists; they are the enemies of righteousness. Don't trust the internationalists; they are the enemies of nationalism and Americanism.

"Therefore, by next spring we should have thousands of our own field guns and scores of thousands of our own airplanes at the front, and an enormous ship tonnage in which to ferry across the ocean so many troops that by April we may have 4,000,000 trained fighting men at the front. . . ."

In opening the fourth Liberty Loan campaign on September 27, 1918, President Wilson further clarified his international aims. He made five points about the peace and the League of Nations:

"First, the impartial justice meted out *must* involve no discrimination between those to whom we wish to be just and those to whom we do not wish to be just. It *must be* a justice that plays no favorites and knows no standard but the equal rights of the several peoples concerned;

"Second, no special or separate interests of any single nation or any group of nations *can be* made the basis of any part of the settlement which is not consistent with the common interest of all;

"Third, there can be no leagues or alliances or special covenants and understandings within the general and common family of the League of Nations;

"Fourth, and more specifically, there can be no special, selfish economic combinations within the League and no employment of any form of economic boycott or exclusion except as the power of economic penalty by exclusion from the markets of the world may be vested in the League of Nations itself as a means of discipline and control;

"Fifth, all international agreements and treaties of every

kind must be made known in their entirety to the rest of the world."

Now came the note that Ludendorff had insisted be sent:

Berlin, October 3, 1918

The German Government requests the President of the United States of America to take steps for the restoration of peace, to notify all belligerents of this request, and to invite them to delegate plenipotentiaries for the purpose of taking up negotiations. The German Government accepts as a basis for the peace negotiations, the program laid down by the President of the United States in his message to Congress of January 8, 1918, and in his subsequent pronouncements, particularly in his address of September 27, 1918.

In order to avoid further bloodshed the German Government requests to bring about the immediate conclusion of an armistice on land, on water and in the air.

MAX
Prince of Baden, Imperial Chancellor

In Washington the President, seeing that Max's note referred to the Fourteen Points merely as the *basis* for negotiations, had no intention of being trapped, but instead carefully laid a subtle trap for his opponents. "Does the Imperial Chancellor mean," he inquired in a reply, "that the Imperial German Government *accepts* * the terms laid down by the President . . . and that its object in entering into discussions would be only to agree upon the practical details of their application?" Further, he wished to know, did the Chancellor speak for the war lords of Germany, or for the German people themselves?

At Oyster Bay, Colonel Theodore Roosevelt dictated a statement to the press:

* Our italics.

I regret greatly that President Wilson has entered into these negotiations, and . . . I earnestly hope that the President will instantly send back word that we demand an unconditional surrender and that we refuse to compound a felony by discussing terms with the felons.

It is deeply discreditable to us that Bulgaria should have been forced to surrender to our Allies, while we remained neutral, and it is even more discreditable to us that we did not long ago declare war on Turkey. . . .

I must earnestly hope that the Senate of the United States and all other persons competent to speak for the Amercian people will emphatically repudiate the so-called fourteen points and the various similar utterances of the President.

These fourteen points are couched in such vague language that many of them may mean anything or nothing and have a merely rhetorical value, while others are absolutely mischievous. . . .

At 8:30 precisely on the evening of October 12th the President and Mrs. Wilson arrived at the 39th Street entrance to the Metropolitan Opera House in New York. It was an Italian celebration and program, for the benefit of the Queen Margherita Fund for the Blinded Soldiers of Italy.

Members of the Presidential party were Admiral Grayson, Joseph P. Tumulty, Margaret Wilson, Colonel and Mrs. House, and the Italian Ambassador and his wife. They made their way to the J. P. Morgan box which had been generously decorated with flags and bunting. At the President's appearance, the audience rose and cheered, and the orchestra played "Hail to the Chief," following it directly with the "Star-Spangled Banner" and the Italian national anthem.

Tumulty was outside the box speaking to one of the Secret Service men when two reporters rushed in and handed him the text of the new German note. Tumulty took it in to the

President who, watched by many in the audience, read it gravely, whispered to Tumulty, and sat back to listen to Enrico Caruso, who had begun to sing "Over There." Tumulty stepped out of the box.

"No comment at this time," he said to the newsmen, but he and Colonel House made their way to the director's office and telephoned Washington.

The text of the note was as follows:

Berlin, October 12, 1918

In reply to the question of the President of the United States of America the German Government hereby declares:

The German Government has accepted the principles laid down by President Wilson in his addresses as the foundations of a permanent peace of justice. Consequently its object in entering into discussions would be only to agree upon practical details of the application of these terms.

The German Government believes that the Governments of the Powers associated with the United States also accept the position taken by President Wilson in his addresses.

The German Government, in accordance with the Austro-Hungarian Government for the purpose of bringing about an armistice, declares itself ready to comply with the propositions of the President in regard to evacuation. The German Government leaves it to the President to bring about the meeting of a mixed commission whose duty it would be to make the necessary arrangements concerning the evacuation.

The present German Government which has undertaken the responsibility for this step towards peace has been formed by conferences and in agreement with the great majority of the Reichstag. The Chancellor, supported in all of his actions by the will of this majority, speaks in the name of the German Government and of the German people.

SOLF
Secretary of State for Foreign Affairs

"The catch is obvious," remarked Colonel House the next morning, when he and the President were discussing what reply should be made. "It's in the sentence about the 'mixed commission' whose duty it would be to make the necessary arrangements concerning the evacuation."

"Yes," said the President, "they would drag on the negotiations long enough to let Ludendorff pull the army together and get ready for more fighting. It won't do, of course. Yet I think we can prevent that by laying down definite terms for evacuation through the military leaders. It's their problem really, not mine."

"But no 'mixed commission.'"

"Of course not. Yet there must be a way to handle it. The whole thing is like a maze—if you go in at the right entrance you reach the center, but if you take the wrong turning, you have to go back and start all over. I've done the same thing in making extemporaneous speeches—started off on the wrong line and had to flounder out as best I could. And I'm still sure I'm right—if Germany is really beaten, she will accept any terms; if she isn't, I don't want to make terms with her."

"I think she is beaten," said House. "But our object now is to disarm her completely, and without unnecessary loss of life."

The Allied armies were getting farther and farther from their railheads. In the territory that had been occupied by the Germans railroads had been wrecked and must be completely rebuilt. The British Field Marshal, Sir Douglas Haig, knowing the British armies had lost heavily in the drive, knowing the French army was exhausted and that the American Army, though it had fought magnificently, had not been entirely ready when the great battles began, believed the drive could not go on much longer. He seemed afraid that the Germans might not accept an armistice. And indeed it was clear that, barring collapse of the German armed forces, the drive must soon slow down. It might take months to get it going again, and in months anything could happen.

Wilson's note was sent on the afternoon of October 14th. It rejected the proposal of a "mixed commission" to negotiate terms of evacuation. This problem, it said, must be left to the military command of the Allies. The armistice terms would include "absolutely satisfactory safeguards and guarantees of the maintenance of the present military supremacy of the armies of the United States and of the Allies in the field." Submarines were to cease their operations against passenger ships at once, and before the armistice could be signed at all. Arbitrary power must be abolished in Germany (which was taken to mean that the Kaiser must abdicate).

Of this note André Tardieu later wrote:

In a single page the whole poor scaffolding of the German Great General Staff is overthrown. The armistice and peace are not to be means of delaying a disaster and of preparing revenge. On the main question itself the reply must be Yes or No! If it is no, war will continue. . . . If it is yes, the military capitulation must be immediate and complete. . . .

Out in New Mexico, where a prosperous Republican rancher named Albert B. Fall was running for re-election to the Senate opposed by a Wilsonian Democrat (and an enterprising if hopeless Socialist), the word came that the President opposed the re-election of Mr. Fall, and opposed it in no mild or uncertain terms. Promptly came a letter from Colonel Theodore Roosevelt to that same Fall: "I earnestly hope the good people of New Mexico will return you to the Senate with practical unanimity."

In Michigan, where Truman Newberry, the Republican Senatorial candidate, had spent $175,000 in the primary and over a million afterwards, and where his opponent Henry

Ford had carefully spent no money and perhaps shrewdly made practically no speeches, except to say somewhat sulkily that he was running because the President had ordered him to do so, the new-old friends Taft and Roosevelt issued a joint appeal to the state's voters to support Newberry. It was probably the only time that two ex-Presidents have ever united to support a Senatorial candidate, and it is also probably true that no man ever spent quite as much money to get into the Senate; or ever got such a bad reception when he arrived.

On October 20th the German Government agreed to all of the President's conditions for an armistice.

Colonel Roosevelt immediately sent identical telegrams to Senators Lodge, Poindexter and Hiram Johnson, saying:

I EARNESTLY HOPE THAT ON BEHALF OF THE AMERICAN PEOPLE THE SENATE WILL DECLARE AGAINST THE ADOPTION IN THEIR ENTIRETY OF THE FOURTEEN POINTS OF PRESIDENT WILSON'S ADDRESS OF LAST JANUARY AS OFFERING A BASIS FOR A PEACE SATISFACTORY TO THE UNITED STATES. . . . SUCH A PEACE WOULD REPRESENT NOT THE UNCONDITIONAL SURRENDER OF GERMANY BUT THE CONDITIONAL SURRENDER OF THE UNITED STATES.

Peace was in the air, but Woodrow Wilson knew that everything for which he was fighting, everything for which he had led this country into war, was balanced on a knife blade. He had told the world America was fighting for a new kind of peace; a peace for all time; a democratic peace. That it would not be easily obtained, but would be bitterly opposed, was clear; that it was worth every ounce of his own energy, he was certain.

The President called in Tumulty. He had the habit of

asking Tumulty's advice on political matters. The secretary had been in politics since his Jersey City boyhood.

"Tumulty," said the President, "I don't like the look of the fall elections. If a Republican Congress is elected, as Hays and Roosevelt and all the rest are asking, it will mean repudiation of my leadership. Just now that must not happen. It would handicap me too much in Europe. It might even mean that a good peace would be impossible. If the Senate gets up on its hind legs everything may be lost."

"What are you going to do, Governor?"

"Do you think I should ask for a Democratic Congress?"

"No. At least not quite that way. Why not have some prominent man write you a letter pointing out the speeches Republicans are making, and asking what you think of them?"

"I don't want to answer their speeches."

"No, certainly not. I should avoid any appearance of answering them. The more indifferent you appear, the more bitter their speeches are likely to get, and by the time you are ready to say something—"

"They will have hung themselves? Well, maybe. But I want to take this somehow or other to the people. I want it to be clear to them what this election means."

Tumulty pointed out that as President, Wilson could not indulge in the kind of appeal Republican leaders had been making. He would have to be much more tactful to avoid resentment on the part of the voters.

"There's something else," he said. "Letters have been pouring in, from Democratic candidates all over the country, asking you to endorse them. You've seen most of them and I put a list on your desk a couple of days ago. You've already expressed yourself on Ford, and against Fall, and a few others. But you obviously can't take them up one by one.

That's why I thought you might do it all at once, with a letter. It has to be indirect, and very tactful."

"I wonder if it does have to be indirect. How about a straightforward appeal to the people to support me? That used to get pretty good results when we were back in Jersey—" He smiled at his old political assistant. "And I firmly believe that I can rely on the people. They've never failed me yet. I don't think they ever failed any statesman who was right and who got his facts across to them."

In the end the President decided on his direct appeal to the people. He knew he had the largest groups behind him and had had since before the war, when his domestic policies had been so well received. He was confident yet somehow regretful that any appeal had to be made.

Tumulty was still unconvinced, and said so. Yet he knew that other presidents had made almost exactly the same appeal. Lincoln in the midst of the Civil War had said, "It is best not to swap horses while crossing the river." McKinley during the Spanish-American War had asked for a Congress to support him.

On a sudden impulse Tumulty rushed to a bookcase, and thumbed through a volume. He read a part of a speech made by President Theodore Roosevelt in 1906:

To change the leadership and organization of the House at this time means to bring confusion to those who have been successfully engaged in the steady working out of a great and comprehensive scheme for the betterment of our social, industrial, and civic conditions. Such a change would substitute a purposeless confusion, a violent and hurtful oscillation between the positions of the extreme radical and the extreme reactionary for the present orderly progress along the lines of a carefully thought out policy.

The President's mind was made up. He sat down at his typewriter and carefully composed a message to the American people. He wrote:

My Fellow Countrymen:

The Congressional elections are at hand. They occur in the most critical period our country has ever faced or is likely to face in our time. If you have approved of my leadership and wish me to continue to be your unembarrassed spokesman in affairs at home and abroad, I earnestly beg that you will express yourself unmistakably to that effect by returning a Democratic majority to both the Senate and the House of Representatives. I am your servant and will accept your judgment without cavil, but my power to administer the great trust assigned me by the Constitution would be seriously impaired should your judgment be adverse, and I must frankly tell you so because so many critical issues depend upon your verdict. No scruple of taste must in grim times like these be allowed to stand in the way of speaking the plain truth.

I have no thought of suggesting that any political party is paramount in matters of patriotism. I feel too keenly the sacrifices which have been made in this war by all our citizens, irrespective of party affiliations, to harbor such an idea. I mean only that the difficulties and delicacies of our present task are of a sort that makes it imperatively necessary that the nation should give its undivided support to the Government under a unified leadership, and that a Republican Congress would divide the leadership.

The leaders of the minority in the present Congress have unquestionably been pro-war, but they have been anti-Administration. At almost every turn, since we entered the war, they have sought to take the choice of policy and the conduct of the war out of my hands and put it under the control of instrumentalities of their own choosing. This is no time either for divided counsel or for divided leadership. Unity of command is as necessary now in civil action as it is upon the field of battle. If the control of the House and Senate should be taken away from the party now in power, an opposing majority could assume control of legislation and oblige all action to be taken amidst contest and obstruction.

The return of a Republican majority to either House of the Congress would, moreover, certainly be interpreted on the other side of the water as a repudiation of my leadership. Spokesmen of the Republican party are urging you to elect a Republican Congress in order to back up and support the President, but even if they should in this way impose upon some credulous voters on this side of the water, they would impose on no one on the other side. It is well understood there as well as here that the Republican leaders desire not so much to support the President as to control him. The peoples of the Allied countries with whom we are associated against Germany are quite familiar with the significance of elections. They would find it very difficult to believe that the voters of the United States had chosen to support their President by electing to the Congress a majority controlled by those who are not in fact in sympathy with the attitude and action of the Administration.

I need not tell you, my fellow countrymen, that I am asking your support not for my own sake or for the sake of a political party, but for the sake of the nation itself, in order that its inward unity of purpose may be evident to all the world. In ordinary times I would not feel at liberty to make such an appeal to you. In ordinary times divided counsels can be endured without permanent hurt to the country. But these are not ordinary times. If in these critical days it is your wish to sustain me with undivided minds, I beg that you will say so in a way which it will not be possible to misunderstand either here at home or among your associates on the other side of the sea. I submit my difficulties and my hopes to you.

The message was made public on October 25th, and was published in the morning newspapers of October 26th. It had not been public an hour before the passage leading to the office of Senator Henry Cabot Lodge echoed with footsteps and rapid conversation. And in the office for three hours, Lodge and other Republican leaders discussed strategy.

"Six weeks ago," Senator New began, "Wilson promised the Democratic National Committee to ask for a Democratic

Congress. *But*—and this is the point—he agreed to do it *only* in case of an emergency."

"That means this is an emergency—they must have decided the election is as good as lost," said Reed Smoot.

"It certainly gives us a wonderful opening," said Congressman Gillett, who headed the House Republican campaign committee.

"What we want to do now," said Senator Lodge, "is to get out a very carefully worded statement taking advantage of this incredibly stupid move. We're the injured, righteous party here. Wilson has practically accused us of treason—of obstructing the war. I think we've got him, all right."

The statement was composed and rewritten and rearranged. For three hours the conferees labored. The final version read (in part):

Some time ago, the President said "politics is adjourned." Now, in the closing days of the campaign—delayed by the united efforts of all parties for the Liberty Loan—now, when all public meetings have been given up owing to the influenza epidemic, the President sends out a direct party appeal calling upon his countrymen to vote for Democrats because they are Democrats without any reference to whether such Democrats have been or are in favor of war measures and have a war record which deserves support. . . .

Republicans are loyal enough to fight and die, as they are doing by the thousands; loyal enough to take up great loans and pay enormous taxes; loyal enough to furnish important men at no salary on some of the great war boards in Washington. But they are not loyal enough, in the President's opinion, to be trusted with any share in the Government of the country. . . .

A few days later Germany's reply to Wilson's latest note arrived:

Berlin, October 27, 1918

The German Government has taken cognizance of the answer of the President of the United States. The President is aware of the far-reaching changes which have been carried out and are still being carried out in the German constitutional structure, and that peace negotiations are being conducted by a People's Government in whose hands rests, both actually and constitutionally, the power to make the deciding conclusions. The military powers are also subject to it. The German Government now awaits proposals for an armistice, which shall be the first step towards a just peace, as the President has described it in his proclamation.

SOLF

Secretary of State for Foreign Affairs

President Wilson made no proposals for an armistice; nor did he call together any meeting to agree upon terms. He turned the entire matter over to the military authorities in France.

In New York, at Republican Headquarters at 452 Fifth Avenue, Will Hays, hearing the keynote sounded in Washington, was speaking for his party:

"A more ungracious, more unjust, more wanton, more mendacious accusation was never made by the most reckless stump orator, much less by a President of the United States, for partisan purposes. It is an insult, not only to every loyal Republican in Congress; but to every loyal Republican in the land. It fully merits the resentment which rightfully and surely will find expression at the polls. . . .

"Mr. Wilson wants only rubber stamps, his rubber stamps, in Congress. . . .

"This is a call to all loyal Republicans, proud in their patriotism, to stand by their country and their candidates and to let the world know that it spurns autocracy no less at home than abroad and will uphold her allies in whatever reparation they may exact for the frightful outrages inflicted upon them by the accursed Huns. We are fighting in France to make certain forever that men may have the right to govern themselves. Here where we have that right we shall exercise it now and always. America was created for that very privilege. America will not be denied it now. America will answer with her vote."

William Howard Taft and Charles Evans Hughes joined in the growing clamor, and finally, at a gigantic rally in Carnegie Hall, Colonel Roosevelt spoke for more than two hours, screaming that Wilson was a cheap politician, and even comparing him to German leaders. "He does not ask for loyalty to the Nation. He asks only for support of himself!"

Austria surrendered on November 3rd; the capitulation of Germany was clearly but a matter of days. The election came on November 5th. It was a decisive defeat for President Wilson. His opponents, controlling both houses of Congress, had him, had the future of the peace of the world, in their hands.

6. Madelon

ON the night of November 1, 1918, the captain of an American machine gun company lay on his belly in the Bois des Loges north of the Argonne and listened to the whispers above his head. The whispers, coming in quick succession, told him much about the enemy's direction and range, for the whispers came from bullets and the bullets came from German Maxims. The captain pressed his body into the earth and turned down his heels.

So this, he thought, is the beaten enemy. Two weeks ago they had told him the German was on the run. It was, they said, only a matter of a day or two. Fourteen days had followed in which his company and the infantry battalion to which it was attached had hung on along the Grandpré–Saint-Juvin road without advancing an inch. Day after day the enemy's 77's had raked the lines, night after night gas shells had filled the valley below with phosgene vapor. Casualties had exhausted the stretchers, wounded Americans were left to die where they fell, and American dead lined the road back into the Argonne forest. Yet the rumors persisted—tomorrow . . . tomorrow they will break. They had already broken at the core.

Last night the report had been definite. Resistance was over. The last battle of the last war was coming to an end.

This morning the whole American army had gone over the top looking like a picture in a Sunday supplement. The sun on the advancing waves had glinted on the bayonets. The infantry major had called out to the captain that it was all over but the shouting, that the advance was going to be a "picnic."

Then they had struck this black patch of woods and the whispering bullets from what seemed like a hundred guns had slithered between the trees and the major's battalion and the captain's company had been forced to its bellies to wait. Through the afternoon and evening they had waited under the cracks, whines, and whispers. The captain thought he would like to see the major then, to ask when the picnic began.

But he could see nothing, not even the messenger who wriggled alongside of him. Into his ear, the orderly called his name.

"Yes," he said.

"Orders from Battalion P.C., sir. A counterattack is expected. You will echelon your guns for defense at midnight."

The captain put out his hand and touched the messenger. The boy was shaking.

"Yes," the captain said. "It's cold. Stick around. I'll need you. My watch gives us fifteen minutes to go."

Echelon defenses. That would be what was called the "sacrifice" defense he had learned about at the school back in quiet Clamecy. Machine guns arranged in a V-shape to hold the enemy infantry back while our own retreated. A suicide formation. It had been easy there at school on the flat field in the sunlight.

The captain gave the orderly some simple directions about finding the sergeants in the dark. Then he talked about dairy farming in the Cherry Valley for the orderly was an "up-state" man too.

"It's time," said the orderly.

"We're late," said the captain, looking at the pale dial on his wrist. He got up and his helmet hit a branch and rang like a bell. He cursed the helmet and was suddenly aware of the silence all about him. The cracks and the whispers had stopped. For four hours, he moved his men and guns about in the woods. When the guns were placed, orders came to pick them up again and advance.

The captain and his men and the infantry battalion advanced for three days. Not a shot was fired against them. They found the enemy's guns—only a handful but perfectly placed—abandoned by gunners who had escaped at midnight on horseback. They found masses of equipment, ammunition, clothing, officers' fine bedding rolls, maps, even field glasses.

Then they came upon deserted barracks which told a puzzling story. On the walls the German soldiers had scrawled obscenities about their officers and their government. Officers' quarters had been methodically, grossly polluted by the men.

On the long advance when the deployed American waves moved so fast that they outran their supplies, the captain tried to figure out the strange sequence of events. For two weeks the enemy had put up as brilliant a rear-guard action as he could imagine. They had covered a full retreat with a few Maxim guns. Yet, at the end, still in good order, the soldiers had cynically revealed to their conquerors their own total moral decay.

The captain spoke about it to the major.

"They're heroes," he said. "And yet they hate themselves."

"They're Germans," said the major.

"Yes, they're Germans. But are the Germans really then a different brand of cat?"

2

On the 8th of November, the Commander-in-Chief of the Allied Armies lay in a special car on a special train and listened to the rain on the roof. He had hardly slept in the night; now in the dawn he was fully awake and thinking.

His thought moved about a focal point, coming back to it again and again impatiently. The focus was the fact that men were being killed too late—after the necessity. Every minute a man died or was wounded somewhere along the 200-mile front—the front which was his personal concern—and the whole urgent concentration of his action from now on must be to lessen the number of minutes. Now that the end was in sight he must force it with all the ruthlessness with which, in the last few weeks, he had ordered the counterpoint of the attack, sparing no man, admitting no fatigue. This time the objective was a word, *armistice*, to be forced on this immediate interval of the enemy's weakness.

Since he had come into command Marshal Foch had encountered many advices, suggestions, arguments from the commanders whom he co-ordinated. Pershing had even refused, at times, to dispose his army according to the Marshal's plan. Pétain had offered slow, pedestrian moves at urgent moments and for a while stuck stubbornly to his theory of limited objectives. Clemenceau, using his constitutional office as head of the French army, came near to ordering Foch to appeal to President Wilson for the dismissal of Pershing. Foch had steered a straight course through these counsels and none of them had caused him to slow his plans. He had listened and gone on.

When the question of the armistice had come before him he had given simple answers to the doubts or fears of Allied statesmen and soldiers. "The conditions," said Sir Douglas Haig, "should be moderate, including only evacuation of Belgium, France, and Alsace-Lorraine, the repatriation of citizens, and the return of captured rolling stock." "Do you want to leave," said Foch, "the obstacle of the Rhine in front of our very noses? It is militarily inacceptable." "Suppose," asked Poincaré, President of the Republic, "the Germans refuse your terms?" "Then," said Foch, "we will con-

tinue the war." Then Colonel House had asked directly
whether the Marshal thought it preferable to continue the
war against Germany or to conclude an armistice with her.

"I am not," said Foch, "waging war for the sake of waging war. If I obtain through the armistice the conditions that
we wish to impose upon Germany, I am satisfied. Once this
object is attained nobody has the right to shed one drop more
of blood."

So Foch, sleepless in the wet dawn of November 8th, came
back to this last answer and was disturbed at the lateness of
his enemy. The train bringing the German delegation was
twelve hours overdue.

But at seven o'clock, he heard, above the noise of the rain
in the thick woods, the sigh of air brakes and General Weygand opened the compartment door.

"Here they are, my Marshal."

Foch raised the blind. The light was vague. Along the
tracks was a morass of yellow mud. Over it and the stretch
of dead leaves, a walk of boards tied together with ropes
had been laid between Foch's special and the dark train
which had just pulled to a stop.

Foch had picked this spot, Rethondes, in the heart of
Compiègne Forest, for the end of the war. There would be
no fanfare, no publicity, no correspondents, no flags or music.
Rethondes with its woods, its two sidings in the mud—built
for heavy artillery to be shunted off and fired—was like a
hundred spots in France in which the war this morning was
being fought by shivering, tired soldiers.

Four men came down the steps of the other train.

"So this," said Foch, "is the German Empire," and pulled
down the blind. "We will meet," he told Weygand, "at
nine."

In the "office car," furnished with a large table in the
center and a dozen square chairs covered with leather and

studded with brass nails drawn up about it, the group of the
Entente assembled. The British Navy was represented by
Admiral Wemyss, Admiral Hope, and Captain Mariott.
With Foch were Maxime Weygand, French chief-of-staff,
Major Riedinger, Captain de Mierry, and Interpreter-Officer
Laperche.

Precisely at nine the Germans—Matthias Erzberger, Count
Alfred Obendorff, General Deatlev von Winterfeldt, the
naval captain Vanselow and two lesser officers—came in and
took the places assigned to them. Foch asked for the creden-
tials of these persons and with Wemyss and Weygand exam-
ined them. Then Foch said,

"What is the purpose of your visit?"

Erzberger looked up, startled; his eyes moved from one
to another of the delegates as if he had not heard the question correctly and expected someone to explain. But there
was silence.

"We have come," he said and stopped. "Why we have
come to ask for—to receive the proposals of the Entente
Powers—looking to an armistice . . ."

"I have no proposals to make," said Foch.

Obendorff leaned across the table.

"What do you want us to say?" he said. "I do not stand
on form. I am ready to say this German delegation asks the
conditions of the armistice."

"I have no conditions to offer," said Foch.

There seemed to be an impasse.

Erzberger read aloud the last note from President Wilson.

"You see," he said, "President Wilson authorized Marshal
Foch to make known to us the armistice conditions."

"Only if," said Foch, "the German delegates ask for an
armistice. Do you ask for an armistice?" he added as if the
idea were new to him. "If you do, I can inform you of the
conditions subject to which it can be obtained."

"We ask for an armistice," said Erzberger and his eyes cleared.

"We ask for an armistice," repeated Obendorff in a lower voice.

The Marshal reached for his papers.

"The details are rather long," he said. "So I will read only the principal paragraphs."

Foch read and the interpreter took his notes.

"The immediate evacuation of lands unlawfully invaded, Belgium, France, Alsace-Lorraine, and Luxemburg, and the immediate repatriation of their inhabitants.

"Surrender by the enemy of 5,000 cannon, 30,000 machine guns, and 3,000 minenwerfer.

"Evacuation by the German army of all territory on the left bank of the Rhine; occupation by the Allies of bridge-heads on the right bank, drawn with a radius of 18¾ miles, at Mayence, Coblenz, Cologne, and Strasbourg and the creation on the right bank of a neutral zone 25 miles wide running east of the river.

"Prohibition of any destruction or damage by the enemy in the area evacuated.

"Delivery of 5,000 locomotives and 150,000 railway cars in good condition.

"Delivery of 150 submarines, withdrawal of the surface fleet to Baltic ports, occupation by the Allied fleets of Cuxhaven and Helgoland.

"Maintenance of the blockade during the period fixed for the fulfillment of the above conditions."

Erzberger, whose face had darkened during the reading, made a sharp gesture at the end. Then he spoke and the passion grew in his voice as he extended his lament.

He asked for a suspension of military operations during negotiation. The German army, he admitted, was demoralized. There was disorganization and lack of discipline. Even he and his fellow delegates had found difficulty crossing the lines, arranged and ordered as it was. And among civilians, the spirit of revolution was spreading through Germany.

Herr Erzberger then played what the Marshal recognized as a trump card:

"All these circumstances," he said, "lead me to believe that Germany may soon fall into the grip of Bolshevism, and once Central Europe is invaded by this scourge, western Europe will find the greatest difficulty in escaping it. Only cessation of Allied attacks would bring about the return of discipline to the German army and save the country by the restoration of order."

The Marshal instantly replied:

"At the moment when negotiations for the signing of the armistice are just being opened, it is impossible to stop military operations until the German delegation has accepted and signed the conditions which are the very consequence of those operations. As for the situation described by Herr Erzberger as existing among the German troops and the danger he fears of Bolshevism spreading in Germany, the one is the usual disease prevailing in beaten armies, the other is symptomatic of a nation completely worn out by war. Western Europe will find means of defending itself against the danger."

General von Winterfeldt read a statement which Foch knew had been prepared in advance protesting again that there must be a truce before the signing. Again Foch refused. The German delegates asked for a delay. Foch remained fixed upon November 11th, at eleven. The deadline would not be changed. The delegation sent a wireless message and a courier to Spa, the German headquarters.

The reply did not come for more than two days. On the 9th, the Marshal sent orders to all his commanders-in-chief in the field to intensify their military efforts against Germany. On the evening of the 10th, he reminded the Germans that less than twelve hours remained. The reply from the German Empire came during the night accompanied by a long telegraphic protest from Hindenburg.

The plenary session met in the dark—at 2:15 in the morning. The armistice was signed at five. Firing ceased on all fronts at eleven.

On the 12th, Foch issued a general order to all the Allied armies:

"You have won the greatest battle in history," he wrote, "and rescued the most sacred of all causes, the Liberty of the World."

3

In the early dawn of November 11th the ancient heart-shaped city at the junction of the Marne and the Seine seemed to heave and sigh after the long interval of its pain. From the white Sacré Cœur standing like a spiritual sentry on its Mount of Martyrs, across the Tuileries and the Seine and the Luxembourg gardens south to the Observatory, the wind blew the news of peace. Out of the labyrinths surrounding the Place de la Bastille and the Place de la République and in the Faubourg St. Antoine, the little people of Paris came while it was still dark to feel the new trembling in the air of *"le jour de gloire,"* arrived at last at the end of the long parade of ghosts: of fear, despair, hunger, endurance. And in the freer spaces along the boulevards, the avenue de l'Opéra, the rue de Rivoli, and the rue Royale, café and restaurant men opened their cellar hoards concealed for years against this very occasion and prepared for formidable business.

Paris had taken the war without hysteria and with little sense of virtue. War, for most Frenchmen, was a practical matter, likely to occur in each generation. It was not a game or a parade. It was not a romantic episode. It was reality, an essential part of life. French soldiers did not play football in nomansland and their young subalterns did not make targets of themselves on the parapets of trenches to provide moral examples for the men. Officers and men endured the trenches with undramatic courage and as their souls burned away at the front, they watched the lights go out with cynical detachment. At home the people watched disaster without surprise—"it is war; what can you expect?"—but the acceptance was no less bitter and the bitterness became a part of the body and will of the people.

The enemy at the Paris gate had been met, in 1914, not with panic but with practical measures. He had been there before within the memory of thousands of Parisians. The city simply prepared for siege, the taxis were mobilized and sent out to bring back the wounded from the Marne. When the Boche had come in the spring of 1918 he had set up a gun with a 75-mile range and dropped shells into the heart of Paris at quarter-hour intervals. One shell had hit a church whose congregation were gathered on Good Friday and brought it down on their heads. But wherever the shells landed, board fences were quickly put up to hide the damage and the boards plastered up with bright pictures of Mistinguet or the dancers of the Folies Bergères, and the city continued about its business.

The people of the city had made no sacrifices for the sake of sacrifice. Conduct was not guided by war conventions. If a pleasure was ripe for the picking it was picked, war or no war. Thus Colonel House had written in 1917:

Dinners are being given in Paris that would be considered a scandal in America not to mention England. To rebut this I was told that if restrictions were placed upon the French people they would rebel. That the only way they could be kept going at the top notch was to let them have their way in this direction.

The Colonel had moved, of course, in upper circles which somehow found wine, butter, coffee, and sugar on the darkest days and with Latin realism used it.

But November 11th was not a fete designed for upper circles. It was a holiday mainly for the lowest. White-faced and thin, the people came pouring out into the light, sad children with soft bones and rickety legs were dancing in the streets in the first dawn, women put on liberty caps and tricolor rosettes and ecstatic poilus in faded blue uniforms drank red wine for breakfast. Music sprang up everywhere, little bands and ballad singers played "Sambre et Meuse" and sang "Madelon." Students who had sung all night in the street of the Panthéon and the Boul' Mich' formed columns and marched across the river.

Traffic stopped in the Place de la Concorde. People climbed on the tops of the cars. They climbed the statues and the fences, straining upward to see. But there was nothing to see but joy. Nothing but weeping, laughing, singing people; people stunned to silence by the prospect of eternal liberty, the end of war; peace, bread, and wine; the little events of repair and rebuilding in a world without fear. Some could only shout and wave their arms and some must kiss or pray and many sobbed for the absent who would have enjoyed this moment of *la victoire*.

There were many British uniforms in the crowd in the Place de la Concorde, but fewer American. No leaves had been given in the A. E. F. The American drive in the Argonne had pushed through to Sedan, and from there all the way back to Sainte-Menehould reserve divisions were strung, waiting their turn at the front. The rest of the two million were in the Service of Supply, at GHQ in Chaumont, at ports of debarkation or scattered over Europe in special services. A regiment had been with the Italians the week before at the final victory of Vittorio Veneto and with the Italians had celebrated another armistice.

But wherever an American appeared in Paris, he was surrounded. He was kissed in public, by brazen but often lovely girls who were provoked by his giant youth or his blondness or what they called his "savagery" in the midst of an exhausted manhood. But mainly he was a focus because he was American, part of the miracle which, at her crisis, had saved France. He was kin to those great armies who had swept through the incredible impasse of the Argonne, news of which in Paris was still vague but incandescent with glory. It mattered little that a particular soldier had lived in Paris through the war doing paper work or police duty. His uniform was a symbol. It was a symbol of last-minute reprieve. It was a symbol of mystic intervention. Most of all it was a symbol of future security, for behind the American soldier was the god who would save the world, keep it safe for democracy and France, and make new war impossible.

So, in Paris, Americans had their hour. Their late coming into the war was forgotten. The desperate stands of the French at the Marne and at Verdun, the million and a half dead French soldiers, the exhaustion of reserves and food were not compared, on Armistice Day, with the dashing exploits of fresh, well-fed Americans in three months of fighting. The immense French money debt which stood on the American books was not recalled. If, after being plied all day with expensive whisky by hosts who drank wine, and told a dozen times that his country had saved France, an American admitted winning the war, his exuberance was forgiven.

These things could not last. The excesses of the day of glory would be followed by a colder reckoning until, at last, there would remain only the vaguest memory of the fleeting warmth.

4

Pure gaiety came less easily to the Londoner. Each Englishman needed either the support of many other Englishmen or the softening of internal restraint at a pub before he could loose himself to full celebration. Otherwise his conscience marched beside him. "In all time of our prosperity . . ." ran the warning in the English Litany, "Good Lord, deliver us," and Englishmen were loth to forget it.

On Armistice Day in London, however, both bitter beer and mob concert came to his aid. So the crowds swept down the Mall with its three rows of captured German cannon; cheered the army through Whitehall and the government in Downing Street; listened to fierce speeches by orators standing on the heads of the lions in Trafalgar Square; and packed the pubs in Whitechapel. And crowds along the Embankment burned hundreds of effigies of the Kaiser and roared round the houses of Parliament for vengeance, and still other crowds, numb with emotion, thronged the churches and stood in the silent concert of prayer.

In the evening a car slowly forced its way to Number 10 Downing Street. A few of the boys and men who jumped on its running board and peered through the windows recognized the man inside—a face as British as the face of John Bull himself—watched him chew the end of his enormous cigar, and, when he smiled at them with his big lips and his stubborn, fighting, North Sea eyes, cheered him. When the car stopped policemen saluted and made a path for him through the crowd, men drew back and touched their caps, and, when the word ran about that the Minister of Munitions —once First Lord of the Admiralty—was calling on the Prime Minister, the cheers roared out for Lloyd George and Winston Churchill.

Churchill found his host and dinner waiting for him in the large paneled room where, for nearly two centuries, prime ministers had dined. In the somber formality of the room, under the portraits of Pitt and Fox, Nelson and Wellington and (as Churchill observed) the somewhat incongruous portrait of Washington, Lloyd George was wholly informal. He was always so; "always natural and simple" and "one could say anything to him, on the terms that he could say anything back." Churchill relaxed in his presence.

But as Churchill said of their meeting, alone, on Armistice night, there was no exuberance between them; none of the fierce joy of the singing, cheering multitudes outside which could be "remotely heard like the surf on the shore." In the muffled quiet of the house in Downing Street, "the magnitude and absolute character of the victory induced a subdued and detached state of mind."

The thoughts of the two ministers had been running through the day in much the same channel. They were not, of course, new thoughts for either. For many months they had been a steady background behind the strenuous practical effort of winning. But today, immediate and all pervading, was the sense of the tremendous work which lay ahead.

There was the home-coming of millions of men. There was the fitting of these men into the pattern of peace. It must be slow but not too slow: there must be kept the fine balance between the overcrowding of normal, peace-time society and the holding back of men under arms after the fighting was over. The dangers were hunger in the home community and mutiny in an army held in discipline against no enemy. There was the job of closing factories, the vast dump of goods for which there was no peaceful purpose. Factory conversion would be slow while workers waited. There would be a huge residue of jobless men.

Across the Channel the problems seemed even larger. The

English people could be counted on to meet events on the home front with tolerance and sense. But what of France? The cry for vengeance would, perhaps, be less than the demand for future security. But the insistence on security might permanently cripple the German people. Could Europe be rebuilt for peace and endure in peace without German aid? If Germany were pushed too far, might she not "slide," as Churchill expressed it, "into the grisly gulf that had already devoured Russia"?

It seemed as if the traditional Anglo-Saxon conscience had entered the room in Downing Street even on the night of the Armistice. For four years Britain had devoted every thought, every effort of will and body to crush Germany by every possible means including starvation, but now Churchill's mood "was divided between anxiety for the future and desire to help the fallen foe." The talk turned to "the great qualities of the German people," to "the tremendous fight they had made against three-quarters of the world." To relieve the famine which was undoubtedly at this moment setting in, Churchill suggested rushing "a dozen great ships crammed with provisions into Hamburg."

Churchill pointed out that there were practical reasons for this as well as moral ones. In what sort of goods and services could Germany pay? In coal? What would this do to the British coal fields? In manufactured articles? How many of these would Englishmen want to receive? England was a highly industrialized nation and would not welcome a dumping of cheap German goods. In services? If Germans manned all the merchant ships they would presently gain all the carrying trade of the world. Slave labor? And what would that do to the British labor market? It was not a simple matter.

So the two men talked late into the night while outside the illumined people saw only the path of glory ahead.

Churchill left with one full conviction.

Three men must meet. Immensely different as they were in experience and temper, they must meet as soon as possible after victory; meet face to face and take the realities hardily in their hands. For, as he wrote,

on that November evening the three men at the head of Great Britain, the United States and France seemed to be the masters of the world.

Behind them stood vast communities organized to the last point, rejoicing in victory and inspired with gratitude and confidence for the chiefs who had led them there. In their hands lay armies of irresistible might, and fleets without whose sanction no vessel crossed the sea upon or beneath the surface. There was nothing wise, right and necessary which they could not in unity decree. And these men had been drawn together across differences of nationality and interest and across distances on land and sea by the comradeship of struggle against a dreaded foe. Together they had reached the goal. Victory absolute and incomparable was in their hands. What would they do with it?

5

The rue de l'Université, which ran parallel to the Quai d'Orsay, following all its curves, had as much quiet distinction as any street in Paris. On it one might meet anyone of importance from a provincial deputy crossing the Place du Palais Bourbon to the Chamber, to the great Marshal himself on his way to the Invalides, or even the little "Tiger" with his skullcap and great white mustaches getting in and out of his car at Number 78. Along it, at his furious pace, often walked David Lloyd George who liked to move under his own excessive steam or, more sedately, in embassy cars, Lord Milner, Balfour, Orlando, Sir William Wiseman, Venizelos, or the Baron Sonnino.

In Number 78, a house large and comfortable enough to hold all of these notables at once, lived the native of Houston, Texas, who, according to Lloyd George, *was* the government of the United States. Perhaps the only relics of Texas which still clung to Colonel House were his drawl—the slow, gentle way of argument which had charmed innumerable cowboys before the Colonel had ever encountered Europe—and a humor as dry and sharp as the cactus desert. But these things had come to delight European statesmen as well as frontier Texans; there was in a conversation with House the excitement of a poker game plus a basic confidence in his honesty, so that none who lost to him ever felt cheated. Keeping always his unofficial appearance, he softened what seemed to be the hard lines of American policy; he welcomed discussion and especially information; he met the European approach halfway and if, in the end—as he usually did—he turned opinion into his own channel, he rarely left the feeling that he had forced it.

So, from October 26, 1918, when he had arrived at Paris, ministers and generals had got the habit of dropping in at Number 78. What happened there would be informal and off the record, yet the Colonel's words would be authentic, for he was in constant code communication with his chief. Colonel House did not make mistakes. When he stated the American position, either he had documentary proof or he was certain of being able to adjust the position to fit his statement.

Thus he gained the respect even of the Italian, Sonnino, who often irritated him almost beyond endurance with his stubborn convictions on balance-of-power politics, and the warm friendship of the ironic Clemenceau to whom Wilson's idealism made not the faintest sense. House's advice was sought, as his brilliant young assistant Walter Lippmann wrote, "because it is believed to be a little nearer this world than the President's and a good deal nearer heaven than that of Lloyd George and Sonnino."

On Armistice Day when, overcome with emotion, he cabled Wilson, "In this great hour my heart goes out to you in pride, admiration and love," Colonel House was conscious also of personal triumph. He was aware of it before Lippmann wrote him, "I did not believe it was humanly feasible, under conditions as they seemed to be in Europe, to win so glorious a victory." He was peculiarly aware of it when, on Armistice Day, he read the note from Clemenceau, whose patience he had strained over long discussion, "I cannot restrain the desire to open my arms to you and press you to my heart."

It had been an exhausting fight. Already the Colonel's aging body had been so weakened by it that he would soon be driven to his bed. But on Armistice Day the victory was sweet, running parallel as it did with the victory of democracy in all the world. House's private victory was the triumph of the Fourteen Points. To these, as the basis of armistice, he had bent the will of all Europe. To do it, he had fought British tradition, French realism, and Italian avarice. To the astonished statesmen who woke suddenly to discover that all the chips lay piled on his side of the table, it seemed that he had done the job alone.

He did not do it alone though the will and the direction were his. Behind him stood a large informed and trained staff. A year before, he had organized a board of experts called "The Inquiry." To him and to the President this board made constant reports. So, when the Colonel came to Paris, he was not foolish enough to leave the whole of the Inquiry in New York.

Among those he brought with him were Frank I. Cobb, editor of the New York *World*, and Walter Lippmann. He used their flexible and persuasive minds to full capacity.

Arriving in the middle of the correspondence between the Germans and Wilson, he met the battle of the Fourteen Points on his doorstep. The military questions of the Armistice, on the details of which Entente generals and statesmen consulted him, he wisely conceded to the military experts. His own expert, Tasker Bliss, could be counted on to uphold whatever American point of view might enter into the military arrangements. But the Germans had asked for a settlement on the basis of the Fourteen Points and Colonel House was determined, come hell or high water, that Entente political minds should be in full agreement on this basis. They must state this, definitely, in their final note to the Germans —the note in which they would instruct the Germans how to ask for an armistice. Otherwise, in all the peace negotiations which might follow, they would be able to keep faith neither with themselves nor with the enemy and the honor of Wilson and of the United States would be sacrificed. So this was House's flaming banner and to him all the military victories of Foch, Pershing, Haig, Diaz, d'Esperey, and Allenby would count for nothing if it were sullied.

He began by setting Lippmann and Cobb to writing an "interpretation" of the Fourteen Points. He was taking no chances on a captious British or Italian statesman saying he did not understand the meaning of this or that point. So these adroit minds, under his direction, anticipated every question. They gave the most elementary explanations and thought up far-fetched examples. They told, almost as if to a child, the numerous things each point did not mean. Almost to the breaking point, they stretched the latitude of each separate principle. Everywhere rhetoric was sacrificed to clarity. When it had been cabled to Wilson and approved by him it became, according to Charles Seymour, "the closest approximation to an official American program ever drafted."

It was soon needed. The Colonel had hardly unpacked his trunks when the opposition began.

"What are we committed to?" asked Lloyd George who, from the start had been frightened by the correspondence between the Germans and Wilson.

"We are committed to nothing yet," said Balfour, "but if an armistice goes through without our stating our position we will be committed."

It was the second point on freedom of the seas which stuck in the British throat. Here Wilson seemed to have rushed in where, for centuries, the angels had feared to tread. And the Germans from the start had leapt at this very point, calling it a principle "with which the whole world would agree."

To the British, freedom of the seas meant freedom under British control. The control had been hard earned. In this very war, not yet ended, the British blockade of Germany had been one of the main causes of imminent German defeat. Was Britain to abandon this weapon for all future wars? Lloyd George could already hear the angry roar of his sea-minded people. "They would throw me out," he insisted, "and a week later another prime minister would repudiate what I had accepted!"

It did no good for House, commentary in hand, to explain that Point II must not be read out of context with the rest; individual cases would be settled by the League of Nations, provided for by Point XIV. Lloyd George stuck to his guns, and Clemenceau and Sonnino to whom the point was of little concern applauded him, for they too had sticking points.

Clemenceau behaved as if he had never heard of the Fourteen Points. They were a speech, weren't they? How did they bind anyone? He had never thought of them till Lloyd George had brought them up. And Pichon and Sonnino thought they had nothing to do with an armistice; it would be time enough to discuss them in the peace conference. An armistice, said Sonnino, was a military and naval thing.

Colonel House said they would be discussed now. He knew that if they slid out of the armistice they would slide forever into limbo. Once the war was over, the power of the United States would weaken in Europe. And his President had already committed himself to the Germans.

"Let's read them, then," said Clemenceau, seeing the set of his friend's jaw.

He stopped the reading after Point I. Open covenants, openly arrived at. Never! That meant that he could not, at any stage in the proceedings, speak privately or agree behind closed doors.

It meant, said House, consulting the interpretation, nothing of the sort. There could be unlimited private conversation provided end results were given full publicity. So the argument passed on Point I.

Clemenceau interrupted again at Point III to ask what "equality of trade conditions" meant. But the commentary whose writers perhaps had American as well as European readers in mind, was explicit. A nation, it said, could maintain a tariff against the whole world providing it did not discriminate between the members of the League of Nations.

Sonnino saw in Point IX the scrapping of his Treaty of London. If House really meant to force acceptance as a basis of armistice terms, Sonnino would write an elaborate reservation into the pre-armistice agreement which was to be sent to Germany. Lloyd George, Clemenceau, and Hymans of Belgium would do the same.

So Colonel House, after the talk had gone on four days, saw a note to the enemy so cluttered with reservations that it would be robbed of all dignity and would prove to the Germans that disunity prevailed among the victors. And it would, moreover, dishonor Wilson in their eyes.

Through the night of October 29th the Colonel lay wakeful listening to the motorcycle messengers in the street bringing and taking messages. In the house below him his staff worked at their coding and decoding. Then, suddenly, at three o'clock, his trump card appeared before him. "I turned over," he wrote next day in his diary, "and went to sleep."

At the conference the next day it appeared that Clemenceau and Sonnino were in the act of preparing their reservations. Clemenceau's, he found, was a most elaborate brief which objected in detail to the President's principles. So he took Clemenceau aside and played his big card.

It would be unfortunate, he explained, if the President, seeing all these reservations, should feel it his duty to take them before the Congress of the United States. It would make a curious impression on Congress if the President should be obliged to explain to it precisely what Great Britain, France, and Italy had been fighting for in the war. Such an explanation, he added, would "place the responsibility upon Congress for the further continuation of the war by the United States in behalf of the aims of the Allies. . . ."

The effect on Clemenceau was electric. He not only tore up his own brief but he exerted such pressure upon the Italians that their reservations were never considered.

There remained, then, only Lloyd George's objection to freedom of the seas and Lloyd George's insistence on stressing the full meaning of "restoring" evacuated territory in Points VII and VIII. House admitted the reservation on restoration—it was not, in fact, an objection but only a clarifying emphasis. But he fought the British concept of freedom of the seas until Lloyd George, under House's threat that it would destroy Anglo-American friendship in the future, agreed to a concession. "Will it do," he asked, "if we merely reserve the right to discuss this matter further at the peace conference?"

"I think it will do," said Colonel House.

So, after the week's struggle, the Colonel won. There had been bluff, courage, and persistence in his playing. Yet he had had behind him, too, in addition to his own peculiar genius of knowing precisely what cards lay in every hand, the strong support of able and studious men. And, most of all, he was heartened by the certainty that among the peoples of Europe in this last phase of the war, his President held an incomparable prestige.

So, on Armistice Day when all had been said and done and the enemy, in the Forest of Compiègne, had accepted the terms with the full understanding that the Entente Allies were agreed upon the Fourteen Points, the Colonel felt satisfaction that the first round was over. He did not discount the troubles which lay ahead. But he knew that in all the controversy he had lost not a single friend and that in the longer battles to come he would have the respect of every statesman in Europe.

7. Now They Will Come Home

CITY HALL PARK, New York City, November 7th. Lunch-hour crowds milled slowly. Streetcars on Broadway ground their way along, occasionally clanging a bell. On benches in the park men sprawled as ever, or gathered in little clumps of three or four, hands in pockets, lazing and talking. A dog trotted across the grass intent on some dog business.

A man in the window of the Associated Press overlooking this scene yawned and stretched, then turned to get back to his desk. Yet as he turned, something caught his eye diagonally across the park under the Brooklyn Bridge elevated station. He looked again. A knot of people seemed to have formed around something, and others were running in. An accident? A fight?

He glanced at the Broadway side of the park. There was another little knot, gathering faster than a snowball, but without rolling. A newsboy ran shouting across the grass, waving a sheet, holding a sheaf of papers under his arm. Men got off their benches and ran to buy.

The man in the window turned. "Boy!" he called. "Get the extra that just came out!"

The groups were dissolving and reforming, and there was a growing murmur that quickly swelled into a roar. Papers just bought were thrown into the air. A trolley motorman, stalled by the crowd in the street, rang his bell furiously. Auto horns began to blow.

An amazed editor ran with a message just off the wire to

Jackson Elliott, chief of the News Department, and put it on his desk. It was from an AP bureau:

"UNITED PRESS FLASHING ARMISTICE SIGNED."

Elliott took a quick look. "Cable London and Paris," he snapped. "Get me Frank Polk at the State Department on the phone. Bring me a map!"

Below, people were running, waving, shouting, dancing in the street. Others were pouring out of buildings, coatless in the Indian Summer day. The mob filled the streets; traffic stopped. From windows came first a trickle, then a cascade of paper. Whistles blew. Bells clanged.

In the office of the Associated Press there was gloom. AP had been beaten on the biggest story since the beginning of the war.

Yet as Elliott pored over maps and over earlier cables giving details of the German armistice commission, where it had to travel and how long it had had to get there, it seemed physically impossible that the trip could have been made and the armistice signed in the time elapsed. London cabled no confirmation, nor did Paris. The State Department had no information.

So the AP carried nothing on its wires except an acknowledgment of the fact that the United Press had reported an armistice. If there had been no confirmation that the story was true, neither had there been any positive statement that it was not true. Faster and faster came the complaints of member newspapers. Mayor Rolph of San Francisco called; he had been asked to lead the celebration in that city, but wanted absolute assurance that the story was true. The Associated Press couldn't help him.

In New York police were called upon to guard the AP building when threatening crowds stormed it, calling the editors "pro-German," because they had not reported the armistice.

At 2:15 the official word came through, and the AP tossed the largest wet blanket in history, covering an entire country:

> WASHINGTON, NOV. 7.—IT WAS OFFICIALLY AN-
> NOUNCED AT THE STATE DEPARTMENT AT 2:15 O'CLOCK
> THIS AFTERNOON THAT THE GERMANS HAD NOT SIGNED
> ARMISTICE TERMS.

But it was not many days later that the galleries of the Hall of the House of Representatives were filled with men and women to hear the President announce the real armistice. Mrs. Wilson was there as usual, with Mrs. McAdoo. The cabinet was there, and General March, the Army Chief of Staff, and most of official Washington. One member of the House, Representative La Guardia of New York, was in the uniform of an army aviator.

When Sergeant-at-Arms Joseph Sinnott announced the President, the entire company rose, and in a growing, spreading cheer voiced approval of the vigorous figure in the cutaway coat, light trousers, and gray cravat. The President did not look his sixty-one years as he shook hands with Vice-President Marshall and Speaker Clark.

As the applause slowly died away Woodrow Wilson pulled several typed sheets from his pocket. He read simply, without any effort to dramatize, but his voice was low and husky at first. Mrs. Wilson leaned forward in her seat and the President glanced at her momentarily as he turned a page.

The announcement that the Germans had accepted the Allied terms brought applause, but it was nothing to what followed when President Wilson read the decisive, binding terms.

There was applause when he announced that Belgium, France, and Luxemburg were to be evacuated at once, but when he announced the evacuation of Alsace and Lorraine the audience jumped to its feet and cheered without restraint.

Approval of the terms of the Armistice was clearly demonstrated by the congressmen and senators and by the galleries. But Mr. Wilson's pleas for humane treatment and a charitable and helpful attitude toward the defeated enemy brought only studied silence. His hearers were in no mood to feed and clothe the German people or to help them get back on their feet. For the German people nothing; but for Woodrow Wilson now that victory had come, tremendous, resounding cheers as he stepped down from the platform and left the hall. And the sound of the cheering followed him until it was engulfed and lost in that of the thousands who lined his path outside, all the way back to the White House.

2

Reporters can tell what people do when a war ends. How they feel is something else—and the outward expression of it is only an inadequate attempt on the part of each to prove to all the rest that he feels as they do. It is a universal burden replaced by a universal joy. No one wants to be alone with such a joy.

San Francisco when the news came had in force an ordinance intended to prevent the spread of influenza—the wearing of small cotton masks over the nose and mouth in public places. It had been rigidly enforced by police, but on Armistice Day—how could it be? As one maskless woman said to a cop who had told her to cover her mouth, "Don't you see I can't blow my horn and keep my mask on too?" Whether the masks did any good no one really knew; but the general feeling was that there was an armistice with influenza too, and Market Street was packed with milling, shouting people and bands suddenly appeared from nowhere. It was like a thousand Main Streets everywhere.

In Oakland shipyard workers found the great gates closed and draped with flags when they reported for work. They hurled high their lunch boxes and hats and snake-danced toward the center of town. There Mayor John L. Davies met them, turned and led them through the swelling crowds marching past the closed stores and factories. The Kaiser was shot, hanged, stabbed, burned, decapitated, and torn to pieces in effigy, and coffins assigned to his use were carried aloft by thousands of willing hands.

Ferryboats crossing the Bay were jammed with people going to San Francisco, and every boat on the water was blowing every whistle aboard.

The great news had come to San Francisco shortly after midnight, and the delirious celebration had started then, and it grew all through the night and all through the next day, and the next evening, twenty-four hours later, it was still going on.

Extemporaneous parades [wrote a gleeful *Chronicle* reporter] as frequent as the Mayor's speeches, but shorter, marched the streets and took right of way by virtue of the law which provides passage for those who know where they are going. It was a wonderful moment when that throng swept down Market Street at 2 o'clock yesterday morning from the City Hall to the Ferry Building. Mayor Rolph, with a soldier on one arm and a sailor on the other, was supposed to have headed the procession. He was somewhere in its merry midst. In the delirium of the moment the Municipal Band had marched away with the North Beach contingent of the general joy.

There never was such a purpose for celebrating before. Please God, there never will be again.

It was the same everywhere. In Jersey City a soldier on leave climbed to the top of a five-story building and to the top of a flagpole on the roof, lost his hold and plunged 125 feet to the cloth top of a touring car. He was bruised severely, but went on celebrating.

On hilltops everywhere bonfires burned. Whistles blew, bells rang, sirens screamed, politicians made speeches. In Hartford the employees of the Maxim Silencer Company joined a parade and made more noise than anyone else. In Cheyenne and Pueblo and Amarillo cowboys rode breakneck through the streets whooping and shooting. In Washington forty-nine bonfires crackled in the Ellipse between the White House and the Potomac.

Men and women who had never seen each other before shook hands, embraced, wept for joy on each other's shoulders. Strangers danced together and sauntered arm in arm along the streets. Soldiers and sailors of all Allied nations were cheered, wined, fed, carried on shoulders through the mobs. In churches thousands knelt and prayed.

A hundred million people, tearful with joy, with one thought above all others, one marvelous, thrilling realization —"the boys are coming home!"

Now it was over. The killing was finished.

Now the men would all come home—all that were still alive. They would come marching down the streets with the bands playing and the confetti and the flowers and surrounded by full hearts, and the close-packed columns would dissolve and the men would enter four million homes which they had left to fight.

Now we could breathe freely about our sons and brothers and sweethearts not yet drafted—the draft boards were cleaning out their offices and shipping records to Washington.

Now we could settle back into the easy, old ways of life and think no more on the torn, burned world.

We had repaid our debt to France and Lafayette, and France and America would forever be the closest friends.

We had saved England from defeat and the English would be full of gratitude.

We had saved the disillusioned German people from autocracy and made them free.

We had helped the freedom-loving Czechoslovaks build their new republic.

Now we could drive into the country on Sunday and picnic in the woods and meadows. No need to save gas.

Now there would be plenty of sugar, and coal, and butter, and all the other things we had lacked.

No more saving peach pits or tinfoil or old iron.

No more volunteer work on draft boards or bond-selling drives. No more knitting for the Red Cross.

The advertisements promised bigger and better automobiles at lower prices for the new postwar America.

There would be no more of George Creel's four-minute men in the theaters to harangue us with patriotic fervor, and we could relax and watch Douglas Fairbanks or Mary Pickford.

Families would be together again; children would see their fathers for the first time; sweethearts long parted would be reunited; no longer was there reason to postpone weddings.

Now we could read the sports pages and the comics instead of the foreign news about the far-off places with unpronounceable names and the unknown statesmen with the sinister purposes.

The Americans who had moved into Bridgeport and Norfolk and a hundred other towns to make guns and ammunition could take their families out of the miserable, expensive makeshift quarters they had lived in, and go home.

Now Europe was merely a place Americans could go with Baedekers and dark glasses to look at cathedrals and feudal castles, or to buy clothes. Or perhaps to take a cozy villa near the sea and mingle with quaint peasants.

At last, at last, the world was in order, for always, and we Americans had put it that way.

There would be no more wars. President Wilson had said so. Now men would be brothers and Peace would rule. Peace on earth, forever and forever. . . .

The details? They were for the experts to work out. They would be too complicated for ordinary folk anyway. They could be left to Woodrow Wilson—and to the United States Senate.

3

Back in September, 1917, Colonel House had foreseen the need of marshaling a tremendous mass of facts, and consideration of a great number of problems likely to arise at the peace conferences. It was obvious that there would be conflicting claims and that there would be potent arguments on each side of nearly every question, and clearly the American Commission must be armed with all the facts that might apply.

The Colonel had asked his brother-in-law, Dr. Sidney E. Mezes, president of the College of the City of New York, to organize a staff for study of these matters. One of the first staff members to go to work was Walter Lippmann, who toiled alone in a little room at the New York Public Library. The staff, however, had rapidly expanded and soon moved to the spacious and well-equipped building of the American Geographical Society, where the head of the Society, Dr. Isaiah Bowman, extended all the society's facilities and himself took over much of the burden of administration.

The growing group of specialists under Colonel House came to be known as "The Inquiry," not because that was a good name, but because it was a poor one. House did not want its work widely known, although it was no secret that the work was going on—in fact the New York *Times* published a front-page story about the Inquiry very early in the game. As it was, the personnel was besieged by special pleaders for various European groups.

There were . . . transient visitors such as Premier Hughes of Australia, who gave us a foretaste of his diplomatic technique at the Peace Conference by laying his electric ear-trumpet on the table when he didn't want to hear any objections to his point of view [relates Dr. James T. Shotwell, historian for the Inquiry]. More picturesque still were the personalities from Eastern Europe, from Macedonian bandits to the Lithuanians whose claim rested partly on linguistic affiliations with Sanscrit!

The members of the Inquiry were not attempting to design a new European order. They were merely figuring out what questions were likely to arise during the peace conferences and getting data to answer them. Since geographical boundaries would obviously be the subject of discussion, much of the Inquiry's work was devoted to maps. Every town anywhere near a disputed border was analyzed to find the national origins of its people and their national sympathies where these had been expressed. Historical maps, showing the changing borders of European countries since the earliest days, and noting the wars and other causes of boundary changes.

Iron, coal, copper, oil, and the other riches of the earth were mapped and listed and counted up. Strategic natural barriers—rivers, mountains, swampland—were considered. Industrial plants and their needs were listed and catalogued. Languages and dialects were studied and mapped, and cultural traits which might make for a cohesive society or might on the other hand make for friction.

Compromises would be made, of course, in re-establishing

border lines. But it was Colonel House's aim to have not one inch of border decided arbitrarily or by opposing pressure groups.

International lawyers like David Hunter Miller worked out knotty legal problems. Economists like Bernard Baruch worked closely with the Inquiry on financial and industrial research. Linguists, historians, anthropologists, geologists, engineers, diplomats—all gave freely of their time and training to make the Inquiry's world study accurate, complete, and practicable.

For the men who were working at the American Geographical Society's building had soon realized what it was that they were doing. They were ferreting out and listing every cause for friction between European nations, every complaint, every historic injustice, every difference, and seeking ways of eliminating each. At the same time they were listing all cohesive elements, everything in tradition, language, customs, and mutual economic interests which might have been neglected but which might now become a part of a plan to bring the nations together and keep them together.

This was their responsibility and their opportunity. It had never been done before on such a scale by a purely objective body three thousand miles away and having no special interests in any of the countries or any of the problems. Always before, such problems had been settled by the threat of war, by secret agreements and combinations, by economic pressures and devious diplomatic maneuvers. This time it could be different. This time disputes could be settled on the basis of scientific and historical fact. The old Europe had been melted down and was in flux. If the molds could be designed correctly, the pouring done by an expert molder using the most scientific methods, might not a Europe emerge free from the frightful stresses that had so often resulted in the strain of war? And as for new stresses arising, might these

not be taken care of by a world organization designed especially to adjust and remove them—a flexible, disinterested
organization basing its decisions also upon facts and not upon
emotions?

It had never been tried, of course. For two thousand years,
as the historians of the Inquiry had shown, the ordinary
people of Europe had been prey to one conqueror's ambition
after another, one war after another. For the conquerors
themselves it had been exciting and gratifying; for the helpless people of Europe it had been hell.

The new structure might not work. There would be many
to oppose it in Europe—all those whose power was threatened, or whose ambitions would be frustrated. But the men
of the Inquiry recognized the opportunity. Here was America, now the most influential nation in the world, led by
Woodrow Wilson before whose picture candles burned in
Europe, a man loved by victors and vanquished as no man
had been loved in nineteen centuries. A man millions stood
ready to follow wherever he might lead, for they believed
he sought the road of peace and freedom and human rights—
and they were sure he sought nothing for himself and nothing for the country he served.

This was reported by hundreds of shrewd and accurate
observers all over Europe, by newspapers and the speeches
of leaders, by the ecstatic letters of American soldiers in
France and of the people of Europe to American relatives
and friends. It was no partisan fancy; it was observable fact,
fact to be reckoned with and applied. This was the opportunity of all time, the one great chance in history to make
reason serve the needs of man, to organize Europe on a
rational basis for the human beings who lived in Europe and
not for a handful of men whose families had misruled
Europe for an age.

The opposition, the Inquiry workers could see, would come

from certain quarters which could be spotted with ease. The arguments against Wilson's concepts of the rebuilding of Europe could be listed and analyzed and foreseen on the basis of the speeches and writings of Europe's statesmen. But what could all the statesmen do if the people of Europe were united behind Woodrow Wilson? The fear of strikes, of angry resentment, of revolution—the Bolshevism which already threatened to sweep westward—these fears would make the anti-Wilson statesmen stop and think. And not only these, but the realization that Wilson was President of the most powerful country in the world, with an army which had proved its prowess in the fields and woods of France.

This chance might never come again. There might never again be so fortuitous a combination of all the necessary elements. It could hardly be expected to repeat itself. If failure was the result this time, could there ever be success, except perhaps after an upheaval similar in pattern but even more terrible in scope and magnitude?

But to the men of the Inquiry staff there seemed to be no reason for failure. Everything pointed to success. And it was success with a solid basis, a democratic basis. Wilson had the backing of the people. It was true that he had asked for a Democratic Congress and had not got it. Yet the Inquiry staff could see that in many Senate contests local issues had prevailed over the national issue—in Michigan fantastic amounts of money had beaten a rather weak Democratic candidate; in New Jersey and Delaware Democratic senatorial candidates had been beaten at least partly because they had opposed women's suffrage while their Republican opponents had happened to be prosuffrage; in Missouri a Democrat had been opposed by very powerful German-American and liquor interests; in Illinois a local situation and a growing isolationist feeling had helped McCormick beat Lewis. And if the President could tell people how to vote, then local issues, which ought to be important factors, would always be put into the background. And Wilson supporters pointed out that the voters were not voting for or against Wilson, but for or against other men, candidates they knew and liked or disliked as individuals. Perhaps the appeal to the voters had been an error; certainly the result of the election had been a blow; but the President had not lost everything by it, and there was still plenty of evidence that the vast majority of the nation was behind him. If the election had been a slap at Wilson, then the almost unanimous joy and approval over the Armistice had been a much harder slap at the Republicans who had wanted the war to go on, had wanted to sacrifice many more American lives in a march to Berlin which could not have given the Allies a firmer grip on their defeated enemies than they got through the Armistice terms which Foch had read the whipped Germans in the car at Compiègne.

No, there was no reason to despair. It might be hard to do, but it could be accomplished. The experiment could be tried now. And tried honestly, it had certainly a good chance of success.

4

The time drew near for the Peace Conference, and many questions arose. Should the President himself attend? Who should the American delegates be? Should Senators be selected, since the Senate had to ratify or reject any treaty made? At length it was settled: the American delegates would be Colonel House, General Tasker H. Bliss, Secretary of State Robert Lansing, Henry White, and the President himself, who would go to Paris, although leaders in France and England had made it clear enough that they were not anxious to have him there except perhaps for the opening sessions. Many Americans also strongly opposed his leaving the country during his term of office. It was even suggested that upon leaving these shores the President gave up his position and was necessarily and automatically succeeded by the Vice-President. George Harvey wrote:

the underlying purpose [is] . . . to project in striking fashion a virtual candidacy for President of the League of Nations, which is destined to Dominate the Earth and ensure a Durable Peace for All Time—if it comes off.

The Fourteen Points, which Harvey had cheered in January, were now the "Fourteen Commandments," and were vague and indefinable. There was

a great deal to be said on both sides of every one of them, so far as any of them present sides, top or bottom on which to erect arguments of any kind.

It had become increasingly clear that France and Great Britain wanted a harsh peace: high indemnities from Germany, and stern conditions. Many in America agreed, and in doing so opposed President Wilson and his plans for a new world order. On November 27th, a week before the President sailed, Theodore Roosevelt made a statement. He said:

Our allies and our enemies and Mr. Wilson himself should all understand that Mr. Wilson has no authority whatever to speak for the American people at this time. His leadership has just been emphatically repudiated by them. The newly elected Congress comes far nearer than Mr. Wilson to having a right to speak the purposes of the American people at this moment. Mr. Wilson and his fourteen points and his four supplementary points and his five complementary points and all his utterances every which way have ceased to have any shadow of right to be accepted as expressive of the will of the American people.

He is President of the United States. He is a part of the treaty-making power; but he is only part. If he acts in good faith to the American people, he will not claim on the other side of the water any representative capacity in himself to speak for the American people. He will say frankly that his personal leadership has been repudiated and that he now has merely the divided official leadership which he shares with the Senate.

America played in the closing months of war a gallant part, but not in any way the leading part, and she played this part only by acting in strictest agreement with our allies and under the joint high command. She should take precisely the same attitude at the Peace Conference. We have lost in this war about 236,000 men killed and wounded. England and France have lost about 7,000,000. Italy and Belgium and the other Allies have doubtless lost 3,000,000 more. Of the terrible sacrifice which has enabled the Allies to win the victory, America has contributed just about 2 per cent.

It is our business to act with our allies and to show an undivided front with them against any move of our late enemies. I am no Utopian. I understand entirely that there can be shifting alliances.

But in the present war we have won only by standing shoulder to shoulder with our allies and presenting an undivided front to the enemy. It is our business to show the same loyalty and good faith at the Peace Conference. Let it be clearly understood that the American peoples absolutely stand behind France, England, Italy, Belgium and the other Allies at the Peace Conference, just as she has stood with them during the last eighteen months of the war. Let every difference of opinion be settled among the Allies themselves, and then let them impose their common will on the nations responsible for the hideous disaster which has almost wrecked mankind.

Henry White was a Republican, the only one on the American Peace Commission. He was also an old friend of Theodore Roosevelt's, and on hearing of his appointment the Colonel wrote to Henry Cabot Lodge—"I am simply overjoyed that Harry White is to be on the Peace Commission. . . ."

Senator Lodge too was apparently pleased, and had several talks with White before the latter left for Paris with the President. In fact, the Senator wrote a nine-page memorandum to Henry White on December 2nd, urging that the conferees demand heavy indemnities from Germany, that Germany be split up into many small countries, that Poland should be given Danzig and also East Prussia, that Turkey should be thrown out of Europe, and Constantinople and the Straits be neutralized. In a follow-up memorandum dated the same day Senator Lodge attacked a number of the Fourteen Points, and was emphatic on delaying in every possible way the formation of any League of Nations.

The League of Nations [he wrote White] to preserve and enforce peace presents a conception which must appeal to every right-thinking man, but like many other general ideas when we pass from theory to practise the terms and details are vital. It need only be said here that under no circumstances must provisions for such a league be made a part of the peace treaty which concludes the war with Germany. Any attempt to do this would not only long delay the signature of the treaty of peace, which should not be unduly postponed, but it would make the adoption of the treaty, unamended, by the Senate of the United States and other ratifying bodies, extremely doubtful.

This memorandum was intended only partly for White's information. With complete frankness Senator Lodge made clear what its real purpose was. Henry White was to show it, in confidence, to Balfour, Clemenceau, and certain others, to give them a picture of what Lodge said was the real American viewpoint. It gave, he said, "the real feeling of the people of the United States and certainly of the Senate of the United States." Then he went on to explain that the document was really a potent anti-Wilson weapon he was placing in the hands of Balfour and Clemenceau. "This knowledge," as Lodge put it, "may in certain contingencies be very important to them in strengthening their position."

Henry White never showed the memorandum to anyone until after the war. But he must have wondered what would have happened if Wilson had yielded to pressure from certain quarters and taken Senator Lodge with him to Paris as a member of the Peace Commission. . . .

5

December 4, 1918, was an exciting day in Hoboken, New Jersey.

Early that morning a flag-draped locomotive had drawn a special train into town, and the train had been immediately surrounded by soldiers, Secret Service men, and Army and Navy Intelligence officers. River Street, opposite the piers, was closed to all traffic, and no one was allowed within shouting distance of the special train. Promptly at eight o'clock the President and Mrs. Wilson stepped from his car and the Camp Merritt band, brought down from Tenafly, beat out the "Star-Spangled Banner." The President stood calm and dignified, holding his hat over his chest. When the music stopped he waved and smiled to the soldiers and started through a tunnel of decorations, including flags of all the Allies.

As he started up the gangplank of the *George Washington* the naval band aboard the ship struck up "Hail to the Chief," and followed it with the "Star-Spangled Banner."

At exactly 10:15, the *George Washington's* whistles blew, the Camp Merritt band, standing on the pier, struck up the "Star-Spangled Banner," and the ship pulled out. The five escorting destroyers thundered out a twenty-one-gun salute, answered by the guns of the *George Washington* itself. Now every ship in the Hudson River and New York Bay let loose with whistles. Crowds on both shores waved and cheered, though they could not have made out the slim and wondering figure standing with the captain on the bridge. Airplanes flew over the ship, one following it far out to sea to get a news photograph. The President was off to Paris.

With him were the people of the Inquiry, and a number of other experts. A few days after the ship had left American shores, the President called a conference of his advisers and discussed with them the job to be done. Dr. Isaiah Bowman, then Director of the American Geographical Society, took careful notes.

The President was gay and frank. "We will be the only disinterested people at the Peace Conference," he said, and added that the men with whom they were about to deal did not represent their own peoples. He thought an Allied Commission should determine carefully the just claims against Germany for indemnities. Otherwise, he pointed out, the matter would be settled according to which set of politicians applied the most effective pressure.

"This is the first conference in which decisions depend upon the opinion of mankind," he said. Unless the Conference was prepared to follow the opinions of mankind and to express the will of the people rather than those of the leaders of the Conference, we should soon be involved in "another breakup of the world, and when such a breakup comes it will not be a war but a cataclysm."

The President, after having told his advisers that he was going to accept their information without question and apply it as best he could, ended by saying, "Tell me what's right and I'll fight for it; give me a guaranteed position."

One evening after dinner the President walked the deck with George Creel.

The ship was in the vicinity of the Azores, and the night was balmy, the sky clear and full of stars.

"Mr. President," Creel said, "I've never had an opportunity to tell you what a help your speeches have been in getting the American point of view before the world. The response to them everywhere was downright incredible. We could get over any point we wanted to make, anywhere in the world, if we could find it in your speeches. I suppose you're the most popular author in the world—everyone hangs on the expectation of hearing from you."

"How did you make out in Germany and Austria?" Wilson asked.

Creel's face fell.

"If the war had lasted a little longer we might have Americanized Mitteleuropa," he said. "We were about to distribute pamphlets—most of them your speeches—over half of Germany from balloons. You know we spread a lot from airplanes, and a few were shot from guns and sent by rocket. But we never managed to get enough stuff into Germany."

The President stopped and leaned thoughtfully against the rail, gazing at the stars, as Creel warmed and with growing enthusiasm told the President how the Committee on Public Information had spread his picture, his speeches, and his writings all over the world, and how they had filtered into the Central Powers and into the armies of the nations on both sides. The longer he talked the more thoughtful the President looked. Then Woodrow Wilson turned, and Creel thought he looked bleak and gray.

"It is a great thing that you have done," he said slowly, "but I am wondering if you have not unconsciously spun a net for me from which there is no escape. It is to America that the whole world turns today, not only with its wrongs, but with its hopes and grievances. The hungry expect us to feed them, the roofless look to us for shelter, the sick of heart and body depend upon us for cure. All of these expectations have in them the quality of terrible urgency. There must be no delay. It has been so always. People will endure their tyrants for years, but they tear their deliverers to pieces if a millennium is not created immediately. Yet you know, and I know, that these ancient wrongs, these present unhappinesses, are not to be remedied in a day or with a wave of the hand. What I seem to see—with all my heart I hope that I am wrong—is a tragedy of disappointment."

8. Americans in Paris

DECEMBER 14TH was a holiday in Paris. Shops, offices, and factories were closed as on the day of rest. But, in the dawn, no one slept. Long before daylight, the people began to move. They dressed in their best black and dressed their children in solemn, well-brushed, discreetly patched Sunday clothes. They gave each child two flags, a barred tricolor and a striped tricolor, and uttered terrific warnings against dropping or losing them. They made little bundles of food for the long watch.

From all the fringes of the city, these people moved. They stopped to rest, shifted their burdens, and moved on until the little black streams converged into big streams and the big streams poured into the heart of the city.

When light came in the back streets, people would stop to read the big placards on the walls which, under crossed flags, told the purpose of the holiday. One, which appeared oftener than the rest, spoke to the "Workers of Paris." The democracies, it said, wished to have "the curse of war forever banished, so that labor in its sovereign right may develop in peace." It said:

For having affirmed these principles of action, for having placed them in the center of the stage of the world, President Wilson has .nerited well of humanity.

France of the workers and the peasants who have so often fought for liberty will thank President Wilson at the hour of his arrival among us.

For the task which remains to be accomplished, may President

177

Wilson feel near to him the hearts of millions of men and women!

In the streets on the 14th of December the workers of France will be assembled in force.

To President Wilson their presence will cry aloud:

For international justice, for the League of Nations, which will make all people equal in rights and duties—for the peace that endures.

Some read this quickly and hurried on but others read it twice and explained it to their children. "You will see him," they said.

When light came in the Rond-Point des Champs-Elysées and in the rue Royale and in the rue Monceau, the parts of Paris seemed to have shifted and thousands of people stood there who had never been seen outside the factory district of Clichy or the Quartier du Marais. So they stood in all the distinguished streets along the line of march—strange visitors from far faubourgs and even from the provinces.

When light came in the Place de la Concorde, horizon-blue mixed with the black as the soldiers came. The soldiers lifted the children to vantage points on the statues or on their own shoulders, for above all, the children must see. The children would have long memories and their grand-children, perhaps in another century, would retell the story.

Americans, watching the Place de la Concorde from the windows of the Hôtel de Crillon, were surprised at the quiet-ness of the crowd. There were no yells or whistles, no shouted comedy, no gaiety. A hundred thousand people simply stood as if they waited to celebrate a gigantic Mass.

At ten o'clock the watchers saw the soldiers try to make a path in the crowd. It seemed for a time as if they could not push the people back. They would give and surge again. But when those on the statues saw the plumes of the Garde Ré-publicaine on the bridge, the people themselves made a path.

In the quiet the watchers at the windows could hear the

hoofs of the Garde's horses as they rang on the pavement. But as the Garde passed, the flags rose over the dark heads of the people and waves of color swept the immense square. Then the first carriage, coming at a space behind the Garde, seemed to bring the sound with it.

Men who heard the cheer said it came out of the earth. They said it was not human, that it could not have come from separate voices. They said it was unbearable, that the dead were crying in it too. Afterward the watchers contradicted one another and some said there was no cheer, only silence and the flags.

But seeing the square from above, the watchers saw the levels break when women knelt as the carriage passed. They saw men who had stood since the dark to see, hide their faces, sobbing in their folded arms. They saw children on men's shoulders throw roses over the bayonets of the soldiers into the path before the carriage. All along the line of march they saw arms stretched out, fingers reaching across the dignity of the parade as if to touch the man who brought salvation.

He had not come, the workers of the Confederation had said, simply to save France. The men who made the labor placards understood this and the understanding seemed to pervade the people who watched from the street—whatever those might think who watched from the windows. When "Wilson the Just" spoke, he talked always of "mankind." He had come to Paris for "international justice." In every corner of the world working folk had instantly understood his words and his words had united them across the frontiers. If men and women were united across frontiers, there could be no war. So the people did not greet him as they had greeted Foch or Haig or Pershing or Georges Clemenceau who had saved France. They met him in a different mood.

Clemenceau himself understood this difference. "I knew

Paris," he said, "in the glitter of the Second Empire. I thought I knew my Paris now, but I did not believe she could show such enthusiasm. I don't believe there has been anything like it in the history of the world."

When all the carriages had passed and the crowd closed behind them, the people were reluctant to go home. They seemed to cherish the spot where they had felt the mystic strangeness.

But as the noon passed, the austerity of their mood softened and they drifted away to the boulevards where, for the day, there was fraternity and equality. In the afternoon they spread over the avenues and the parks as the day warmed into a fête. At night, when the pink and yellow lights pricked on along the streets and the gas floodlights circled the dome of the Panthéon; when the white fingers from the searchlights on the Eiffel Tower swept across the sky and electric signs long dead remembered Chocolat Menier or Pernod in tricolor, the people sang and danced, loved or slept in the new music of the world.

Mrs. Woodrow Wilson, walking between the tables in the Elysée Palace on the arm of little President Poincaré, was struck by the immense number of servants in bright livery, the chic of the chattering women, the lavishness of flowers and dainties, and the elaborate social ritual at this first state banquet of the Peace. Coming here so soon after the drive through Paris, the change of scene was arresting.

She and President Wilson had had scarcely a moment to inspect their luxurious new home—the Murat Palace in the rue Monceau. In their brief moment there, a frantic emissary had arrived to say that on no account must the President come to the banquet in the cutaway he had worn in the carriage. Now, at the Elysée Palace, she scarcely recognized her husband in the funereal frock coat which some genius had thought to include in the President's baggage.

Yet with all these curious preoccupations with which official Paris, so recently delivered from war, seemed to be absorbed, the war was not long forgotten, even at the gala banquet. The guests had entered the palace flanked by soldiers with bayonets. Drumbeats cadenced the long march to the tables when Mrs. Wilson, her hand in the viselike grip of the little President of the Republic, felt "like a big liner with a tiny tug pushing her out from her moorings." As she took her place at the table, she was impressed to see the great heroes of the war, Foch and Joffre and her own Pershing and Bliss, moving to their places. And even the thousands of violets upon the table had been ingeniously molded into the shapes of airplanes, guns, and ships.

Poincaré spoke of France. For four years France had struggled, endured, suffered, bled at every vein, lost the best of her children. The French government had arranged for President Wilson to see the devastated regions for himself, that he might understand the ruin.

Wilson replied:

"I am sure that I shall look upon the ruin wrought by the armies of the Central Empires with the same repulsion and deep indignation that they stir in the hearts of men of France and Belgium, and I appreciate, as you do, sir, the necessity of such action in the final settlement of the issues of the war as will not only rebuke such acts of terror and spoliation but make men everywhere aware that they cannot be ventured upon without the certainty of punishment."

But Edith Wilson knew the truth behind the grace of the President's reply. He would go, no doubt, to the devastated regions. But he would go after the meetings of the conference, not before, as his French hosts wanted. "*No*," he had said when first the French plan had been told him. "The French want me to see red. . . . I could not despise the Germans more than I do."

After the banquet, the Wilsons were rushed to their palace so that President and Madame Poincaré with whom they had just eaten lunch might call upon them, and the instant the Poincarés had left the Wilsons were whisked back to the Elysée to return the call. These vital ceremonies were so adroitly managed that the afternoon was still young when the Wilsons came back for the third time.

Nor was the President tired. He was silent, as if his mind had separated itself from the complexities through which his body had been moved. Edith Wilson saw, as they came back to the unfamiliar Paris home, that he was not sharing her exuberance or her amusement. She remembered his face at the end of the first drive through the streets. It was an expression she had not seen before—a smile that was not quite his own or even quite human; and others had spoken of it, saying that it had surprised and stirred the people. At the Elysée banquet it had faded.

He asked her suddenly who was waiting to see him. There were several men, delegates from various groups.

"There is a woman, too. She says she is an organizer of working women but she seems to be extremely cultivated."

"Let her in."

"There are others ahead of her."

"Yes, I am sure of it. Let her in."

The woman came in, crying. She had spent many days organizing a parade—it was a body of hundreds of workers who had wanted to march to the Murat Palace to tell the President they believed in the Fourteen Points and ask him to speak to them. They had got their permit long before. Then, suddenly, as the women were assembling, an officer had come and taken their permit away, giving no reason.

The President glanced at his wife.

"You see?" he said. Turning to the woman, he said, "What can I do?"

"But you can do anything. You are the President of the United States."

"I am sorry. I should like to talk to your people. Thank them for me. But I am helpless. I am the guest of your government."

As the days passed, Mrs. Wilson saw her husband grow more restless under his host's demands. With each new day the ceremonies multiplied. There was the Freedom of the City with champagne at the Hôtel de Ville. There was the wreath on the tomb of Lafayette which the President, to the horror of the Florists' Association, had bought independently, and against all custom placed with his own hand on the grave. There was the initiation of Papa Joffre into the Academy. There were the elaborate plans for the President's trips to Rome and to London. There were presentations of golden keys, medals, jeweled doves of peace. There were astonishing quantities of sweet champagne and indigestible food.

The President admitted that these things were pleasant. And he was impressed by his visits to the hospitals. He enjoyed spending Christmas with the homesick American soldiers in the mud of Chaumont. But neither gaiety nor ritual were the things he had come for. Must the peace of the world wait so long upon the etiquette of officialdom?

And as, day after day, he drove through the streets and as the crowds of the people still surged about him, still cheered him, it seemed sometimes, as he passed them close, that in their wondering eyes he saw the same question.

2

On December 14th while Paris welcomed Wilson, the people across the Channel were deeply engrossed in domestic business. In England that Saturday the general election began.

A young American lieutenant in the American Officers Club in London was disturbed because an older American captain said the British election system was more sensible than the American.

"In England," the captain explained, "there has to be an issue before there can be a general election. At home, the election has to meet a timetable. So every four years the bosses have to lie awake nights thinking up an issue. Here they worry whether the issue is big enough to force an election."

"All the same," said the lieutenant, "our system gives the President a chance to mature his judgment. He can think ahead and meet the issues when they come. He is not afraid to work out a program like the Fourteen Points. Wilson couldn't have done that if he believed he might be thrown out of office by any popular whim."

"Did you vote for Wilson in '16?"

"Yes. My first vote."

"All right. You voted for him on a peace-time platform. There was hardly a word about foreign policy in it—only an implied hope that he would keep us out of war. In '17 he was forced to take us into war. In '17 and '18 he was expected to carry on that war without a word of official advice from the people. A month ago, in November, the election bucked him with a Republican Congress, though he and you and I know damn well the election was decided on local and personal issues. No large, important foreign issue was ever presented to the voters. The issues were simply cooked up because an election was coming. Then, after the election, the war stopped. Now, with still no official advice from the people, Wilson is expected to make a treaty in the interests of the United States. When the treaty is all made, the Senate can throw it out the window."

"They can but they won't. You've got to give the Senate

credit for some intelligence. Anyway, we'll be home then. We can force them to take it."

"How? There are no more elections. How can we force them to do anything? If, by the summer, the Senate gets a personal hate on the President they can throw his whole job on the scrap heap. And you and I can't say a word about it!"

In Number 10 Downing Street it was precisely this question about himself which had bedeviled the British prime minister since the signing of the armistice. He had not worried, at the moment, about the American election system. Wilson, he assumed, could take care of himself. Wilson, in any case, was safe in the tenure of his office.

But David Lloyd George had come into office under the British system to meet a particular issue. His party had chosen him specifically to carry on the war. Now the war was over. If the public had changed its mood toward him it might, of course, not make any immediate difference. But if there were any doubt now of the popular feeling, there was a chance of the public throwing him out later at some critical time during or even after the treaty negotiations.

So, as the question plagued him, he had decided to force the issue and ask for a vote of confidence in a general election. He wanted above all things to hold his job. He believed, furthermore, in all sincerity, that England—more than ever in the peace settlement—truly needed him. So he was taking a chance. But his faith in himself as a politician finally convinced him that he could swing the vote against all opposition. And once the vote of confidence was given on the specific issues of peace, there could be no later disaster.

As it turned out, his politician's flexibility had been bent almost to the breaking point. At the beginning of the campaign (which ended with the voting December 14th) he had, to say the least, been startled and distressed by the public temper. He had hoped for a little tolerance toward the beaten enemy. He himself had felt a great deal, and in an exalted mood on Armistice Day he had said so in heedlessly definite terms.

"No settlement," he had said, "that contravenes the principles of eternal justice will be a permanent one. . . . We must not allow any sense of revenge, any spirit of greed, any grasping desire, to override the fundamental principles of righteousness. Vigorous attempts," he warned, "will be made to hector and bully the government . . . to satisfy some base, sordid, squalid idea of vengeance and of avarice. We must relentlessly set our faces against that. . . ."

But when, later, he had met his public face to face, precisely what he had prophesied came true. Indeed, the baseness, squalor and sordidness of the demand for vengeance which was hurled at him by his first audiences topped his darkest fears.

"Hang the Kaiser!" hectored and bullied the enormous crowds. "Make Germany pay every penny of the cost of the war! Squeeze the orange till the pips squeak!"

What was he to do? Dispute with these hardy Britons who had supported him in all his ardent fight for victory? Refuse them compensation for the bitter sacrifices they had endured for its sake? Appear before them (however misguided they might be) as a turncoat, a traitor, a pro-German? Already as the question flashed for an instant in his face, there were murmurs against his loyalty in the darker corners of the hall.

What could he do? Did he, in the wavering moment, think with favor upon a more serene American system which at least permitted a man to hold his ideals? What he thought, the record does not reveal. It reveals only that, after a few attacks of hectoring and bullying, David Lloyd George chose the better part of valor and bowed to the extremely vocal will of the British people.

Perhaps it occurred to him that, later, when men cooled

after the battle, he could return to his tolerance. Perhaps, he argued that others, in the Peace Conference, would support it. But in any case, before many days had passed, he was hanging Kaisers and squeezing oranges with as much vigor as the most fanatic of his hearers.

At the end of the campaign, he had gone even further. He had violently attacked the Labor Party which stood against the hectoring. He had called their leaders Bolshevists—a fighting word in December. "If Mr. Ramsay Macdonald," he had shouted, "and Mr. Snowden and Mr. Smillie had had their way, we should have lost the war and what happened in Russia would have happened here."

That was the last speech. He had gone the whole hog. On the next day, the 14th, he rested. He was confident of victory. If, on the 14th, he relaxed sufficiently to read the *Times'* story of Wilson's landing at Brest, and if, reading it, he took comfort in the thought that Wilson might bring back his old principles of justice to mankind, he did not mention it in his memoirs.

3

In France, Georges Clemenceau also faced an election.

Clemenceau had no qualms of conscience. All his life he had fought for France and only for France. Now, in his aged body, little, strangely shaped, with his great white mustaches bristling his defiance, his skullcap hiding his baldness, his perpetual gray gloves hiding the ugly, painful eczema on his hands, his energy mocking all the signs of his age, he fought for France still. For him there was no tolerance of the hard-beaten enemy who had raped, desolated, all but destroyed his only love. There was no charity, no queasy afterthought, no sentimental retrospect on the great qualities of a misled people. He hated Germany and he hated Germans;

to him they were incarnate bad, all of a piece, the eternal enemy. To him there was only one future, that of a France secure forever against repetition of the assault—not by a change of mind, not by appeals for repentance, or Christian cheek-turning, but by guns and steel.

Clemenceau knew what he knew, had seen what he had seen, unclouded by romance. He had seen the coal mines of Lens flooded by the retreating Boche. He had seen thousands of hectares of jealously parceled land, tended, coaxed, enriched by generations of small farmers who had formed the core of France, seen it with the topsoil blasted off it, perhaps forever, so that not a blade of grass would grow. He had seen streets of houses, each with a wall torn off, the jealous intimacy of the rooms with their cradles and crucifixes naked before the barbarian's leer. Now, with Paris basking in the sunlight of victory, with all the world rejoicing, the peasants on a thousand farms were staring into empty stables and yards, calling to Georges Clemenceau, "Give us back our cows!"

These were not dreams from which a happy world had waked. They were French facts. So was the roll of dead French youth. So was the static French birth rate. So were the bent bones of the underfed French children who would grow, if they grew at all, into deformed men and women, a feeble generation, unfit for a new war. Yet the comparative population figures on the two sides of the Rhine—forty million French to sixty million German—still stood as the portent of another war. Words could not disguise it. Ideals of brotherhood or forgiveness could not obscure it.

For France, then, there must be no next war. If, along the Rhine, strips of French-occupied territory, neutral zones, bridgeheads could prevent it, France must have those things. If reparations, disarmament of the German army, crippling of German industry could prevent it, France must insist that

these be written into the treaty. It was not a question of revenge. It was not a mere desire for repayment of costs. It
was a question above all else of security for the future. That
was the view of the French realist, and if some of the organized workers who had been led astray by Russian philoso-
phies of peace did not subscribe to it, it was undoubtedly the
conviction of an immense majority of Frenchmen.

So Georges Clemenceau met his elections without qualms.
He felt no need to sop his conscience. The tricks of the
politician were not necessary. At the moment he faced his
public, he was with it heart and soul. At that moment he distrusted what seemed to him vague programs of Points and
Leagues. To him, at that moment, the old system of the
balance of power—but more adroitly managed—was a far
better guarantee of security than the "will-o'-the-wisp of
words," and he said so, frankly, before the Parliament.

By the second week of the new year, some of the seventy-
odd Americans attached to the delegation who had come with
the President on the *George Washington* and the hundred-
odd journalists who had trailed him became uneasy. It was
now nearly a month since the President had arrived and the
Peace Conference had not begun. Members of the staff speculated on the delay. Some thought it deliberate, part of the
wily European intrigue which was always suspect in certain
American quarters. The British, the French, and the Italian
delegates, they thought, were waiting for the popular enthusiasm over the President to cool. Others believed that
Lloyd George, Clemenceau, and Orlando wanted time to size
him up, to plan their approach to him. Some Americans de-
tected an inspired effort in the French press to break his
popular prestige. The press seemed to play up the political
news from America, debates among senators, divisions among
the people as to the wisdom and power of the President.
There was no question that the press was severely censored;

the censors, indeed, made no bones about it. There were large blank spaces in all the papers where cuts had been made after the papers had been set up, though what the omissions were only the censors knew.

The British press gave large space to the President's visit to England. The *Times'* editorials continued warm. More laconically, it reported the special enthusiasm of the workers. It raised its eyebrows—so slightly, to be sure, that only habitual readers noticed it—over the President's visit to Manchester to talk to labor groups, remarking that no Head of a State had done such a thing before.

The official attitude of Rome toward the President's visit was something else again. It had singular aspects which men close to the President were quick to comment on among themselves. There was no doubt of the magnificence of the reception, of the graciousness of the King and Queen, and of the hundreds of the nobility who kissed Mrs. Wilson's hand. The President's suite in the Quirinale overlooking the gardens of the Via Venti Settembre, the gorgeous state dinners, the drive to the Villa Savoia under "a dome of sapphire pouring golden sunshine over a radiant world" and the jewels and toilettes of the court were all that could be desired even of Italy, and quite overwhelmed Edith Wilson. But the President was not allowed to speak to the people.

Through delegates he had promised to speak to them in the Piazza Venezia immediately after his visit to the Vatican. On his way to the Vatican, the usual immense friendly crowd had almost stopped his car. But when he came back from his audience with the Pope, the crowd had been broken up and sent home by the police.

The President, unused to the official Italian attitude toward the masses, had been indignant. He had been told that the crowd was unruly. He had replied that it was nothing of the sort; that a gross discourtesy had been done him. It made no difference. He would be permitted to show himself to the people on a balcony, but not to address them.

The reason was obvious to men like George Creel and Gino Speranza and to other, closer advisers of the President. Italian Foreign Minister Sonnino had been terrified lest Wilson mention the peace before the Italian public had been properly prepared for what he might say. Sonnino was particularly alarmed about the Fourteen Points which had been given little publicity in Italy. Sonnino had other plans. When the time came to develop them, the people would have been given the proper build-up.

In Paris, after all the trips and ceremonies, the staff was ready for the Conference. The Inquiry—the group of experts—had settled in their offices in the Hôtel de Crillon and had done a great deal of work. Colonel House, in spite of a severe attack of influenza, had directed it. David Hunter Miller, the expert on international law, had prepared briefs on the freedom of the seas and many other matters. He had also worked on the fifty-six-billion-franc bill for reparations which the French had already submitted. Isaiah Bowman, the geographer, had prepared many maps. Secretaries, members of secretariats, technical advisers had been appointed. And there was a press bureau.

To the press bureau came the impatient journalists. They would be admitted, of course, to all the sessions of the Conference? No. But this was to be an open covenant, was it not? Yes, indeed. Openly arrived at? Yes . . . but. The press bureau would issue statements. Still, the sessions would be secret? No indeed, not the plenary sessions. But the others where the real work was to be done? Yes, they would be secret, sure enough, and without reporters.

A murmur arose among the American journalists and spread to the British, French, Belgian, Swiss, Greek, Chinese, Dutch, Swedish, Brazilian, Armenian, Egyptian, Polish, and other reporters, some of whom had come great distances to the Conference. The murmur became a rumble and a roar. So the first of the Fourteen Points was to be scrapped at the start! What price, then, the others?

The roar got into cables and headlines before it could be explained. The explanation was simple enough. The Treaty would be given out when it was drafted. The process of its drafting would be made known then. This procedure violated nothing. It merely rearranged the schedule of publicity. Obviously the delicate preliminary discussions could not be made public from day to day, before any patterns were formed. Furthermore it would be physically impossible to admit between five hundred and a thousand reporters to a small meeting in a conference room. The more thoughtful journalists saw sense in this, but their first disappointment had already been reflected in the press of the world; the headlines had scattered distrust.

In the two months since the happy Armistice Day, Paris had changed. It had become, in a sense, the Mecca of the world. Into it had thronged countless thousands of strangers. Behind the official delegations of twenty-seven Powers and unofficial groups of neutrals had come their camp followers: businessmen, industrialists, money-changers, entrepreneurs large and small, honest advocates and crooked conspirators, peddlers, buyers, spies, and whores. Every race, sect, and color in the world seemed to be there; every tongue, dialect, and vernacular of East and West was spoken in the streets. Malays, Pont-Euxine Greeks, Montenegrins, Levantine Jews, Mormons, Negroes, disguised Turks and Bolsheviki, Georgians and Khirgises, Quakers and Yogi, all were there. And the Parisian profiteers, hidden during the war, crawled out of the cellars to greet them with bows, smiles, and one-way pockets.

This bright parade of the outlanders brought a festive air

and Paris, welcoming them, remembered its tradition of gaiety. Among the high world, the trappings of grief quickly disappeared. Miraculous stocks of food and wine appeared, surprising the foreigners who had read in their home papers of starving France. Lovely new "creations" from the rue de la Paix appeared not only at Rumpelmayer's, at Larue, and the smarter restaurants of the Bois, but also at the private dances in the houses along the avenues radiating from the Etoile—parties from which the foreigner was rigidly shut out. Dancing became epidemic, a craze, and with the dancing was champagne from shattered Reims and *Foie gras* from recaptured Strasbourg and the celebrated Paris pastry made from sugar for which the women of the Faubourg Saint-Antoine still had to stand in line.

Into this merry whirlpool, ignored or pushed aside, drifted the demobilized soldiers of France. Day after day the men who had twice saved Paris came home to wonder that amid all the splendor about them they could find so little to eat. For four years their government had fed them well. Even in the rat runs where they had fought they had rarely missed their bread and wine and coffee, cheese and good rich soup. Now they walked the streets harassed by the fragrance from the sidewalk restaurants. Now their mothers and their wives were trying to figure how they could feed an extra mouth.

The more they came, the less room for them there seemed to be. Often they could scarcely find a place to stand at the zinc bar of their favorite *bistrot* nor could they pay the new prices for black coffee or Cinzano. Ahead lay the cost of civilian clothes and the dubious prospect of a job. Already round the periphery of the Paris whirlpool factories were cutting down their staffs or closing, and discharged workers were meeting discharged soldiers. Sometimes they would stand together in silent groups—because there was nothing more to talk about—and people who knew Paris well said there was nothing more ominous than a group of silent men.

So it was not surprising that subversive placards were torn by the police from the walls—placards about Russia, about international organizations of the oppressed, about the horrors of peace. Then, where the placards had been, stronger words were scrawled: strike, revolution, capital, words from an old song, "Ça ira . . . if we do not hang them we will burn them. . . ."

Thus, as the winter merged into spring and the black maskers crept in, chilling the dancers, lesser folk began to ask each other if it were still true, now that the wars were over, that America and her President could save the world.

4

President Wilson, as the Conference opened, was not deceived about the bigness of the problem before him. Every day of his impatience, the picture had grown larger, more complex. Into it a Greek delegation had painted Thrace and the Dodecanese Islands; Italians had drawn their brush with a broader stroke along the Adriatic coast, pushing away the brush of the Jugoslavs at Fiume; Poles had showed bloodstains at Lemberg and Posen where they said war was still going on; Rumania had painted in the whole of Transylvania and Bessarabia in her own colors; Japan and China had splashed conflicting shades over Shantung; Albania had put a question mark on Valona, which Italy coveted; and there were question marks also on Memel, Danzig, Trieste, Damascus, Jerusalem, large parts of Africa, and many islands in the Pacific.

And Britain had sketched in fictitious moneybags and a gallows for the Kaiser, and the map of France seemed every day to move farther over the map of Germany. But most insistent of all, wherever the President looked, he saw open mouths and naked bodies.

Into this crowded picture he must bring something else. He must bring the principle of self-determination as far as possible into the conflicting claims—peoples must decide for themselves the nation to which they wished to belong. He must bring justice, so that none should get too much and none too little. He must see that mandates or trusteeships were furnished for the colonies captured from Germany— trusteeships which would guarantee welfare to the people who lived there. And he must bring relief, for only his country was rich enough—but plans for this were already under way and, if Congress would give Mr. Hoover the money, would be carried out.

The President did not suppose these jobs could be done and the picture made harmonious without mistakes. Mistakes were as sure as the little green apples made by God back home. Toes would be stepped on and shins kicked, however you worked it out. People would complain, cry out to heaven, revile him and all the rest of the peace-makers. It was far too soon after the fever of war to effect a cool appraisal of values. But the President had the answer to these things too.

The answer was the League of Nations. That was why he believed the League of Nations must come first of all. Once there was a league, there would be means of arbitration for all the disputes. Once the League stood on a firm foundation it could take the Treaty—which, if there were a league, would only be a preliminary treaty—and debate it over the cooler years. With the United States powerful in the League, the unsettled questions would move always closer to just, unprejudiced solutions. So, however much Lloyd George and Clemenceau and Orlando and Japan's Makino might thwart him in the Treaty, the League would remain as his advocate for the future to keep alive the hope of the world.

Thus if Britain demanded impossible reparations or France pushed the barrier of her security too far, Germany would not give up hope. A treaty, after all, was a living thing, not a final act. If the League dominated the Treaty, was recognized at the start as above the Treaty, then there would be no dishonor if the Treaty proved flexible under its hands. If France, in her present bitterness, grabbed all the Rhine valley and wrote the fifty billion francs into the document, it need not be forever fatal to the peace of Europe. France and England might both, in a few years, change their minds. Italy might discover that healthy trade with Jugoslavia was more profitable than a strip of sterile Dalmatian coast.

So, it was for the very reason that he knew the map of Europe could not be made in a day that the President wanted the League. Given the League, compromises with hate or greed could only be passing phantoms amenable through the tempering years to the pressure of eternal justice.

This was the President's argument and to him it was final. Meanwhile he would fight with all his strength against every temporary injustice. If he failed for the moment, the League would be there to carry on. But on the League itself he would not yield an inch, now or ever, and generations of Scotch-Irish stubbornness stood behind him in his resolve.

5

It is not necessary to explain to anyone who has taken part in a large meeting that such gatherings by themselves rarely settle anything. An attempt to draw up a treaty at a series of meetings in which delegates from all the interested nations took part would have resulted in endless debate over details, bitter wrangles, uneven and unfair pressure from an ill-informed public and press, and very possibly, as one member of the American Commission remarked, in another war.

Also, the interests of some of the smaller states like Brazil or Albania were local matters, and if the time of the full conference were taken up with their discussion, the job would never be finished.

So, even before the first plenary session, it was decided that most of the work must be done by a Council of Ten representing the five most important powers: France, Great Britain, Italy, the United States, and Japan. The first four of these were conceded to have played the major parts in the war in Europe, and Japan had conquered many of the German colonies. In the Council of Ten, two plenipotentiaries sat for each nation. For the United States they were the President and his Secretary of State, Robert Lansing, for the others they were the Prime Minister and the Foreign Minister of each.

The plenary session on January 18th formally opened the Peace Conference with much fanfare and ceremony in the largest room of the Palais d'Orsay. All the delegates were there and most of the journalists. An adroit speech by President Poincaré, which somehow managed to mention everyone and was designed to make everyone happy, was followed by shorter but equally noncommittal addresses by Lloyd George, Clemenceau, and Wilson. Wilson nominated Clemenceau for President of the Conference and was seconded, by prearrangement, by Lloyd George and the Baron Sonnino. Clemenceau was elected by an acclamation which could hardly have been anything but unanimous. A little program business was presented and passed on to committees and the meeting adjourned amid the head-shakings and whispered complaints which always occur when a practical device is substituted for free-for-all debate.

The Council of Ten which had already met in the pleasant study of Monsieur Pichon at the D'Orsay Palace continued to meet there almost daily. The meetings were formal in spite of the seductive atmosphere of the room with its big fireplace continuously burning expensive French logs, its pearl-gray carpet with red roses, the fine Gobelin tapestries which warmed its walls, and its luxurious armchairs in which, durning somnolent passages, council members were said to have lost themselves. Clemenceau sat with his back to the fire and delivered himself in short bursts of what were known in Wilson's country as wisecracks; Wilson, intent and serious, sat at his right. Lloyd George beyond wriggled perpetually in his chair while his maned head shot from right to left. Orlando, large and soft, spread an air of benevolence, to the disgust of Sonnino who distrusted everyone including his boss. On Clemenceau's left sat some twenty secretaries and interpreters.

Wilson's first concern was to get special problems handled outside of these meetings. To do this, he persuaded the Council to appoint commissions of specialists. These commissions studied the local interests of the smaller nations, territorial problems, reparations, relief, anything which required specialized technical knowledge. They could make no decisions; their job was to present the facts in an orderly form to the Council and recommendations based on the facts.

One of the President's first objects in this effort was to clear the way for the League of Nations, to get the League first place on the agenda of the Conference and make sure that the League was made an integral part of the Treaty. By securing the appointment of committees he avoided dangerous delays and, in addition, provided committee machinery for working out the details of the League Covenant.

He had prepared the way by a quantity of personal work which he had wedged in between ceremonies ever since his first arrival in Paris. In informal conversations he had overcome resistance to the principle of the League on the part of the French, British, and Italians. He had then made a new draft of his Washington Covenant and submitted it to David Miller for close legal scrutiny. He had listened to the advice of House, Lansing, and Bliss on the new draft. So by the time the obstructions were cleared from the Council meetings, he had a completed plan for their official approval.

There was a persistent belief in America that Wilson had encountered bitter opposition and intrigue in Paris on the League principle, both in and out of the Council of Ten. This arose, perhaps from the desire to present a dramatic contrast between the pure idealism of America and the "Machiavellian" politics of Europe. In view of events as they matured, it is a curious concept. But the record shows no such antithesis.

The record shows that in the week following the opening of the Conference, Wilson presented to the Council a resolution about the League which was approved. The record shows that this resolution was approved on January 25th, by the entire Conference in its second plenary session.

Here it is:

1. It is essential to the maintenance of the world settlement, which the Associated Nations are now met to establish, that a League of Nations be created to promote international co-operation, to ensure the fulfilment of accepted international obligations, and to provide safeguards against war.

2. This League should be created as an integral part of the general Treaty of Peace, and should be open to every civilized nation which can be relied on to promote its objects.

3. The members of the League should periodically meet in international conference, and should have a permanent organization and secretariat to carry on the business of the League in the intervals between the conferences.

4. The [Paris] Conference therefore appoints a Committee representative of the Associated Governments to work out the details of the constitution and functions of the League.

Thus, in the first official week of the proceedings at Paris the President established his first and most important point.

The rest of the Council's work in the interval before Wilson left for the United States on February 14th reflected the chaos in Europe in the post-Armistice period. Actually, the Council became the new Europe's chief executive. Every disorder, every failure of the enemy to fulfill Armistice conditions, every appeal for relief came before it. It was expected to renew the Armistice when renewal came due. It was expected to restore order when Paderewski brought it the news that war had broken out again in Posen and Lemberg when a Ukrainian army of 80,000, officered by Germans and Austrians, had attacked the Poles there. It was expected to keep track of the intervention which was still going on in Russia and decide on the behavior of the Allied armies there and of their relations to anti-Bolshevik groups. And it was expected to speed relief to all parts of suffering Europe and to arbitrate difficult questions posed by that relief.

It is not surprising therefore that it was delayed in its treaty-making. It is not even surprising that it was not always successful in its immediate administrative functions.

Wilson left with certain obstacles overcome. He left with the assurance that many others obstructed the path ahead. He had been angered by some of the attitudes he had met, saddened by some of the conditions he had seen. He had been perplexed and distressed by the impossibility of solving certain problems and by the difficulty of preserving, in a Europe which changed from day to day, a point of view which was wholly detached, wholly in line with his declared principles.

In this temper, wiser, more conscious of humanity's distress, more fearful perhaps of his lonely power to relieve it, he turned his face toward the homeland where, among his own beloved people as he had so often told them, lay the hope of the human race.

9. Objection Being Made

SENATOR JIM WATSON, of Indiana, was a fairly frequent Sunday dinner guest at Senator Henry Cabot Lodge's house in the winter of 1918-19. The two men were good friends, respected each other highly, and enjoyed each other's company. But one Sunday evening after dinner Jim Watson found his friend with more than casual conversation on his mind as they settled into chairs before the fire.

"Senator," said Lodge (Senators always start their conversations by calling each other "Senator"), "I'd like you to be my special representative in the Senate on the League of Nations fight."

Jim Watson was willing.

"I want you to keep mum on this assignment and report to no one but me."

"Of course, Senator," said Watson, "but I don't see how we are ever going to defeat this proposition. It appears to me that some 80 per cent of the people are for it. Fully that percentage of the preachers are right now advocating it, churches are very largely favoring it, all the people who have been burdened and oppressed by this awful tragedy of war and who imagine this opens a way to world peace are for it, and I don't see how it's possible to defeat it."

Senator Lodge turned his shrewd eyes to his friend.

"Ah, my dear James," he said, "I do not propose to try to beat it by direct frontal attack but by the indirect method of reservations."

"What do you mean by that?" asked Watson. "Illustrate it to me."

"Well, for instance, the question of our government taking a mandate over Armenia, a matter which has been under discussion. We would merely demand a reservation on the subject. We can debate that for days and hold up the dangers that it will involve and the responsibilities we will assume if we pursue that course, and we can thoroughly satisfy the country that that would be a most abhorrent policy for us to adopt."

Senator Lodge and Senator Watson talked for two hours on the strategy of demanding reservations and amendments all along the line. Senator Watson was not entirely convinced that this tactic would really keep the United States out of the League of Nations.

"Suppose," he said, "that the President accepts the Treaty with your reservations. Then we are in the League, and once in, our reservations become purely fiction."

Senator Lodge answered with a smile of unshakable confidence, and the firelight deepened the lines in his face as Watson looked at him.

"But, my dear James, you do not take into consideration the hatred that Woodrow Wilson has for me personally. Never under any set of circumstances in this world could he be induced to accept a treaty with Lodge reservations appended to it."

Watson remained dubious.

"But that seems to me to be a rather slender thread on which to hang so great a cause."

"A slender thread!" said Lodge. "Why, it is as strong as any cable with its strands wound and twisted together!"

2

Woodrow Wilson had left behind him in the United States every shade of opinion about the League of Nations and America's part in it. Former Senator Albert J. Beveridge, of Indiana, for instance, objected to it on practical grounds.

"Consider our position and advantages," he said, "which all the money that ever was issued could not purchase, all the labor that ever toiled could not create. Nature has placed this Republic on the throne of the world—midway between Europe and Asia, from which we are separated by thousands of miles of ocean. We are perfectly situated for defense, and perfectly situated, too, for world trade, world friendship, and world helpfulness. Our forefathers cut with the sword all political relations with the old world, so that, under our institutions of orderly freedom, we could work out American ideals.

"Shall we abandon these advantages? Shall we sacrifice our heritage? Shall we enter into a government which places us in the same position as if we were a physical, integral part of Europe and Asia? Shall we poison American idealism and American aspirations with the age-old racial hatreds, ambitions and intrigues of alien races and distant lands? Can anyone doubt what the answer of the American people will be?"

Beveridge, like Borah, wanted to meet the League head on, to oppose it in principle. He urged Lodge and the others in Washington to put up a more aggressive fight. Painstakingly Lodge explained to him that they had to be careful; and at length Beveridge saw the point. Perhaps delay, after all, was a useful weapon.

The duty of the hour, he now said, was "to make peace, to call our soldiers home, and then in leisurely fashion make the decision on a League. We ought to take plenty of time to decide whether we want to make the United States an insurance company which itself pays the premiums for the insured as well as the benefits to the insured."

Still Beveridge maintained that no possible reservations or amendments changed the basic fact that joining the League involved giving up independence of action in important matters.

Senator Philander C. Knox, of Pennsylvania, wanted not only to delay consideration of a league, but if possible also to detach it from the Peace Treaty. He indicated his feelings by saying quite frankly, "The practicability of such a league in any thoroughgoing sense is, to say the least, most doubtful if indeed it be not altogether chimerical at this period of civilization."

Theodore Roosevelt, confined to bed, agreed with Lodge, and thought the league would be "a war breeder rather than a peace maker." The two men had a conference about the middle of December, and although neither of them knew at the time exactly what the Covenant of the League would be, they agreed on tactics to fight it, and on December 21st Lodge made a very long speech on the Senate floor.

Later he wrote to Theodore Roosevelt, "I am sending you a copy of the speech which I made on Saturday, which was intended chiefly for the benefit of the Allies."

The Senator outlined his ideas about the Treaty. He urged heavy indemnities, the leaving of territorial and border settlements to the European countries involved, and the abandonment of a League of Nations as a part of the Treaty.

Is it not our first duty and our highest duty to bring peace to the world at this moment and not encumber it by trying to provide against wars which never may be fought and against difficulties which lie far ahead in a dim and unknown future?

We are abundantly able to make our opinions known not only

to the President but to the Allies, who have a very clear and even acute idea of the power of the Senate in regard to treaties. They must know that the Senate can and often has rejected treaties. Others the Senate has refused to ratify and held without action. Many others have been vitally amended. The Allies should not be kept in the dark as to the views of the Senate. . . .

But when, on March 9th, Henry White in desperation and on his own initiative, begged Lodge for specific suggestions, the Senator felt differently. White's cable read:

I should be grateful if you would cable, in cipher through the Department of State, to me the exact phraseology of amendments modifying the League of Nations covenant which Senate considers important. It is our desire to meet the Senate's views as closely as it is possible to obtain acquiescence therein of other nations anxious for recognition of their own special interests, which immediately they will insist upon in the covenant if we in addition demand exemptions in favor of ours. Two days ago, I wrote you fully, but feel use of cable desirable time being so important. Please send full report of your and Knox speeches by next courier.

Although Henry White assured Lodge that this was a personal message and that he had not consulted the President about it, and although Lodge would be the last man to doubt White's integrity and good faith, Lodge feared some trap. If he expressed himself in confidence to White, he might be accused of attempting to speak for the whole Senate; and, as he put it, "I should also be committing myself individually to propositions upon which I might wish in the future to make modifications or perhaps very vital changes."

After consultation with Knox, Brandegee, and Elihu Root, Lodge declined to give White any assistance. White, deeply concerned over the threatening outlook, must ruefully have thought of the long memorandum the Senator had prepared in December, giving what Lodge then had called "the real feeling of the people of the United States and certainly of the Senate of the United States," a memorandum he had asked White to show confidentially to Balfour, Clemenceau, and others, as he thought it might "in certain contingencies be very important to them in strengthening their position."

There were a few Democrats in the Senate who opposed the League and some Republicans who favored it. But a lonely figure in the last days of the Sixty-fifth Congress was Senator Porter J. McCumber. Although a Republican, he was the League's most able defender. On January 7th he rose with angry passion written on his face:

"If you justify our alliance with France, Great Britain and Italy in this war [he said] to protect the safety and civilization of the world, then how in Heaven's name can you condemn an alliance with the same and other countries to prevent another assault on civilization? How can you in one breath approve the alliance to make war to save the world and in the next breath condemn an alliance to save the world by the prevention of any savage or brutal war which might threaten it? . . . It will not do in one breath to say that war is wrong and in the next breath that such wrong cannot be checked."

An anti-League Democrat was Senator Thomas W. Hardwick of Georgia. He too asked questions of those who urged the League: "Are you willing to revoke and deny and denounce the Declaration of Independence?" he cried. "Were the Tories good Americans? . . . Do you believe in the fairies? . . . Are you willing to enter into a league for perpetual, unending, interminable and innumerable wars?"

While the Senators were making their speeches, famine and pestilence swept central Europe. Years of war had reduced the crops, stock had been appropriated by the military, little coal was being mined and less was available to the average family. Distribution of what food and fuel and necessities of life there were was chaotic; prices had skyrocketed beyond the reach of any but the rich. Unrest bred disorder everywhere; had there been strong, organized leadership there would have been general revolution. In Russia many Bolshevist leaders were well aware of this and confidently expected Soviet rule to sweep westward.

This neither Henry White nor Henry Cabot Lodge desired, and White, receiving regular reports from Poland and Germany, cabled Lodge urging him to support the $100,-000,000 food relief appropriation urged by Herbert Hoover and Woodrow Wilson. Military occupation of these lands, White indicated, would be enormously more expensive and would not solve the problems of hungry people. It would only anger them and possibly serve to hasten revolution. Paderewski had sent a most urgent appeal for help in Poland where conditions were desperate, but the situation was little better in Germany, where there was also starvation and untold misery. White felt that a stable peace could not be accomplished without immediate help, and the United States, untouched by war, was the only country in the world that could save millions upon millions of human beings from starvation. And only food and help and sympathy would prevent more frightful bloodshed and revolutions and chaos which might be impossible to set right without the further expenditure of billions of Allied dollars and millions of Allied lives. The whole peace was at stake; everything depended upon adequate relief in Germany, Poland, and other countries in Central Europe.

Senator Lodge was unruffled. He wrote White a letter:

The bill for the hundred millions [he told his friend] has passed the House and is now in the Senate. It will go through; but there is a general determination that it shall be carefully guarded, and that the expenditure of the money should be in the hands of officers of the government who shall be responsible to Congress for the use of the money. I think there is also a very strong feeling in this country against giving food or money to the Germans. Reports from all the soldiers who are occupying German territory and from our naval officers who are on the inter-allied commissions to take hold of the ships and who have been in the German seaports, all say that the Germans have a sufficiency of food and are better shod and on the whole better clothed than they are in France or England. I believe our expenditures will be carefully limited to those people who were either our allies or our friends.

On the other hand, Lodge added, the delay in making peace was serious, for this and the continued food blockade were starving German children, killing their aged, and leaving the whole people bloodless and exhausted. To Lodge, the Germans with their "sufficiency of food," better shod and better clothed than the French or English, were starving and dying because Wilson insisted on his League, which delayed making the peace.

Senator William E. Borah objected to the bill for feeding the hungry of Europe mainly because Mr. Hoover's work had been "carried out without thought for the interests of American taxpayers." Borah wrote the Chicago *Tribune* congratulating the newspaper on its fight against the League. "The *Tribune*," said the Senator from Idaho, "was never greater than in these days."

To these may be added the remarks of a Senator from Ohio, Warren G. Harding:

"I do not hesitate to say that I think the world today, trembling under the menace of Bolshevism, owes a large part of that growing menace to the policies and utterances of the Chief Executive of the United States."

3

This was the country, these were the arguments, to which Woodrow Wilson returned in February. He had cabled ahead, asking that Senate debate on the League be postponed until he had had an opportunity to discuss it with the members of the Foreign Relations Committees of the Senate and House. The two committees were, in fact, invited to dinner at the White House. Senator Borah, of Idaho, and Senator Fall, of New Mexico, declined, but Lodge and the rest were quite willing to let the President have his say.

The President had not originally intended to land at Boston. He had intended to speak first to the members of the Foreign Relations Committee. But many people in Boston as well as advisers in Washington wanted him to make his first appeal to the American people rather than to Congress, and it was an approach congenial to the Wilson way of doing things. A speech in Boston would be a bold stroke in the camp of his enemy.

His "enemy" was unhappy about it. He wrote to Henry White:

As he is the President of the United States, of course I accepted the invitation to the dinner. I should not have thought of doing otherwise. I also felt, as a gentleman and man of honor, that having accepted the invitation to dinner I should comply with his request not to discuss the terms of the League as set forth in the draft of the committee, until after the dinner. The President, however, does not seem to look at it in the same way, and is going to land in Boston, my own city, and there address a great mass meeting which is all arranged for while I am reduced to silence because I wish to observe what I think is required of an honorable man.

Wilson's voyage home had been smooth and easy except for heavy fog and a near grounding off the Banks of Newfoundland. Many wounded soldiers were on the *George Washington*, and the President and Mrs. Wilson visited them daily. The Assistant Secretary of the Navy and Mrs. Franklin D. Roosevelt were also aboard, and Mrs. Wilson found them delightful companions.

Boston sensed a fight, and turned out for one. The Wilsons arrived shortly before noon on February 24th. Governor Calvin Coolidge, trying to look happy, and Mayor Peters of Boston were on hand to meet them, and to drive with them to the Copley-Plaza through streets lined with flags and streamers, enormous WELCOME! signs and fully 200,000 Bostonians. Up Summer, Winter, and Park streets to Beacon Street, through Charles, Boylston, and Arlington streets and Commonwealth Avenue to Dartmouth Street and the Copley-Plaza. Grandstands in front of the State House; Woodrow Wilson waved his hat. People leaned out windows; small boys clambered over statues to get a better view; flowers, cheers. Home.

Lunch at the Copley-Plaza privately with son-in-law Francis Sayre. Then straight to Mechanics Hall. Between 150,000 and 200,000 people had tried to get tickets to a hall with space for only 7,000. The hall was lavishly, not to say suffocatingly, decorated with streamers, flags, banners, large pictures of George Washington. The wide lecture stage was nearly filled with chairs to take care of a part of the overflow audience.

Governor Coolidge made a gracious speech introducing the President:

"We welcome him as the representative of a great people, as a great statesman, as one to whom we have entrusted our destinies and one whom we will support in the future in the working out of those destinies as Massachusetts has supported him in the past."

Other preliminaries. A speech by Mayor Peters. The "Star Spangled Banner," sung by John McCormack. At last, the President stepped forward to the center of the stage and spoke:

"Governor Coolidge, Mr. Mayor, Fellow-citizens: I wonder if you are half as glad to see me as I am to see you. It warms my heart to see a great body of my fellow-citizens again, because, in some respects, during the recent months I have been very lonely indeed without your comradeship and counsel. . . ."

No nation, said the President, distrusted our motives in Paris; representatives of every group and nation came first to the United States delegates, because they trusted us.

The crowd showed little interest in all this. They had come to hear what the President would say about Henry Cabot Lodge. The speech they were hearing was good Woodrow Wilson but not good fight. But the fight came later, and the crowd warmed along with the speech.

"I do not mean any disrespect," said Wilson, "to any other great people when I say that America is the hope of the world. And if she does not justify that hope results are unthinkable. Men will be thrown back upon bitterness of disappointment not only, but bitterness of despair. All nations will be set up as hostile camps again; men at the peace conference will go home with their heads upon their hearts, knowing they have failed—for they were bidden not to come home from there until they did something more than sign the treaty of peace. . . . Any man who thinks that America will take part in giving the world any such rebuff and disappointment as that does not know America. I invite him to test the sentiments of the nation.

"We set this nation up to make men free and we did not

confine our conception and purpose to America, and now we will make men free. If we did not do that all the fame of America would be gone and all her power would be dissipated. She would then have to keep her power for those narrow, selfish, provincial purposes which seem so dear to some minds that have no sweep beyond the nearest horizon. I should welcome no sweeter challenge than that. I have fighting blood in me and it is sometimes a delight to let it have scope, but if it is challenged on this occasion it will be an indulgence. Think of the picture, think of the utter blackness that would fall on the world. America has failed. America made a little essay at generosity and then withdrew. America said, 'We are your friends,' but it was only for today, not for tomorrow. America said, 'Here is our power to vindicate right,' and then next day said, 'Let right take care of itself and we will take care of ourselves.' America said, 'We set up light to lead men along paths of liberty, but we have lowered it—it is intended only to light our own path.' "

Again Woodrow Wilson had gone to the people, but the people had not got quite what they had hoped for. Was there to be no rough-and-tumble bout with Lodge? There was disagreement here, but the shape of the battle was not clear. The reception of the speech was mixed, confused, not sharp; the net effect was slight. And it was not a time for quiet stalking or for shadow-boxing. The round was indecisive.

A formal dinner at eight, in the state dining room of the White House, for thirty-six. In purpose, at least, a historic dinner for two billion. Here Woodrow Wilson vainly hoped to win the minds of seven men who stood firmly in his path. To reconcile irreconcilables.

If charm could have done it, it would have been done.

The White House was illuminated inside and out—the first time in two years—as for a state dinner or reception. The dinner was excellent, the repartee lively and amusing. Mrs. Wilson, the only woman present, was at her very best. The President was gay and gracious, laughing and talking.

Senator Lodge escorted Mrs. Wilson from the table into the East Room after dinner. She stayed only long enough to exchange pleasantries, but after she had gone the Senators stood about chatting informally. Meanwhile chairs had been arranged in an oval, and the President asked his guests to be seated. He made a preliminary statement, then said:

"Ask anything you want to know, gentlemen, and ask it as freely as you wish. I will answer you very frankly." He said he wanted to meet every point of view if possible, and he hoped no one would hold back.

The talk was easy at first. Lodge took very little part. Borah and Fall were, of course, not there. Brandegee questioned the President closely; the others talked less. The President was unruffled by cross-examination and answered calmly and as completely as he could all the Senator's questions. But he left his opponents unconvinced. Their minds had been made up before the dinner; that Wilson knew. There was also a question whether they had so far committed themselves against the League that it would be impossible for them to change now, even supposing they were susceptible of changing their convictions.

His friends on the committees remained his friends; his enemies were still his enemies. The dinner was a failure.

4

Tuesday, March 4, 1919, a fateful day in the history of the world. On this day, in something less than four minutes by the Senate clock, the League of Nations was dealt a smashing blow. Everything that came after it was altered by it. For many months, on the Senate floor, in Paris, later in half a hundred cities in the United States, Woodrow Wilson's fight must always be with that beleaguered night at the front of his thoughts.

It began on Sunday morning. Senator Brandegee knocked on the door of Number 1765 Massachusetts Avenue just as his colleague Senator Lodge was finishing breakfast. The two men went into Lodge's study.

"It seems to me," said Brandegee, "that at this juncture some declaration should be made to the effect that the League cannot be passed by the Senate. If possible, we ought to get the signatures of one-third of the Senate on the declaration."

Lodge saw the point at once. Brandegee's plan implemented everything that had gone before. All the speeches opposed to the League, all the arguments against it, had not shown what this would show—that the League could not become reality without concessions to the Senate. For clearly, if the League were to be accepted by America as a part of the Treaty, the Senate would have to pass it, under the Constitution, by a two-thirds vote. And if more than one-third of the senators announced that they would vote against it, the world would realize that Woodrow Wilson must yield his dream or compromise with the practical men of the Senate.

"Let's go see Knox," suggested Lodge.

Knox saw a possible objection. "You can't safely put it to a vote," he said. "It would be beaten. That lets out a Senate Resolution. You might get a third but you couldn't get half the Senate, which you would need to pass a resolution. Yet to carry greatest weight, it should be officially a part of the Senate proceedings."

Senator Lodge found no difficulty on this score. "You draft

the resolution," he said, "and I'll present it. I'll present it clearly out of order. Some Democrat is sure to object to it; so it won't come to a vote. If it doesn't come to a vote, it won't be defeated."

"It's taking a chance. I don't like it."

Senator Lodge was sure the Democrats would make the obvious move to stop such a resolution. So Knox made a draft, Senator Cummins added a few suggestions, and all three signed it. Next day Senator Brandegee led the hunt for signatures.

The Senate was engaged in a fight over appropriation bills. March 4th would be the last day for the Sixty-fifth Congress. The Republicans, wanting to ensure the calling of an extra session, were filibustering. The filibuster, as a matter of fact, was already won: it was obvious that the bills could not be put through in the time remaining. But the Senate was in almost continuous session, far into the night of March 3rd. It was just before midnight that Senator Lodge came into the Senate chamber, followed by Senator-elect Medill Mc-Cormick. They took seats; McCormick signed the resolution which Lodge carried.

At 12:02, Tuesday, March 4th, Lodge rose, and the hand that held the resolution was shaking. The vital import of the thing he was about to do was clearly in his mind. So too was the risk involved. For should the resolution come to a vote in the Senate that night, it would almost surely be defeated, and defeat would be a smashing blow at the plans of the irreconcilables. They were taking that chance; they counted on a Democratic Senator to take the bait—a resolution Democrats would oppose, and one clearly out of order at the time.

"Mr. President," said Lodge, and his voice was now steady, "I desire to take only a moment of the time of the

Senate. I wish to offer the resolution which I hold in my hand, a very brief one:

Whereas under the Constitution it is a function of the Senate to advise and consent to, or dissent from, the ratification of any treaty of the United States, and no such treaty can be operative without the consent of the Senate expressed by the affirmative vote of two-thirds of the Senators present; and

Whereas owing to the victory of the arms of the United States and of the nations with whom it is associated, a peace conference was convened and is now in session at Paris for the purpose of settling the terms of peace; and

Whereas a committee of the conference has proposed a constitution for a league of nations and the proposal is now before the peace conference for its consideration: Now, therefore, be it

Resolved by the Senate of the United States in the discharge of its constitutional duty of advice in regard to treaties, That it is the sense of the Senate that while it is their sincere desire that the nations of the world should unite to promote peace and general disarmament, the constitution of the league of nations in the form now proposed to the peace conference should not be accepted by the United States; and be it *Resolved further,* That it is the sense of the Senate that the negotiations on the part of the United States should immediately be directed to the utmost expedition of the urgent business of negotiating peace terms with Germany satisfactory to the United States and the nations with whom the United States is associated in the war against the German Government, and that the proposal for a league of nations to insure the permanent peace of the world should then be taken up for careful consideration.

"I ask," continued Senator Lodge, "unanimous consent for the present consideration of this resolution."

The bait was out.

Claude A. Swanson, of Virginia, jumped to his feet and sprang the trap:

"I object to the introduction of the resolution!"

Senator Lodge must inwardly have sighed with relief and the sense of victory. But he spoke calmly and his words showed that he had counted on what had happened.

"Objection being made," he said, "of course I recognize the objection. I merely wish to add, by way of explanation, the following:

The undersigned Senators of the United States, Members and Members-elect of the Sixty-sixth Congress, hereby declare that, if they had had the opportunity, they would have voted for the foregoing resolution.

Henry Cabot Lodge	William M. Calder
Philander C. Knox	Henry W. Keyes
Lawrence Y. Sherman	Boies Penrose
Harry S. New	George P. McLean
George H. Moses	Carroll S. Page
J. W. Wadsworth, Jr.	Joseph Irwin France
Bert M. Fernald	Medill McCormick
Albert B. Cummins	Charles Curtis
F. E. Warren	Lawrence C. Phipps
James E. Watson	Selden P. Spencer
Thomas Sterling	Hiram W. Johnson
J. S. Frelinghuysen	Charles E. Townsend
W. G. Harding	William P. Dillingham
Frederick Hale	I. L. Lenroot
William E. Borah	Miles Poindexter
Walter E. Edge	Howard Sutherland
Reed Smoot	Truman H. Newberry
Asle J. Gronna	L. Heisler Ball
Frank B. Brandegee	

Two other names, those of Davis Elkins, of West Virginia, and of Albert B. Fall, of New Mexico, were added the following morning. All the names were those of Republicans;

not one Democrat signed. Eleven Republicans did not sign—some of them, according to Lodge, because they were out of Washington and had not been approached.

On March 4th at noon, Vice-President Marshall, president of the Senate, banged his gavel and with bitterness in his voice, for he was a faithful supporter of Woodrow Wilson and the League of Nations, varied the regular "Adjourned, sine die," which announces the end of a Senate session. He said, and there was no smile upon his face,

"Adjourned, sine Deo!"

That night Woodrow Wilson and William Howard Taft spoke in the Metropolitan Opera House in New York for the League of Nations; and the next day the President sailed again for France.

The news of what had happened in the Senate went before him.

10. City of Light

AT the tip of the Breton peninsula—the thumb of France pointing west across the Atlantic—stands the somber town of Brest, gray, rocky, swept by Atlantic storms and rarely touched by the spring sun. Its harbor, cunningly designed by God and man, had become by the time of the war the chief naval port of France, and during the war it had been ingeniously improved by American engineers for the debarkation of hundreds of thousands of American troops and millions of tons of their supplies.

It was through the port of Brest that General Pershing and his first soldiers had entered France in July, 1917, and the Breton women had put on their bright costumes to greet him, savior of France, and in December, 1918, they had dressed again and dressed their melancholy town with flags and flowers to welcome Wilson, savior of the world. Even this stern and weathered folk had been stirred, that December day, by the cannonade of the fleets in the roadstead; they had put out in their little red-sailed boats to meet the ship of peace.

On the 13th of March, three months later, there was no ceremony. The women, tired of dressing up, shut themselves away from the wind. The wind sobbed in the narrow streets and howled across the emptiness of the Place de la Liberté. In Camp Pontenezen, a wide sea of mud in a fringe of the town, American soldiers played endless games of checkers and craps while they waited for ships to take them home. In the afternoon of the 13th, some of them stood on their duckboards to stare across the gray water, straining their eyes for a sight of the *George Washington*. But it was night when she came into the roadstead. The wind had dropped and the moon appeared suddenly.

In an enormous fur-collared coat which covered everything but his eyes, Colonel House waited for his chief. It was against the doctor's orders, as it had been in December; he had obeyed then but nothing could keep him now from being the first to talk to "the Governor," the first to tell of Paris and the first to hear of Washington. He was not hopeful about what he might see and hear.

But the President looked his fighting best. Never had his smile been so confident, his hand firmer. As he walked from the landing stage to the train, answering the salute of the American honor guard, his face became stern and militant. On the train to Paris, as House watched him and listened to the sharp belligerency of his voice, he almost feared his mood, knowing what lay ahead. It was a peculiar trick of House's genius to keep a jump in advance of his chief; to be a scout on his path, spotting the ambushes so that half his mind moved always in the future.

"Your Washington dinner," said the President, "was a total failure."

"My dinner? . . ." said House, who was thinking of the Baron Sonnino.

"Yes, the one you wanted me to give to the Foreign Relations Committee. Lodge and Knox never opened their mouths. I answered Brandegee's questions. But it didn't get us together."

"It did one thing, Governor. It stopped this talk about your being a dictator. At least, now, you've put your case before the Senate and the people know it. So even if you didn't mollify the Senators you've taken a long step with the people."

"Yes. Of course the people want what I want. They want the League."

"We shall have to amend the Covenant."

"Why? There are only details . . ."

"But to get it by the Senate. They want to include the Monroe Doctrine, don't they? And the right of withdrawal."

"An amendment on the Monroe Doctrine would not be a serious matter."

"If you ask for it, England and France may ask for concessions in exchange. And Japan. The Japanese think they have a Monroe Doctrine of their own in China."

But the President fought the Colonel's thoughtful doubts and premonitions. He would not talk of concessions. As for the Senate, it could not force him. He was as strong as ever with the people and it was the people that counted. It was the people who had made the sacrifices and given their sons and it was the people who wanted a new world without wars.

House went briefly over the course of the Conference in the President's absence. He told him of the delay in the work—though the committees had gone ahead as usual— because of the absence of Lloyd George and Orlando, who had taken advantage of the President's leaving to go home and attend to their domestic politics. He told him the details of the shooting of Clemenceau in February by a communist and of the old man's amazing recovery.

"It was a terrible thing," he added. "It was almost unbelievable that a Frenchman should try to kill him. But there is great unrest everywhere."

That, he explained, was why so many men in the Conference believed that they must hurry to complete the Treaty. The government in Germany was dangerously unstable. The Bolshevik propaganda was gaining ground in Hungary. The people of all the Central Powers were starving under the continued Allied blockade. Unless the terms could be settled quickly, these men believed that the whole of Europe would be swept by anarchy.

"An incomplete Treaty will not help," said the President. "Above all we must keep our minds on the League of Nations. If that delays the Treaty, then the Treaty must be delayed."

But the more the President showed his confidence, the less Colonel House shared it. Constantly, warily, in the last two weeks, he had been searching the future. Down every road he saw an impasse.

The French had not lessened their demands. On the contrary, the figures they had worked out for reparations had grown so fantastic that, if they got in the Treaty, they would weaken its whole validity. They had actually suggested a sum which came to two hundred billions in dollars! Now, on top of that and on top of their Rhineland claims, they were asking control of the Saar Valley in Germany to replace the coal lost in the flooded mines of Lens and Courrières. In Italy a new cry had arisen for the city of Fiume across the Adriatic—a place not even mentioned in Sonnino's Treaty of London. Lloyd George, while he opposed the Italian claim, was committed to his people for reparations and, as the French figures grew, he kept looking over his shoulder at England hoping for a softening of his people's vengeance. But he never found it. The British public was still listening for the squeak of the orange pips.

Each of these questions was soluble only by compromise. There was no other way. The President must learn to understand this. It would be hard for him. Even for Colonel House, familiar as he was with European government, politics, and statesmen, it was bitter enough. But House could not deceive himself. Once he had seen the clear lie of the cards on the table, he knew that no trick could alter the outcome of the game. And he knew, now, that one of those cards had been played by Washington.

It is now evident [he had written in his diary eleven days before] that the peace will not be such a peace as I had hoped, or one which this terrible upheaval should have brought about. There are many reasons why it will not be one. . . .

The American Delegation are not in a position to act freely. The elections of last November in the United States have been a deterrent to free action by our delegates. The British elections and the vote of confidence in the French Chamber of Deputies, put the finishing touches to a situation already bad. If the President should exert his influence among the liberals and laboring classes, he might possibly overthrow the Governments in Great Britain, France, and Italy; but if he did, he would still have to reckon with our own people and he might bring the whole world into chaos. The overthrow of governments might not end there, and it would be a grave responsibility for any man to take at this time.

Two days after House had written his forebodings, the French press had played up the March 4th "Round Robin" of the American senators. Yet the American Commission in Paris had been curiously unmoved by the news. They were so deeply absorbed in their work, so single-minded in their desire for a just peace! They were fine Americans, these workers, especially the experts, who were so interested in the truth that the evil winds of politics and intrigue rarely touched them. Almost hourly they had come to House with their reports and their problems: statistics of the precise damage—so grossly exaggerated by the French and the British examiners—to the towns of France and Belgium, to the precious forests of France and Italy; reports on the dead-end in Russia, on the stalemate between Japan and China, on the ethnic and strategic tangle along the Adriatic, on the Arabs and Jews in Palestine, on the food situation as it affected the various countries of Europe. There was, for instance, the magnificent work of Hoover, hampered by the Washington senators who were content to let children starve if they happened to be German. . . .

But with every day that passed, House became more certain of the hopelessness of finding clean-cut "American" solutions to these things; there were so many crosscurrents, human, racial, religious—from streams whose sources were lost in the dark before the dawn of history. These were not the material of a fixed and frozen treaty. Their flow could only be guided by an agency which remained forever fluid. The League had been such an agency—House caught himself thinking in the past tense and got up.

"We're both tired, Governor," he said. "We can talk in the morning."

2

Paris was a town for walking. Its variety kept the mind divorced from the legs. A dark, narrow street, bending to hide the surprise ahead, would open on a square of trees and fountains with a church of complex shadows rising from its center or it would turn suddenly into a telescopic vista or a curved sweep of arched river. And within walking compass were many eras of time and all conditions of men.

In the spring of the Peace, many Americans walked in Paris. When the day's job was over the workers of the Commission left the monastic atmosphere of the Hôtel de Crillon where the offices had seemed like the cells of monks, and late into the night tormented themselves with the vague nostalgia of the streets. In the streets there was no one to watch, listen, or interrupt, and these Americans, tramping for miles in twos and threes, over bridges, along quais, or straight garden paths, gave up their secret burdens and struggled for light.

The younger men had the most need of walking. Some had fought in the crusade of war; nearly all were still searching for the Grail. They were afflicted with passionate loyalties, some to the President, some to the ideals which now seemed to be moving beyond his reach. Over these men, in mid-April when the thick fog closed round the meetings of the Council, hung the menace of disillusion—most frightening of all bogies to Anglo-Saxon youth. Was the cosmic romance dead? Had the glamour faded from the beautiful abstractions: "mankind," "freedom," "equality," "democracy"? Was humanity with all its sweat and pain, its leather aprons and overalls, its bloodstained uniforms, still in the hands of a few frock-coated plotters in a palace? And was the western sun setting on Europe after its brief, hopeful warmth, returning it to medieval darkness?

These were the questions to which the discreet Paris night gave no answer. Yet there were ups and downs in the talk of the walkers.

"Clemenceau won again today. He has got his way in the Rhineland. Now he will get a fifteen-year control over the Saar Valley."

"Why not? France must have security. And coal, too. I have seen the mines the Boche have destroyed at Lens. Eight million tons a year."

"You can't get security by breeding wars. Here you're putting hundreds of thousands of Germans under French control. From now on those Germans will think of nothing but revenge—to fight their way back to Germany. And the Saar —yes, France needs the coal, but why can't there be an agreement for Germany to deliver it? And after fifteen years, France will never give up the Saar."

"Yes, she will. The League of Nations will see to that."

"Ah, the League . . . The League died when Wilson let in the Monroe Doctrine. What has the Monroe Doctrine to do with a world society of nations? It is just the American brand of imperialism—hands off South America! No, that amendment simply starts a long train of reservations. The Japanese will insist that everybody but Japan must keep his hands off China. Soon the whole thing will degenerate into a balance of power. No, I've lost hope in the League. It's gone the way of the Fourteen Points."

"I've lost hope in it too if the United States stays out. And the Senate will never ratify a league without the Monroe Doctrine."

"I tell you the League is dead. It doesn't matter whether it's ratified or not."

"I can't believe that. There's got to be compromise. Five governments can't be expected to agree on every detail on the basis of fighting a war together for four years—less than two in our case. You can't scrap the whole of history—all the past traditions and commitments."

"You've got to scrap it. That's what the Fourteen Points did. With the Fourteen Points, we could start from scratch in a new world. But what happened to the Fourteen Points? The British killed freedom of the seas with a reservation. The French killed self-determination with the Rhine and the Saar. The Italians are killing Point IX with the Brenner line and Dalmatia, and Point I on open covenants by sticking for the London Treaty. And Wilson himself has killed the League with the Monroe Doctrine. There go five points. And Wilson has agreed to them all."

"He hasn't given in to Italy yet. He's made a compromise with France because he had to, but he hasn't given the French half of what they asked. I think he ought to give them more than they ask. Until we get rid of the German threat to France, there will always be new wars."

"All right, fine. Cut Germany up, then. Disarm her entirely. Smash the whole empire. But come out openly first and abandon your Fourteen Points and the 'subsequent speeches.' If you want, occupy Berlin. It'll be expensive, but go ahead. But you've got to do one thing or the other. Either make a just treaty with Germany or don't make any treaty at all—dictate your terms and go on with the war to enforce them. But this job they're patching up at the Quai is pure hypocrisy. It's a breach of faith with Germany and it's a war-breeder. It's an announcement to the world that all the Allies except us were in this thing to get new territory. Britain and France get Asia Minor, Britain and Japan divide the German colonies, France gets the Rhine and the Saar valleys, Italy gets the Tyrol and the pure Greek Dodecanese—"

"Wait a minute. Part of those are mandates of the League."

"Mandates! That's just a word. You know what a mandate with Japanese administration means."

"Not if the League is on the job. But you can't say England and France were in this war to get territory. France was attacked and England was bound by a treaty. Italy and Rumania were bought just as Germany bought Bulgaria. But that's the way wars were fought in 1915. When we came in we brought a new concept. Wilson showed that the war went beyond nationality, that it was really a revolution of peoples against old formulas of government everywhere. At the end of it he saw the vision of a new formula introduced and carried out by a community of the nations of the world. And when he told this thing in words, all the peoples of the world recognized it."

"Are you telling me something?"

"I'm going to tell you something. I had to say that first. Wilson produced a new trend in the thinking of the world. The facts were there; he simply threw the light on them. Now you can't change a structure of world politics which is a century old in one year. The structure must change itself as the thought of the peoples is brought to bear on it. But Wilson has turned that thought on the old structure and what's more he has worked out a device to keep it turned there. As the years go on, the peoples, working through the League, will break down the old structure until it is gone. We're only at the beginning of the revolution now. But we, the United States, must stay in it and see it through. Wilson showed the truth to our soldiers and they fought for it. If Americans abandon the League now they will break faith with the dead."

"But Wilson has broken faith with himself."

"Never. He has fought for every word of his belief with all his power. He has been beaten sometimes. We've gotten the strange idea here that Wilson is all-powerful—a kind of god. Actually, I can't imagine how he's got the power that he has—with us only eighteen months in the war. But he can't control governments whose people have lost a million dead. The amazing thing to me is that he's won the concessions he has—not that he's given a few."

"But he shouldn't have given any. The British and the French signed the Armistice with Germany on the basis of the Fourteen Points. If they don't keep their word, he should withdraw from the Conference."

"And give up the League? Give up every point he has won? What kind of a treaty do you think there would be if he got out? No. This treaty with all its faults will be the best treaty that could be written—and ten times as just as anything that we would have had if Wilson hadn't been here. And the League will remain to straighten out the rest over the years."

"There will be a league whether Wilson goes or stays."

"Yes, and what kind of a league will it be, for God's sake,

with the United States out of it? Will the British keep their faith in such a league? Will the Japanese respect such a league? How long will such a league stand out against the old diplomacy, the separate secret agreements, the hidden kegs of dynamite, and the hidden fuses? Will it be a league of peoples or a league of rulers?"

"Norman Angell says it is a league of governments now. He says that the Council provided by the League constitution is a cabinet—an executive instead of a representative legislative body—yet it is expected to make laws."

"Yes, there are holes in the Covenant. There were terrible holes in the Constitution of the United States, too, in 1789. Any constitution has to grow. What good was our Constitution until it was amended by the Bill of Rights? Without that it might have become an instrument of tyranny. The United States is experienced in such things. If we are in the League, we can force that kind of growth because the whole spirit behind the League is the spirit of the New World."

So the talk went in the nights. Sometimes a young Englishman, such as the intense liberal, Harold Nicolson, who called his love for Americans a pleasant "vice," would join a group. Nicolson's bitterness against Wilson came not from disapproval of the Wilson doctrine but because he believed it so passionately. To Englishmen of his kind who had seen the light briefly and accepted the godhead, it was a shattering disappointment to discover the clay feet on which a common human, subject to doubts, defective eyesight, and indigestion walked among the Council.

Frenchmen did not join the walkers. The younger French specialists of the Conference were engrossed through the day in what they called the "realities" and, of an evening, they had more immediate concerns than walking on cosmic clouds. Their time, perhaps, was more profitably spent, for the restless Anglo-Saxons found neither relief to themselves nor solution to the gigantic problems which faced the lonely four in the heavy air of the Council rooms.

3

By mid-April, the hopeful gang of American journalists who had followed the President to Paris in December had lapsed into the mood of alternate mischief and boredom which affects persons of the press in the long absence of catastrophes. There was, too, an absence of official news. Only rumors could be reported in the doings of the Council. The few plenary sessions had been dull. The papers at home were sick of the local color and human interest which the reporters had spent many warm evenings collecting.

Most of the correspondents had been unfitted for the job. Many of them had never been to Europe. When they had arrived in France they had been furious at the food, the drinks, the bathrooms, the telephones, and the fact that Parisians talked French. In the first newsless weeks they had stormed about the city, scolding waiters, tram conductors, elevator boys, and hotel concierges. They had crowded the Folies Bergères and Harry's Bar and talked in loud voices about the benighted French. In those days they were not popular. But they made friends as time went on.

As the violent anti-Wilson campaign began in the French press, certain correspondents saw ways of combining it with the anti-Wilson campaigns of their home papers. They became more friendly with such French reporters as spoke English. They supplied these reporters with rumors, reports, and "inside stories," which, when printed in French papers, would make useful quotes for the home public as showing the French point of view. They cabled synchronous dispatches home. Lacking specific advices on the course of the Conference, they invented for it a course which was likely to please the politics of the home editors.

Through the ending of March and the first half of April, they became especially popular with the Italians who, at this time, seemed to be increasing in Paris. English-speaking Italians kept asking the American press boys to parties, talking to them at length in cafés, introducing them to the Hôtel Edouard VII where the Italian delegation had its luxurious headquarters. The talk was mostly on a town called Fiume, a town with an Italian name, Italian population, and Roman traditions, though across the Adriatic from Italy. By a tragic misfortune, they explained, this totally Italian town had come under the sway of Austria-Hungary, whose defeat by Italy had finally liberated it. Now, in a shocking access of injustice, the Peace Conference was assigning it to the new bastard state of Jugoslavia!

Did Americans realize who these Jugoslavs really were? Croats and Slovenes! (The Americans winced at the ugly names.) For four years they had fought against Italy. They were barbarians. To give this beautiful port to such scoundrels was a slap in the face to a brave ally who had lost 600,000 men killed. It was unbelievable. And it was against self-determination, for the people of Fiume had determined themselves Italians. Ninety per cent were Italian-born.

On April 10th, the *Herald* in New York published an editorial which read:

Mr. Wilson's high regard for the rights of small nations has certainly brought him up against Italy, whose claims under a treaty made at the time she entered the war seem likely to be disregarded, with the result that she may have to give up her ancient port of Fiume to a small nation which bitterly opposed her when she was fighting for liberty and civilization.

This editorial was surprising to those who knew that Sonnino's Treaty of London had specifically assigned Fiume to the Croats, and that Italy's "ancient port" had been under Hungarian and Austrian sovereignty since 1471, that its hinterland was entirely peopled by Jugoslavs, and that the Italians who had settled there had done so because it was a profitable trading center.

The American reporters were not told that up to the Armistice the Fiume question had not arisen in Italy, that in April, 1918, a love-feast called the Pact of Rome had been celebrated between the Italians and their hated Jugoslav "enemies" who were then called an "Oppressed Austro-Hungarian Nationality," and that the cry for Fiume had been stimulated among the Italian people since December by their government because their government feared the commercial competition of a foreign port against their own new port of Trieste.

By mid-April, however, even the Italians no longer relieved the boredom of the correspondents. By mid-April, the Conference seemed to have settled into such an even stride that it might well finish without further disaster.

Then, on April 23rd, a bombshell dropped in its midst. On that afternoon, the President himself gave a story to the press of the world. A few hours later *Le Temps* published it in an extra. In the afternoon a statement was issued from the Hôtel Edouard VII.

"As a result of the declaration by President Wilson on the Adriatic question," it said, "the Italian delegates have decided to leave Paris tomorrow."

And on the 24th Vittorio Orlando, amid a cheering crowd of those Parisians among whom the anti-Wilson campaign had been a success, boarded the train for Rome.

The President's declaration had rocked the old diplomacy on its foundations. In London and Paris, ministers, ambassadors, and suave secretaries trembled at the shock. Tories in the clubs shook their heads and spoke in whispers. But in the factories of Manchester and Saint-Cloud, the workers laughed with joy.

For Wilson, following an old conviction that the war had been a revolution of the peoples of the world against an old order, had appealed directly to the Italian people over the heads of their government. If, as the ministers said, it was a violation of the Council's secrecy, it was, nevertheless, a vindication of the principle of open covenants openly arrived at.

And Wilson remembered how the people had crowded the Piazza Venezia in January to hear him speak and how his hosts had adroitly maneuvered him out of it. The government had been afraid then of his influence with the masses. Well, if he could not speak, at least he could write for the masses to read.

In the appeal, the President told the people of the rights of small states, of the scrupulous safeguards which we of the League of Nations must give them. He told them of the necessity of access to the sea by the new small state of Jugoslavia. He told them that Fiume had been specifically assigned in the Treaty of London to the Croats, one of the peoples of that state. He told them of the great concessions of territory the Conference was prepared to make to Italy in the Tyrol and in the Istrian peninsula. He spoke of the American part in the Conference and of Italy's unbreakable ties with the American people which had been "drawn, millions strong, from Italy's own fair countrysides."

The whole appeal was a colossal diplomatic blunder, though, as many believed, a magnificent one. As Harry Hansen—a striking exception to the run of Paris correspondents—wrote in 1919:

In the history of the Peace Conference this appeal will always stand out as marking a turning point in diplomatic procedure. It will become one of the great papers of the conference; it will be consulted again and again not alone for its content, but for the moment that gave it birth and for the influence that it subsequently had upon the whole subject of Italian expansion on the east coast of the Adriatic.

But in its implications to Orlando and Sonnino the gesture was not pleasant. It implied a split between government and people, and this was a serious implication. In effect it denied the right of the delegates to represent the people of Italy at the Conference. So the Italian delegates went hastily to Rome to set themselves right.

They had no trouble. The politicians at Rome had done their work well throughout Italy. Appealing to the slogan-loving Italians with mob-rousing oratory, they had given the cry for Fiume an impetus which could not be stopped. It had been put into poetry by d'Annunzio. Its repetition in a violent Milanese newspaper had already raised an obscure editor named Mussolini out of his obscurity. And what objections there were from the socialist workers whom this Mussolini had betrayed were drowned in the uproar.

So Orlando, arriving in Rome, met an ovation which rivaled that given Wilson three months before. Papers, placards, speeches, reviled Wilson—the hero of January. Cartoons showed him in a spiked German helmet. Wilson's gesture toward Orlando was pointedly characterized by an antiphonal cheer, "Long live America: Down with Wilson!"

So the gesture failed. But Fiume was withheld. Lloyd George and Clemenceau, shocked as they were by his *faux pas*, stood behind the President. And, after their rage had cooled, Orlando and the Baron Sonnino came back to Paris just as the Germans were arriving at Versailles to examine what they called the "Diktat" which had been prepared for their acceptance.

The appeal to the Italians was the President's last great defiance to the old Europe. But as April turned into May and Paris bloomed in the first full spring of peace, the news from home was sinister enough and increased his belief that he must repeat his gesture at home, carrying the League of Nations over the head of the United States Senate to the people of America.

To save the League in the Old World he had made what were called "shameful" compromises and diplomatic mistakes. He had won a point in the French controversy over the Rhine and Saar valleys but in return he had had to commit the United States to an alliance with Britain for the defense of France in case of a new German attack. Yet surely the people at home would support that! Even some of the irreconcilables were weeping about poor bleeding France, which Colonel George Harvey had said must be assured "the fullest possible protection against another attack that it is possible . . . to enforce upon Germany with all the coercive forces of the allied and associated powers."

He had agreed to give Japan a limited economic control in the ancient Chinese province of Shantung. This had been a German concession since 1898 until Japan had taken it over in the war. In 1917, the Allies had promised to back the Japanese claims at the Peace Conference. But Wilson's concession at Paris was branded by his critics as an outrage against a weak nation and the Chinese delegation refused to sign.

And he had made other, lesser, concessions. But he had kept the League.

In the spring a coolness had grown up between the President and Colonel House. Some said this was because House had been too friendly with the European statesmen, too conciliatory toward Italy, too much lured by his love of intrigue. Perhaps the cause does not matter. The fact was sad enough, for it altered an old and a warm friendship and, to some extent, it split the American delegation.

But as May came, the President showed signs of fatigue. His friends said that no human being could have supported the strain without it. Night after night he had worked till midnight. He had had one serious illness with high fever, yet the Council had sat in the room next his sickroom and he had been in constant communication with it. He had continuously met the double burden of his principles and the complex detail of the Conference. His appointments had sometimes numbered eighteen in a day, in which he had listened to the complaints of woodcutters from the Tyrol, Jews from the Levant, Arabs of Hedjaz, Poles from Teschen and Lemberg, Chinese from Kiau Chiau, Greeks, Koreans, and Albanians, and workers from France and England. He had stood on a pedestal before which grieving women and children knelt in prayer and he had been called traitor, coward, megalomaniac, and even lecher in the press or in the clubs of Europe. He had gone home, once, warm with hope, and met political hate in his own capital. Was it surprising, asked the loyal, if lines showed in his face by the end of April?

But on May Day, when the unrest beneath the gaiety of Paris had risen to the surface in a general strike, when the army bivouacked in the streets to prevent disorders, many hundreds of French workers defied soldiers and police to show their persistent loyalty to their hero by gathering in front of the Hôtel de Crillon. "*Vive Wilson,*" they shouted through the long afternoon. "*A bas Clemenceau!*" The President could not answer them. But as he heard their cry he must have recognized in it the same trusting faith that he had met in the same Place de la Concorde on the 14th of

December, 1918. Had he answered their prayer in deed or only in word? Would the League which he had fought for these hard months ease their burdens through the years, bring them endurance of peace, increasing justice, security from hunger and fear?

In their mood of bitterness against their own statesmen, he could not tell them. He could not tell them, then, the truth he knew himself, that the completion of his answer must come now not from him, or from Lloyd George or Clemenceau, but from the people of the United States.

4

By invitation of the Conference, the German delegates, led by Count Brockdorff-Rantzau, arrived at Versailles for a meeting on the 7th of May. Their reception was cool. Barbed wire was drawn round the hotel assigned to them and the grounds in which they were permitted to walk. Guards were stationed outside the wire. On the 7th, they occupied a table in the midst of the Conference at the Grand Trianon palace.

The men of the Conference rose as the Germans entered, a courtly gesture by the victors to the defeated. The Germans did not respond. After Clemenceau had addressed them, Count Brockdorff-Rantzau began to speak. He had not been expected to speak. No speech from the Germans was on the agenda of the Plenary Session. But it was not the speech which brought a unanimous gasp from the members. It was the fact that the German delegate spoke sitting in his chair.

Colonel House wrote charitably in his diary that this might have been due to the Count's nervousness. But to most of the men in the room it was a studied insult and whispers ran round the fringe.

"A last slap in the face from the beaten enemy."

"It's characteristic. There's no decency and no dignity in them."

"But why do they injure themselves so? They haven't hurt anyone else by this stupid gesture."

As the Count went on, reading his long protest through his thick spectacles, while his beard moved slowly up and down with his words, it seemed to the Conference that his whole look and attitude, his voice and what his protest said all seemed part of the old regime, a proof that nothing new had come to Germany. What faith could be put in a government represented by a man like that? Even Kühlman, even Prince Max himself, could not have been a clearer symbol of the Germany the world had fought!

To the minority which had hoped and worked for tolerance to Germany it was a sad demonstration.

"It is demanded of us," the Count read, "that we confess ourselves to be the only ones guilty of the war. Such a confession in my mouth would be a lie. We are far from declining any responsibility that this great war of the world has come to pass. But we deny that Germany and its people are alone guilty."

In the days that followed, Brockdorff-Rantzau added to his protest a series of notes covering more than four hundred pages. He went back swearing that Germany would never sign the Treaty.

On the 29th of May arrived the official *Comments by the German Delegation on the Conditions of Peace and Counter-Proposals*. It was a long and repetitive document. To the Council it read almost as if Germany had won the war—certainly as if she stood on a level of equality with the powers which had beaten her.

It began with the Fourteen Points, on the basis of which Germany had agreed to ask for an armistice.

"This discussion," it said, "can only extend to the application of the Fourteen Points and the subsequent proclamations of Mr. Wilson."

Having said this, however, it began on the next page to quote from the speeches of Asquith, Robert Cecil, and Winston Churchill and on subsequent pages from those of Painlevé, Pichon, Balfour, Bonar Law, Lloyd George, Lord Grey, Ribot, Milner, and Orlando. It quoted from a book of Wilson's, *The State*, published in 1889.

From this variety of springboards it launched an attack on the Fourteen Points and subsequent declarations by Wilson. It protested almost every territorial change with the argument that it violated the principle of self-determination —including Alsace-Lorraine and the Polish corridor, for which the Fourteen Points had specifically provided. It called the League of Nations a "hostile coalition" in the concept of which reappeared "the fatal idea of the Holy Alliance of 1815, the illusion that world peace may be secured from above by way of diplomatic conferences with diplomatic organs."

It dwelt on Wilson's distinction between the German government and the German people, it referred to Wilson's note asking for a government in Germany which would represent the people, and it told of the answer to this demand in the German people's overthrow of their old autocratic rulers and the total regeneration of Germany. But now, the *Comments* said, it was the people which were forced to bear the burden of these terms. Even if the government had remained imperialistic "it would be difficult to imagine how harder terms could be imposed."

By June 16th, a committee of five—Tardieu for France, Philip Kerr for Britain, Manley Hudson for the United States, Vannutelli Rey for Italy, and Saburi for Japan—had drafted a reply. Meanwhile Paris was alive with the wildest rumors: of German mobilization, of new German revolution, of Bolshevism—always of new Bolshevist epidemics.

The special committee's reply to the German *Comments*, dispatched on the 16th, took instant note of the curious approach of the German Delegation.

"They seem to think that Germany has only to 'make sacrifices in order to attain peace,' as if this were but the end of some mere struggle for territory and power."

It explained then the judgment which had been passed upon the war by "practically the whole of civilized mankind."

"In the view of the Allied and Associated Powers the war which began on August 1, 1914, was the greatest crime against humanity and the freedom of peoples that any nation, calling itself civilized, has ever consciously committed."

It went on in a crescendo of accusation:

That, to attain dominance in Europe, Germany's rulers had taught their subjects that might was right in international affairs and indoctrinated them in the belief that all Germany's neighbors were jealous of her prosperity and power;

That these rulers had built colossal armaments in their plan of conquest;

That they had "developed a system of espionage and intrigue which enabled them to stir up internal rebellion and unrest and even to make secret offensive preparations within the territory of their neighbors whereby they might, when the moment came, strike them down with greater certainty and ease";

That they had kept Europe in a ferment by threats of violence;

That they had finally encouraged a subservient ally to declare war against Serbia at forty-eight hours' notice knowing that this "almost certainly meant a general war";

That, in the war which followed, they had violated Belgian

neutrality guaranteed by themselves in a sacred treaty and by frightfulness in promiscuous shootings and burnings had terrified Belgians into submission;

That they had begun the use of poison gas knowing its appalling effects in human suffering;

That they had attacked innocent women and children by bombing non-military targets from the air;

That they had driven the innocent passengers and crews of ships into the sea by ruthless submarine attacks;

That they "drove thousands of men and women and children with brutal savagery into slavery in foreign lands";

That Germany's conduct throughout the war was "unexampled in human history" and that the seven million who had died and the twenty million more who lived wounded and suffering "because Germany saw fit to gratify her lust for tyranny" bore witness to the "terrible responsibility which lies at her door."

The reply then turned to the people's share of the blame:

"It is said that the German revolution ought to make a difference and that the German people are not responsible for the policy of the rulers whom they have thrown from power." The Allies "welcome the change." But "the German revolution was stayed until the German armies had been defeated in the field and all hope of profiting by the war of conquest had vanished. Throughout the war, as before the war, the German people and their representatives supported the war, voted the credits, subscribed to the war loans, obeyed every order, however savage, of their government."

This Treaty was a war settlement. It could not be based on postwar promises of regeneration. To be a just settlement, it must carry such punishment as would restore at least part of the losses inflicted on the innocent and which would stand as an example to potential aggressors of the future.

The reply went on into the details of the German protest.

Here it was evident that the Anglo-Saxon conscience (which to the French seemed pathological) had been at work. For it was not the French who conceded changes in the Draft Treaty's frontier to meet the German protest. Nor was it the French who, in close adherence to the principle of self-determination, had suggested a plebiscite in Upper Silesia, or who had met the convenience of the Germans in the reduction of their armed forces.

A memorandum giving detailed defense of the Fourteen Points was attached to the reply. And an ultimatum gave the German Delegation five days in which to decide to sign.

But on the fifth day no decision had been made and Marshal Foch made military preparations in the Rhine Valley. On the sixth, the German government fell, and to make allowance for this, the Council gave an extension. But on the 23rd of June, word came that the new government had capitulated and that it would send two delegates whose names no one outside of Germany had ever heard, to sign the Treaty. So, on the 23rd, flags waved anew in Paris.

There was still a small minority in the Conference—with Americans among them—who felt that the Treaty's treatment of Germany had been prejudicial to eternal peace. They felt that Germany should have been allowed to take part in the Conference. They believed that the fantastic reparations demands—still vague in figures, but colossal in implication—weakened the whole Treaty. "If you ask a man," they said, "to agree to a set of conditions one of which is impossible, he will presently think of the others as impossible too, and eventually delay and quibble and perhaps refuse the lot." They believed that Germany should be immediately admitted to the League in spite of the Committee's (and Wilson's) reasonable argument that she must first prove stability and good faith. They thought the Polish Corridor was full of dynamite. They saw many breeders of long hate in some of the territorial clauses.

In the last few days, events in Paris moved fast. The Austrian, Bulgarian, Turkish, and Hungarian treaties were completed. The signing of the German Treaty of Versailles was set for the 28th.

So Paris prepared for a fete. The great palace at Versailles was made magnificent with red carpet. Troops of cavalry polished their sabers and their horses. The flags of the Allies were draped with the charming French taste which despises bunting. The Hall of Mirrors where Bismarck had forced the French to sign in 1871 was swept and dusted. Exclusive invitations were issued, which, however, admitted even the experts of the Conference and certain dignitaries who had taken no part in it. The great gardens were turned over to a gay public. The Germans signed at four. One of the pens broke down and another was hastily supplied from the pocket of a French secretary. The instant the last pen was lifted from the parchment the great fountains of the gardens of Versailles, dry through the war, began to play, all the guns in the circle of forts round Paris boomed the news, and in the remote *bistrots* of Clichy and Saint-Denis glasses were raised to the Peace.

On the 29th Colonel House wrote in his diary:

I am leaving Paris, after eight fateful months, with conflicting emotions. Looking at the Conference in retrospect there is much to approve and much to regret. It is easy to say what should have been done, but more difficult to have found a way for doing it.

The bitterness engendered by the war, the hopes raised high in many quarters because of victory, the character of the men having the dominant voices in the making of the Treaty, all had their influence for good or for evil, and were to be reckoned with. There seemed to be no full realization of the conditions which had to be met. An effort was made to enact a peace upon the usual lines. This should never have been attempted. The greater part of civilization had been shattered and history could guide us but little in the making of this peace.

How splendid it would have been had we blazed a new and better trail! However, it is to be doubted whether this could have been done, even if those in authority had so decreed, for the peoples back of them had to be reckoned with. It may be that Wilson might have had the power and influence if he had remained in Washington and kept clear of the Conference. When he stepped from his lofty pedestal and wrangled with representatives of other states upon equal terms, he became as common clay.

On the 29th, too, President Wilson boarded the *George Washington* at Brest. "His nerves were worn," said Charles Seymour of the Inquiry, "and his physique was shaken, but his spirits were high. If he guessed anything of the struggle that lay before him in the United States, he concealed the suspicion. The feeling of those that accompanied him on the boat was that the Senate must and would ratify the Treaty; that the country would enter enthusiastically upon the venture of the League of Nations."

So, as the rocks of Britanny faded forever before the President's eyes, his deeper thought was hidden. But the ship was gay enough to draw him out of any melancholy. It was packed with singing soldiers. Behind them lay the blood and the misery, the cold, the mud, and all their dead friends. Behind them lay Europe with its *vin blanc*, its "mademoiselles" of whom they still sang, its box cars, its incomprehensible language, and its effete customs. Ahead lay home, freedom, folks, civies, and ice cream. So, late into the night they sang of God's country,

"Where the ash and the oak and the bonny willow tree
All grow together back in North Amerikee."

11. The Pastures of Peace

THE campaign of the irreconcilables was expensive. Pamphlets were distributed, especially in the Middle West and in states where it was thought a strong campaign might develop enough pressure to win over one or two wavering senators. There was newspaper advertising. There were mass meetings to be paid for, there was much high-priced traveling by speakers and publicists, there were all the other expenses naturally connected with an elaborate and extensive campaign of this type.

In the spring of 1919 the Hearst papers all over the country, the Chicago *Tribune*, the Kansas City *Star*, and the New York *Sun* were all holding up their end and banging faithfully away against the League, but other phases of the job were slowing down.

And so, in May, 1919, there was a meeting of glum anti-Leaguers at the Washington home of Senator Brandegee. The irreconcilables, so far as funds for their campaign went, were broke.

Senator Medill McCormick thought he could raise twenty thousand dollars back in Illinois, where isolationist feeling was strong and growing stronger. But this was clearly not enough. By chance, one of the men present mentioned that he was going to a dinner to be given by Henry Clay Frick, the Pittsburgh steel multimillionaire, in honor of General Wood. Senator Knox shouted eureka.

"Why not take Mr. Frick aside," he suggested, "and give him the story? He and Andrew Mellon usually act together on things like this, and if you manage to get something out of Frick, I'll talk to Mellon at once, and we ought to get something out of him too."

George Harvey, telling this story several years later in his book *Henry Clay Frick; The Man,* leaves the reader with the impression that the irreconcilable representative was himself, though he calls him "the eager propagandist," "the delegated conspirator," "the New York member of the cabal."

Harvey, if it was he, found his task remarkably easy. In fact Mr. Frick opened the subject himself, asking his visitor to give him the irreconcilable side of the League question. Harvey gave him the "stock arguments," and Mr. Frick was apparently convinced at once.

"As I understand it," Frick said with some amazement, "the proposition is to pledge the United States, now the richest and most powerful nation in the world, to pool its issue with other countries, which are largely its debtors, and to agree in advance to abide by the policies and practices adopted by a majority or two-thirds of its associates; that is, to surrender its present right of independence of action upon any specific question whenever such a question may arise."

"That is substantially it."

"Well, I am opposed to that. Of course I am. I don't see how any experienced businessman could fail to be. Why, it seems to me a crazy thing to do."

"That is what Senator Knox and the rest of us think. Now the question is, Will you help us beat it?"

"What do you want me to do?"

Same thing people were always asking Mr. Frick to do, of course. Harvey described the needs of the anti-League group. Frick wanted to know why Mr. Mellon hadn't been approached.

"For some reason or other Senator Knox seemed to think it might be well for me to pull your leg first."

"Come now, do you consider that a compliment or a reflection?"

"Oh, a compliment surely. In fact, my only objection to his program was that Mr. Mellon might feel aggrieved."

Frick, in a happy mood, chuckled over the joke.

"Well, I'll go along. How much do you want?"

Harvey suggested a sum.

"That won't go far."

Harvey recovered quickly. "Only for a starter of course."

"It will be sent in the morning."

Senator Knox immediately approached Mr. Mellon, who made a similar contribution. The expenses of the anti-League campaign were very largely covered by these two Pittsburgh multimillionaires.

2

As the end of the Sixty-fifth Congress drew near the Republican leaders found that control of the new Congress was going to be a matter of touch and go. In the Senate there were forty-nine Republicans and forty-seven Democrats. But Senator McCumber, a Republican, was definitely pro-League; and Senator La Follette was a man of extraordinarily independent disposition. Henry Cabot Lodge couldn't count on him as he might have liked. It was true that Democratic Senator Reed, of Missouri, usually followed the Republican line on matters concerning the League. But the balance was too close for comfort, especially when it is remembered that Vice-President Thomas Marshall, whose vote decided in case of a tie in the Senate, was a Democrat and a faithful Wilson follower. Yet, as Republican leader, Senator Lodge was determined to maintain control.

Because the balance was so close, every single seat was of exaggerated importance. One member of the new Senate, Truman Newberry, of Michigan, had been elected over

Henry Ford after the expenditure of fantastic sums of money in both his primary campaign and the election. In the closing days of the Sixty-fifth Congress, Democratic leaders, especially Senator Pomerene, of Ohio, had attempted to get a thorough investigation. In the end they had failed. The Republicans had threatened to filibuster to the close of the session if it were attempted.

When Newberry was sentenced by a United States court to two years in Leavenworth (the sentence was later reversed by the United States Supreme Court) for violation of the election laws it was embarrassing to such Republicans as Senator Medill McCormick, who had begun his public career with denunciation of a similar scandal in Illinois. But it would have been too risky to permit the Newberry seat to be lost. And the fact that something over $175,000 had been spent to gain Senator Newberry his seat seemed much less important to his colleagues than accusations of wasteful expenditure by the Wilson administration during the war.

Without the aid of Senator Newberry, the Republican leaders might not have been able to dictate the membership of the important committees. With his vote they were able, for instance, to organize the Senate Foreign Relations Committee as follows:

Republicans	Democrats
Henry Cabot Lodge, Mass.	Gilbert M. Hitchcock, Neb.
Porter J. McCumber, N.D.	John Sharp Williams, Miss.
Wm. E. Borah, Id.	Claude A. Swanson, Va.
Frank B. Brandegee, Conn.	Atlee Pomerene, Ohio
Albert B. Fall, N.Mex.	Marcus A. Smith, Ariz.
Philander C. Knox, Pa.	Key Pittman, Nev.
Warren G. Harding, Ohio	John K. Shields, Tenn.
Hiram W. Johnson, Calif.	
Harry S. New, Ind.	
George H. Moses, N.H.	

Of the Republicans on the Committee, all except Senator McCumber had signed the Lodge-Brandegee-Knox Round Robin of March 4th.

This was the committee to which Henry Cabot Lodge had referred when, during the President's stay in Washington, he had said, "If the Foreign Relations Committee approves it [the Treaty] I feel there is no doubt of ratification." It was of course a perfectly correct statement. As one wit said, "He might as well have said that if the Foreign Relations Committee approves it the Senate will drop dead." Lodge, Brandegee, and Knox, the framers of the March 4th resolution; Johnson and Borah, the western isolationist senators whose sincerity the entire nation recognized; Albert B. Fall, who had his own set of reservations to the Treaty; Harding, New, and Moses, generally regarded as reliable Republican yes-men who could be depended upon to take party orders. What were the chances of approval here?

Yet the fight was far from over when, on May 19th, the Sixty-sixth Congress met for the first time, in extraordinary session. There is no need to review in detail the debate as it continued from these first meetings until President Wilson's return from Paris. It was not all concerned with the League. Republicans, whose control of the Senate rested partly upon the presence there of Truman H. Newberry, accused the Wilson administration of corruption and waste of public funds. There was much criticism of the income tax, a measure particularly unpoplar among New York City's wealthy. German-American elements were told that the League of Nations was aimed at Germany; Irish-American elements were told that it would force America to fight to keep Ireland under the British; Italian-Americans were aroused by the Fiume controversy.

Wilson, in Paris, gave little evidence of concern about these debates and arguments. Perhaps he thought them unimportant beside the work he was trying to do. Even after his arrival in America in July he made few attempts to answer his critics, but pressed only for ratification of the Treaty with the Covenant of the League as a part of it. He denied nothing, argued no points, made no accusations. He had one weapon, a weapon he had found effective in the past, a weapon in which he believed implicitly. It was not yet time to use it.

3

Woodrow Wilson landed in New York on July 8th. The New York *Tribune*, a leading Republican paper, vividly described his reception. Thousands had been waiting for him for hours. He had hardly left the Twenty-third Street Ferry on his drive to Carnegie Hall when the cheers brought him to his feet in the touring car and kept him there the full distance.

They saw in him [reported the *Tribune*] the symbol of the victory and the peace, therefore the children shouted and white-haired women leaned from the boarding house windows with tears streaming down their cheeks to throw him a "God bless you!"

But the shouts and cheers of West Twenty-third Street and Fifth Avenue were as nothing to the prolonged din that came from nearly four thousand throats as he entered Carnegie Hall . . .

Next day, in Washington, the Treaty was before the Senate. There was very little debate now on any parts of the Treaty except the League. The strategy of the Republicans now became more clearly defined and changed to a policy of attacking each Article of the League Covenant, using every argument imaginable, and in general portraying the League as something which would take away all American rights and make more wars certain, with American participation in each and every one inevitable. Article 11, for instance, which provides a mechanism for thorough discussion of minor disputes by all powers before they come to a head, and which was designed to prevent small wars which might develop into great ones, to the opposition became dangerous and threatening. "Under this provision," argued the Republican Publicity Association in an article later printed in the *Congressional Record*, "the United States . . . immediately becomes involved in every war of the future, no matter how far from our shores. . . . Our soldiers and sailors, to all intents and purposes, automatically become hirelings of the League, subject to orders to proceed to the scene of bloodshed and fight against the country that the council may deem to be in the wrong. Do you want to send your boys off on such a mission?"

Article 10, however, loomed as the most controversial of all. The article read:

The Members of the League undertake to respect and preserve as against external aggression the territorial integrity and existing political independence of all Members of the League. In case of any such aggression, the Council shall advise upon the means by which this obligation shall be fulfilled.

Mr. William Howard Taft pointed out the fact that the strength of this article lay in its acceptance by the United States. If this nation, with its tremendous power, prestige, and moral influence, accepted it, was there one nation that would dare to enter a war which might bring the United States in against it? Mr. Taft thought it extremely unlikely. So, of course, did Mr. Wilson. Most French statesmen, fearing another attack by Germany, considered Article 10 of primary importance—in fact without it they considered that the League could not succeed. Small nations regarded it as their protection—and their main reason for joining the league.

In the weeks ahead, Article 10 was gradually to take its place as the keynote of Republican objection to the League and the Treaty.

The importance of the fight that seated Senator Newberry of Michigan became clearer than ever during the debates that followed immediately upon the presentation of the Treaty to the Senate. On July 17th, Rhode Island's Republican Senator Colt came out for the League. The forces were lining up into three main groups: irreconcilables, mild reservationists, and those who would accept the Treaty without change. Each day the balance got more delicate; as it teetered, the invective on both sides of the question got stronger.

The hot Senate debates of July and August centered mostly on the reservations which Senator Lodge proposed to attach to the Treaty. As the Senator had told Jim Watson, President Wilson would not be likely to approve of these reservations. Thus the blame for the defeat of the Treaty and of the League could be switched from the Senators who had originated the reservations and had said frankly that their intention was to defeat the Treaty, to the President who had worked and fought for it.

The reservationists in their many speeches and their nearly continuous succession of strategic parliamentary maneuvers sought to represent the President as stubborn and willful, unable to accept even the slightest change in his handiwork. Mr. Taft's explanation of the importance of Article 10 did not have any effect. Nor did Senator Key Pittman's reminder that if one nation could adopt reservations to suit itself, so could any other nation. If the United States could make certain parts of the contract inapplicable, Brazil could also void sections objectionable to her, and so could all the other twenty-odd countries, and if they did, what use would the

Treaty be? Each nation would agree only to the parts that pleased it, and it was quite unlikely that these would prove the same parts in all cases. Furthermore, Senator Pittman pointed out, if the United States adopted reservations, all other signatories would have to accept these or the Treaty would not bind them. It would result either in a hopeless deadlock or in interminable negotiations. Meanwhile the nations of Europe faced the superhuman task of bringing order out of unprecedented chaos. They needed to know what our stand was. Senator Pittman implied that his opponents knew perfectly well that the reservations they proposed were impossible and that they were meant to be impossible from the beginning. It would be better for the world, he thought, to settle the matter quickly one way or the other, and without reopening the contention and strife that was inevitable if reservations were attached. "If you are against the League of Nations," he said, "then say so and vote against it; kill it openly and quickly, but do not give it a slow poison that must result in its death."

The President had offered to appear before the Senate Committee on Foreign Relations but had not been called. At length, on the morning of August 19th, he asked the Committee to meet with him at the White House.

The conference was carried on with frankness and politeness, but it settled nothing. The President answered innumerable oral questions and accepted a long list of written queries from Senator Fall to be answered at his leisure. His answers apparently did not sway the feelings of a single Senator, nor did his extended accounts of how certain parts of the treaty were formulated. No action was decided upon, no later conferences were planned for the following weeks. Little was said that had not been said before. The senators who had said before the conference that they could not understand certain provisions of the treaty still said they could not understand them.

Perhaps the conference was not intended to settle anything or change anything; perhaps the President, who had called it, did not expect that it would. Was the purpose of it merely to put certain things on record? Was it merely to avoid charges that he had not been frank in answering questions or in meeting with his opponents? Or were the stenographic notes which were rushed through and released to the press in sections while the conference itself was still going on intended to inform the American public? Whatever its purpose, the meeting passed into history practically without notice. It was another vain effort.

The President tried another approach. He asked fourteen of the reservationist senators to confer with him individually at the White House. One by one they came and one by one they left, and the President knew that he had accomplished nothing. The fourteenth was Senator Jim Watson of Indiana. Watson, though a League opponent, had a profound respect for the President and an honesty and frankness which Wilson, in turn, respected and valued.

When Jim Watson arrived at the White House he was shown to the Red Room by Mr. Tumulty, and the President joined him at once. The President and the Senator, members of the same college fraternity, shook hands.

"Senator," said the President, seating himself in a comfortable chair, "they tell me you know how this fight in the Senate is going, and furthermore, they tell me you will give me the truth about the situation."

"I'm flattered by the suggestion," said Watson. "I can't say I know exactly what the situation is, but I'll certainly tell you the truth if I tell you anything."

The President hesitated a moment. Then, leaning forward with the air of a man about to exchange confidences with an old friend, he asked,

"Where am I in the Senate on this fight?"

"Mr. President, you are licked."

"By what majority?"

"That varies with the reservations—on some you will be better off than on others. I can show you the votes if you want to see them—"

The President waved away the suggestion.

"I don't want to see the votes," he said, "I just want your résumé of the situation."

"Well, take the subject of mandates. You will get twenty-four votes in the Senate in favor of that proposition."

Wilson's jaw dropped in amazement. For a moment he was speechless, then he slowly measured out his words.

"You mean to tell me that twenty-four votes is all I can get on the mandates?"

"Mr. President, that is the sum total."

Wilson shifted in his chair, stared for a moment at the floor, then looked up boyishly.

"I heard a story today—and you are probably one of the last men in the world I should repeat it to."

"I'm a sucker for a story," said Watson, "and I hope it's one on me!"

"Don't take it personally," said the President. "It's about the little boy who told his teacher that his father was a pickpocket."

"Yes."

"The teacher called the father on the telephone and reported what the little boy had said, but the father didn't seem excited. The teacher was shocked. 'But you aren't *really*, are you?' she asked.

" 'Well, no,' said the father. 'But you wouldn't have me let him know I'm a Senator, would you?' "

"Wait till I tell that one to Warren Harding!" Watson said, slapping his knee.

"But, seriously, Senator, is there no hope?"

"Mr. President," said Watson, "there is just one way by which you can take the United States into the League of Nations."

"What way is that?"

"Accept it with the Lodge reservations."

Wilson jumped to his feet.

"Never!"

Jim Watson got up slowly, and as he watched the President's angry face he thought of Lodge's words by the fire-light. This hatred was indeed "a cable with its strands coiled and twisted together," but that did not, of course, take into account whatever objections the President might have about the reservations themselves. Jim Watson credited Wilson with sincerity and intelligence, however much he disagreed with him. Now the President was striding with quick nervous steps to the window. Suddenly he turned.

"I'll appeal to the people!" he said, and there was firm decision, but Watson thought little confidence in his voice. Suddenly Wilson looked frail and discouraged. Watson hesitated before he spoke again.

"It is too late," he said. "You are like a man in quick-sands now, and every struggle you make will only sink you the deeper. People are not for the League now, and you cannot bring them around. And if you will pardon the suggestion, you had better reconcile yourself to the situation, go on with your administration to the end, preserve your health, and save yourself for future greatness in private life."

Wilson offered his hand and Watson took it as they walked to the door.

"Thank you, Senator, for your friendliness and frankness. But it is to the people I must turn now."

"But you can't!" said Mrs. Wilson that evening. "You are too worn out. What you need is a long rest, and instead of a rest you plan one of the most exhausting trips you've ever undertaken."

"There's no other way."

"Cary—you mustn't let him. As a doctor you must see that he's in no condition to do it."

"She's right, you know," said Dr. Grayson. "Think a little about what you will have to face. The terrific heat in the Middle West—the continuous heat on the train—the smoke and cinders and dust. The cumulative discomfort, day after day, week after week—it's really quite beyond you."

"It's dangerous—and where will the League be if you break down?" Mrs. Wilson was plainly frightened.

"You'll have to make dozens of speeches under difficult conditions. You'll have to shake hands with at least five thousand people. The horrible food at the official luncheons and dinners. There'll be parades and receptions—you'll spend most of your time standing up in the back seat of touring cars."

"It makes me ill to think of it," said Mrs. Wilson.

"You needn't go. There's no need for you to—"

"You don't think I'd let you go alone, do you?"

The President gave her an affectionate look.

"Think of the mental strain," said Grayson. "They'll schedule every minute of your time and you'll be under pressure to stick to the schedule and at the same time to do things local groups will want you to do. They'll want to show you the sights and want you to meet local committees and talk to schoolchildren. They'll feed you lunch and they'll all have brass bands blaring away at you."

"That's all true," said the President, "but I feel it's my duty. My own health is not to be considered when the future peace and security of the world are at stake. If the Treaty isn't ratified, the war will have been fought in vain, and the world will be thrown into chaos. When I asked our soldiers to take up arms, I promised them that this was a war to end wars. If I do not do everything in my power to put the Treaty through, I will never be able to look those boys in the eyes. I must go!"

Mrs. Wilson and Dr. Grayson looked at each other helplessly. To what the President had said neither could find an answer.

Tumulty, with a map in one hand and a copy of the *Congressional Directory* in the other, sweated out the strategy of the tour. Perhaps the anti-League senators would not be impressed by the longings for peace of an aching Europe, perhaps they cared little for the soldiers who had died in France and Belgium or the widows and families they had left behind, perhaps they cared nothing for the aspirations of humanity toward a better world, perhaps the brotherhood of man was to them a stupid, sentimental phrase, but threaten them with the loss of their jobs and they would surely come round. And Tumulty had sublime faith that once a recalcitrant senator's constituents had heard "Governor" Wilson make one of his impassioned speeches, that senator would be buried under letters. This tour was the thing that would do it—if it were planned to hit just the right spots. Senators on the edge—senators already under some pressure from home —those were the ones to squeeze. To Tumulty it was a beautiful strategic operation. No point in talking to Illinois—it was lost anyway. No point in talking to Mississippi, on the other hand, for John Sharp Williams was a strong pro-League man and had the firm support of his people. A talk at Columbus would put the thumb on that fellow Harding. Jim Watson, a pretty good scout but an unregenerate League opponent, would get a lot of mail following a Presidential appearance at Indianapolis. From there to St. Louis—give that renegade Jim Reed the business! Hitchcock's support was wavering a little—and as one of the pro-League leaders he must have a boost if he needed it—so the President had better speak at Omaha. That might jar George Norris too. It wasn't off the route to California where Hiram Johnson's home folks needed to be told a few things.

4

The Presidential special left Washington on the night of September 3rd, with the private car *Mayflower* the last on the train. Dr. Grayson of course came along, and the faithful Tumulty, and Mrs. Wilson, and Brooks, the President's valet, and Mrs. Wilson's maid. Jackson, White House messenger, a favorite of the Wilsons', had been substituted for the regular porter by Tumulty as a prank.

There were Secret Service men of course—practically a battalion of them. There were a hundred-odd newspaper correspondents on the forward cars of the train.

As Grayson had predicted, every possible moment of the President's time was scheduled, and the whole party had to move with military precision to keep up to schedule. Wilson had not written his speeches ahead of time—he had to make notes and work them up on the train in odd moments and on the move.

It was not a placid country that Woodrow Wilson traveled across. Over a hundred major strikes and lockouts were on. During the twenty-three days of the tour nearly 300,000 steel workers left the plants at Newcastle, Farrell, and the other hill-perched sooty towns of western Pennsylvania. Steel workers in Gary and Pueblo and a dozen other cities fought with police and guards and soldiers. The Great Lakes seamen voted to strike in sympathy, so did firemen in Cleveland, switchmen in Youngstown. The coal country was in almost continuous turmoil. There were race riots in Chicago, Knoxville, Washington, and other centers. In Boston, policemen had struck, and Governor Coolidge had belatedly called out 5,000 state troopers to maintain order.

Hard masters, the American people, but appreciative of a good fight and full of sympathy for a fighter clearly game and determined. Woodrow Wilson, having fought hard in Paris for six months and in Washington for two, was a groggy fighter. The slim, frail, sixty-three-year-old champion—according to his lights—of human rights and freedom had fought too long without rest; yet he knew that this next-to-last round must be one smashing punch after another or the fight was lost. He had supreme faith in his countrymen; he was certain that if he could complete this tour and then face Congress with the nation behind him, he could win. That would be the last and decisive round—Washington after his tour.

Grayson—Tumulty—Edith Bolling Wilson—all could see how near he was to the end of his rope. He knew it himself. Yet time, he could see, favored his opponents. Give them a few weeks more to pound away at the League day after day; to repeat countless times their arguments and threats and warnings to a people confused and weary of Europe and her problems—let them do this without answering them effectively, and the cause was lost. His side of the debate must be given them—given them dramatically and in human terms, given them by him. Nothing mattered but this. If you believed in Democracy you believed in the ability of the people as a whole to make the right decision and to stand back of the right decision. It should be necessary only to give them the facts, the clear answers, to plow through the welter of confusing statements, misleading statements, downright pernicious statements which Woodrow Wilson knew were coming from his enemies. Only he could do it. Hitchcock—a splendid fellow; John Sharp Williams, brilliant, biting, erudite; Pittman, Swanson, Robinson—and all the others in the Senate who were for him—all good, but the League was not theirs, it was his. In the minds of the people he was the symbol. A junket by pro-league senators, most of them less effective speakers than the anti-league Borah and Johnson, could only neutralize the opposition. But with these men behind him in the Senate taking care of the business of the day, he could draw far more attention than a few senators holding meetings here and there. Some of the top correspondents of the day would follow him and report his speeches and his reception. His tour would be projected in headlines to cities he could not visit.

First night out he must get some rest. These confounded headaches that had plagued him for weeks—it seemed years —perhaps he could get rid of them if he could sleep on the train. Speeches would have to be written—nearly a hundred of them in less than a month, and some would be long, and only a few could be wholly extemporaneous. Well, he would get them done some way, with Tumulty's help, perhaps. There was no doubt he could manage them so far as composition was concerned. He was full of his subject; he knew all his arguments. And writing was easy enough when you knew what you wanted to say. But these headaches—these awful headaches. The stiffness in the back of the neck, the tired, twitching eye muscles. . . . Ah, well, Grayson would keep him going somehow . . . he must . . . he must . . . but it was like an endless, grinding, destroying dream.

Columbus, September 4th—Not too large a crowd. They liked the speech well enough, but were obviously not carried away by it. Not really a bad start, but it could have been better. Four thousand people. . . . Later that day, a talk from the rear platform of the train at Richmond, Indiana. . . . First dig at Senators Harry New and Jim Watson . . . probably useless—neither of them vulnerable. . . .

Indianapolis, September 4th—The President spoke in the Coliseum of the State Fair, which was in full swing. This had looked like a good idea to Tumulty when he was working out the itinerary, but it worked out badly. In competition with ferris wheels, shooting galleries, and stock contests; the crowd was in a gay, sight-seeing mood, looking for something exciting and unusual. Thousands were in the Coliseum; more thousands tried to get in; the confusion as Wilson spoke made it impossible for those in the rear of the hall to hear him at all. Hundreds wandered in, got a glimpse of the President, and wandered out to look at a two-headed calf. About 12,000 people were in the hall during all or a part of his address. Reporters noted frequent applause, but the confusion was distracting. The Presidential party returned to the train and sped silently across Illinois. No use talking with the isolationists who had elected Lawrence Y. Sherman and Medill McCormick to represent them in the Senate. . . .

St. Louis, September 5th—Missouri, home state of the hostile Democratic Senator James A. Reed, gave the President a good ovation. He talked first to members of the Chamber of Commerce and their guests—1,200 in all. In the evening his speech was to 12,000 who cheered him lustily before he could start. The reports of this meeting would make Jim Reed squirm!

Now things were beginning to click. As the train pulled out of St. Louis, the President, exuberant and feeling better than he had for several days, sat down at his typewriter to make notes for his next speeches.

Kansas City—Des Moines—Omaha—Sioux Falls—Saint Paul—predominantly Republican territory. Good receptions everywhere, but little evidence of effectiveness. Meanwhile, debate in the Senate went on along the regular lines—except for one thing: there were a few senators missing. Borah, McCormick, and Hiram Johnson had set forth in the wake of the President to speak against the League as he had spoken for it. . . .

Senator Ashurst, of Arizona, counting Democratic votes in the Senate, reported that he could find only twenty-seven Democrats who would stand to the end against reservations. Ashurst thought the country was against the Treaty unless radical reservations were attached, but he added, "The future is what President Wilson must look to for his vindication." As a Democrat at heart, even though a reservationist, Senator Ashurst added wistfully, "We may be winning elections about 1940 on the strength of Woodrow Wilson's memory, but not in the near future."

Helena and Billings, Montana, September 11th—Here, and at Coeur d'Alene, Idaho, the following day, the people listened and applauded. But Montana's Democratic Senator Walsh, perhaps angry at what he considered the President's pressure tactics, seemed now to be for stronger reservations than before. Perhaps the President's Montana speeches were backfiring. And certainly nothing he said at Coeur d'Alene next day made any impression on Senator Borah, though Borah's constituents applauded with enthusiasm.

As the President had sped by night across the high plains of eastern Montana, the Senate's greatest spellbinders were in Chicago. Ten thousand people were gathered in the great Auditorium Theater. They were not there to cheer the President. They were there to hear Senators Borah, Johnson, and McCormick, who were following him, though not along the same path, because, said the President's friends, they did not want their drawing power directly compared with his. In Chicago they had been sure of a full house.

Borah strode back and forth across the platform on which McCormick and Johnson sat, in the city which elected William Hale Thompson mayor because he promised to "punch King George in the snout." He had his audience with him and he could do what he would with them. And as he slowly moved across the stage, hands grasping his lapels, he spoke in reasoned tones:

"He started, as you recall, with open covenants of peace openly arrived at. You and I echoed the sentiment. All America applauded." Now Borah stopped and shouted at his listeners: "Who quit? Who was the quitter?"

"Wilson!" bellowed the crowd.

Borah looked profoundly satisfied, and resumed his pacing.

"There shouldn't be a boy in Russia today," he shouted, "except by unanimous vote! England has suggested—all England has to do now is to suggest—that we send a hundred thousand men to Constantinople!"

"Impeach him!" screamed the crowd. "Don't let them go!"

"They say we are killing time," Borah went on. "I am killing time for just one reason—to let the American people know the facts that have been withheld from them—facts that Wall Street knew two months before the Senate or the American people."

Wilson was standing the trip well up to this point. He still had headaches; he still was miserably tired. Perhaps he was disappointed by his reception, although it had nowhere been negative. Mrs. Wilson was invariably at his side, smiling, gracious, watchful. Dr. Grayson too was careful of his patient; these two worried people gave the President every possible attention, eased everything for him as much as they could. And the public, so far, had seen only an alert, smiling Wilson with an attractive, attentive wife; had heard only the strong-voiced orator, speaking with sincerity and urgency in ringing phrases.

The Pacific Coast. It was vitally important, the climax of the trip; success or failure depended to a considerable extent upon what happened here. In the state of Washington, Senator Miles Poindexter had signed the Lodge Round Robin resolution of March 4th; and Senator Jones too was a Republican. In Oregon, Democratic Senator George Earle Chamberlain, Wilson's former friend, had said "the military establishment of America has fallen down because of inefficiency in every bureau and department of the government of the United States." And Chamberlain's colleague, Republican Charles L. McNary, who had not signed the Lodge resolution—a young man and, Wilson thought, an honest and just man. These two might be won over if their people were won over. They *must* be won over.

Seattle, Washington, September 13th—The streets lining the path of the President were packed with a roaring crowd. This was the kind of reception he had found in Paris and Rome, the kind that could leave no doubt, that could mean only overwhelming enthusiasm for the man who stood lithe and smiling in the slowly moving open car. These people cared; they believed in him. It grew as the car moved forward; a wave of sound moving along ahead of him and dying away behind him.

An armory full of cheering humanity heard the President speak and would not let him go when he had finished.

And in Tacoma, near the foot of Puget Sound, 30,000 people jammed a stadium, and at Portland it was much the same. The Northwest, at least, was won. The newspapers, most of them Republican, nearly all supported him, and it was obvious how the people felt.

South through the Cascades of Oregon and the Sacramento Valley of California to Oakland and a terrific reception at

San Francisco—the kind of loud and hearty western welcome for which San Francisco is famous.

The Wilsons' suite at the St. Francis was barely large enough to hold the flowers that were sent. The grape growers sent a basket twelve feet high filled with chrysanthemums and enormous clusters of beautiful grapes.

He was paraded through cheering crowds, as bands blared. There were meetings and greetings and speeches and buckets of flashlight powder in the crowded hotel lobbies and in the ballrooms where he was lunched, dined, and feted and where he was, of course, always expected to speak. Luncheon at the Palace Hotel, where the President made his most important address, was torture. A very brassy orchestra sat almost in the President's lap. He had caught cold the night before on the train. There were too many people in the room and too little air. His head had ached all morning. For half an hour, moving slowly through the packed streets, he had had to stand in his automobile and smile and wave at the crowds.

"They are killing me!" he whispered to Mrs. Wilson. "They mean only to please me, but they are killing me!"

However, he managed to get through the speech.

His exuberant hosts had planned a long drive for that afternoon, and a visit to wounded men at a Presidio hospital. But Mrs. Wilson and Dr. Grayson said no. Tumulty reported to the press that the President had a slight cold and sore throat and that Dr. Grayson had ordered him to rest in his hotel room that afternoon and to see no one.

Oakland, Berkeley, and Palo Alto all caught glimpses of him during his two days in the Bay area. Nowhere had he seen such enthusiasm. Some reporters thought there had never been such a welcome. Yet California had been much concerned about Japanese immigration—anti-League senators had said that if the United States joined the league there would be no way to restrict it. There was also sentiment against the Shantung agreement, which many people thought indicated strong favoritism on the part of Woodrow Wilson toward Japan.

But as he spoke in California these doubts disappeared. Except for the Hearst papers, he had an excellent press; even the San Francisco *Chronicle*, which had not up to then favored the League, devoted page after page to pictures and stories about his visit. And he left behind him seeds of rank discontent in the home city of Hiram Johnson. A few days later thirty-eight prominent Californians including Benjamin Ide Wheeler, once President of the University of California, and Ray Lyman Wilbur, sent Senator Johnson a telegram protesting his attitude and his tactics in the League fight. It was a list of people not to be ignored, even by Hiram Johnson. . . .

San Diego, California, September 19th—The President spoke, through amplifiers, to what was said to be the largest audience ever addressed by a Chief Executive—fifty thousand people, more than one-third of San Diego's total population. He was frequently interrupted by thunderous applause, and he left town for Los Angeles a victorious conqueror. Los Angeles too was eager to be taken by storm. The town's Republican newspapers went all out for the President and the League. Lyman J. Gage, a Republican who had been secretary of the treasury under McKinley, said, "I think I express the sentiment of the great mass of people when I say, 'God Bless President Wilson. Go on with the work!' "

The trip was beginning to have real impact. Word came that Senator McNary of Oregon had joined with Senator McCumber in a move to offset radical amendments to the League which Hiram Johnson was trying to put through. McNary was not unaware of the President's reception on the Pacific Coast. And David Lawrence, in syndicated articles published in newspapers from coast to coast, wrote:

President Wilson leaves the Pacific Coast triumphantly. That is an extreme statement to make and will be disputed by those who look at the League of Nations as a political question or as somehow akin to the prestige or political fortunes of Woodrow Wilson.

But the idea, not necessarily the man, has triumphed. . . . In many respects the speech which President Wilson made at the auditorium in Los Angeles was the best of his whole tour. Not because so many Johnson men stood with him and cheered, not because Republicans predominated in the meeting, not because California felt proud that she had cast the deciding electoral votes which made Woodrow Wilson President, but because the sheer force of his explanations on Shantung, on the question of six votes for Britain to America's one, and the policy of isolation or partnership caused a deep reaction against the men who are now believed to have misrepresented the contents of the treaty itself, an unforgivable thing in an intelligent electorate like California's.

Hiram Johnson was still on his tour through the Middle West, where he was drawing large and enthusiastic audiences. But in Washington his associates were plainly worried and telegraphed him that he had better come back to help with the fight.

But on President Wilson the pace was beginning to show. Every ounce of his energy was going into his speeches and appearances. As one writer put it "he seemed to grow older by years with the passing of each day." Grayson counted the days ahead with apprehension, but still hoped his patient might return to Washington intact. Yet to Grayson the worst of it was that victory in the West would have to be followed instantly by more hard battles in Washington—the advantage must be pressed. And when there was talk of following up the successful western tour with an invasion of New England, Grayson threw up his hands. In Washington there might be short periods of rest between battles; without these the President was sure to crash sooner or later.

Salt Lake City, Utah, September 23rd—The President was met by Governor Bamberger, Mayor Ferry of Salt Lake City, and most important of all, by President Heber Grant of the Church of Jesus Christ of Latter Day Saints. President Grant had already told his followers that the League was perfectly compatible with their bible, the *Book of Mormon*. Now the fact that he accompanied Wilson through the packed streets of Salt Lake City through crowds almost uncontrollable in their enthusiasm, with people hanging from windows and roofs and filling every inch of available space, was taken by many as official approval by the church of what Wilson stood for.

The President spoke in the great Tabernacle, and President Grant delivered an invocation. Fifteen thousand people had crowded into the edifice—far more than its capacity. At least as many had been turned away. Mrs. Wilson reported later that the air was so close that only smelling salts kept her from fainting, but the President managed to speak smoothly.

Crowded and uncomfortable as they were [reported the Salt Lake *Tribune*, a Republican newspaper] the immense gathering by their attention and applause gave overwhelming evidence that a vast majority of them agreed with what the President had to say about the Covenant. They interrupted him time and again with handclappings; they shouted favorable answers to his questions and demonstrated at every climax which the President reached that they wished to see the ratification of the treaty and the League of Nations. . . . The President's sincerity, the care with which he weighed his words, and the ease of his address made his message simple and at the same time tremendously effective.

Politically, the Salt Lake City visit was aimed at Utah's Republican Senator Reed Smoot, one of the senators who had signed Lodge's March 4th Round Robin resolution.

Smoot, a Mormon, was put clearly in the position of opposing the Mormon Church policy, since President Grant so obviously was pro-League and pro-Wilson. There had been no secret about this conflict, but the meeting in the Tabernacle brought it to the attention of everyone in Utah—and Utah is almost all Mormon.

The President, stopping briefly at Laramie and at Cheyenne, home of Senator Francis E. Warren, continued his relentless program of going direct to the constituents of the senators who opposed the League. *Rocky Mountain News* headlines read, "A wild welcome given Wilson at Cheyenne." More word of tangible results came through. On the 24th Senator Lodge, fearing defeat of Senator Albert Fall's thirty-five amendments, had barely managed to get a vote on them postponed, forty-three to forty—a closer margin than he had been accustomed to and closer than he expected. He failed to prevent the setting of a day for their consideration. Senator Hitchcock commented:

The outcome . . . was highly satisfactory to treaty supporters. We defeated the effort to postpone consideration of the Fall amendments and accomplished our purpose of having a definite day set for their consideration and decision. . . . We have the votes to defeat these amendments, and we accomplished our purpose in having the matter so arranged that the decision will come this week. The only Democratic vote we lost was Senator Reed's, which had been lost for months. We only gained two Republican votes yesterday on the question of fixing the date, but many Republicans on the merits of the question will vote against the amendments. That is the reason Senator Lodge attempts to delay the vote.

There were more urgent calls for the return of the barnstorming irreconcilables: Borah, Johnson, and McCormick. They would be badly needed when the vote came up.

Denver, Colorado, September 25th—The *Rocky Mountain*

News reported that more than half the adult population of the city waited to see and cheer Woodrow Wilson on his way to the auditorium. More than 32,000 school children were on hand, waving flags and shrilly sounding their delight at the gaunt but bravely smiling figure waving the tall silk hat. Seventeenth Street on the way to the Brown Palace Hotel shook with the impact of the city's welcome. And when he stepped upon the platform to begin his speech, he was delayed for many minutes by the crowd's enthusiasm. The *News* reported later that

a demonstration even greater than he received when he first entered the great hall was accorded the President when he asserted that, because the treaty embodied American principles, he felt that he had a right to say that he had the support of the people of the United States. Cheers broke loose, women waved handkerchiefs and flags, the enthusiasm mounting until it took expression in a tumultuous outbreak.

But the *News* reported that Wilson "spoke dispassionately, earnestly. He appealed almost not at all to the emotions of his hearers."

The wave was clearly still on the rise. As San Diego had outdone San Francisco, and Los Angeles and Salt Lake had outdone San Diego, so Denver outdid them all.

The morning before the President's Denver speech, the New York *Times* carried a front-page article headed: "SENATORS LINE UP AGAINST AMENDING TREATY—Votes in Both Parties Swing over to Opposition to Johnson Proposal—REPUBLICAN CHIEFS DELAY." The article began:

Washington, September 24—Owing to a sudden change in the Senate situation involving the opposition to the Versailles treaty, Republican leaders today admitted they were beginning to doubt that any part of the amendment program of the Foreign Relations Committee could be carried out.

The Republican leaders secretly admitted that within the last few days they had lost considerable of the support upon which they had counted for the Johnson amendment to equalize the votes of the United States and the British Empire in the League of Nations Assembly. Not alone had the opposition forces lost Republican votes during the last week, it developed, but a number of Democrats whose support had been confidently expected gave unmistakable evidence that they were going to vote against all the amendments.

Pueblo, Colorado, September 25th—Greater enthusiasm than Denver's seemed impossible, yet Pueblo, a much smaller city, gave him one of his most tremendous welcomes. When he stepped to the stage of the new auditorium, the entire audience rose and cheered for ten minutes.

He had seriously doubted, just before the speech, whether he would be able to go on. Never had he felt so desperately weary and ill. It took supreme determination and a mighty effort of will to make his speech, and he poured into it all the conviction and the passion he was capable of giving:

"What of our pledges to the men that lie dead in France? We said that they went over there not to prove the prowess of America or her readiness for another war but to see to it that there never was such a war again. It always seems to make it difficult for me to say anything, my fellow citizens, when I think of my clients in this case. My clients are the children; my clients are the next generation. They do not know what promises and bonds I undertook when I ordered the armies of the United States to the soil of France, but I know, and I intend to redeem my pledges to the children; they shall not be sent upon a similar errand.

"Again, and again, my fellow citizens, mothers who lost their sons in France have come to me and, taking my hand, have shed tears upon it not only, but they have added: 'God bless you, Mr. President!' Why, my fellow citizens, should they pray God to bless me? I advised the Congress of the United States to create the situation that led to the death of their sons. I ordered their sons overseas. I consented to their sons being put in the most difficult parts of the battle line, where death was certain, as in the impenetrable difficulties of the forest of Argonne. Why should they weep upon my hand and call down the blessings of God upon me? Because they believe their boys died for something that vastly transcends any of the immediate and palpable objects of the war. They believe, and they rightly believe, that their sons saved the liberty of the world. They believe that wrapped up with the liberty of the world is the continuous protection of that liberty by the concerted powers of all the civilized world. They believe that this sacrifice was made in order that other sons should not be called upon for a similar gift—the gift of life, the gift of all that died—and if we did not see this thing through, if we fulfilled the dearest present wish of Germany and now dissociated ourselves from those alongside whom we fought in the war, would not something of the halo go away from the gun over the mantelpiece, or the sword? Would not the old uniform lose something of its significance? These men were crusaders. They were going forth to prove the might of justice and right, and all the world accepted them as crusaders, and their transcendent achievement has made all the world believe in America as it believes in no other nation organized in the modern world. There seems to me to stand between us and the rejection or qualification of this treaty the serried ranks of those boys in khaki, not only those boys who came home, but those dear ghosts that still deploy upon the fields of France.

"My friends, on last Decoration Day I went to a beautiful hillside near Paris, where was located the cemetery of Suresnes, a cemetery given over to the burial of the American dead. Behind me on the slopes was rank upon rank of living

American soldiers, and lying before me on the levels of the plain was rank upon rank of departed American soldiers. Right by the side of the stand where I spoke there was a little group of French women who had adopted those graves, had made themselves mothers of those dear ghosts by putting flowers every day upon those graves, taking them as their own sons, their own beloved, because they had died in the same cause—France was free and the world was free because America had come! I wish some men in public life who are now opposing the settlement for which these men died could visit such a spot as that. I wish that the thought that comes out of those graves could penetrate their consciousness. I wish that they could feel the moral obligation that rests upon us not to go back on those boys, but to see the thing through, to see it through to the end and make good their redemption of the world. For nothing less depends upon this decision, nothing less than the liberation and salvation of the world.

"Now that the mists of this great question have cleared away, I believe that men will see the trust, eye to eye and face to face. There is one thing that the American people always rise to and extend their hand to, and that is the truth of justice and of liberty and of peace. We have accepted that truth and we are going to be led by it, and it is going to lead us, and through us the world, out into pastures of quietness and peace such as the world never dreamed of before."

For a moment there was complete silence in the hall; then the clamor burst forth like thunder in the mountains. It was as though every man and woman in the audience had begun it at a signal; it was deafening and it went on and on. . . .

But for Woodrow Wilson, the end had come.

The valley of the Arkansas lies between low rolling hills where once grew tall and waving grass. The buffalo had rubbed and bellowed in the round wallows on the dry land nearby. These were the high plains, the northern end of the *llanos estacados* where the Lipan Apache had hunted and Spaniards had died of thirst and hunger and of disappointment because there was no gold. The covered wagons followed this shallow sandy river upstream plodding westward along the Santa Fe Trail.

On these plains the makers of America had built their rude sod houses or their tiny wooden shacks, dug wells, and started out with plows to make their homesteads. The dry furnace heat of summer days gave way to harsh unyielding winter winds that drained the body warmth like death and took it southward. Along the Arkansas and its tributaries the scattered cottonwoods and willows, the few scrub pines, were the only fuel there was to warm the porous walls and floors of homes where these Americans lived and worked, bore children of the plain and died.

Then high-wheeled noisy tractors had come, and dragged their plows and harrows across this land to finish off the grass, to make wheat for men at war and hay for cattle to feed a hungry world. Barbed wire had come, and rails and roads and towns. Farms still clung close to streams, and cattle grazed where there was little moisture in the soil.

This was a valley in America, Woodrow Wilson's land.

5

It had been a hot as well as an exhausting day, and the President sank into a chair on the train and leaned his head forward on his hands, grateful for privacy at last but unable to think of anything except the murderous aching in his head. Mrs. Wilson brought him a glass of water and he leaned back and closed his eyes.

Dr. Grayson hovered over him, obviously worried as the

President stayed motionless in his chair. He was not asleep, yet he hardly looked awake either. The train rolled on through rocky hills where cattle munched sparse grass. A few farmhouses appeared, and fields of stubble with grain or hay piled in them. As daylight faded Grayson grew alarmed, and took the President's pulse. He found it weak and slow, hard to count. He sat next to his patient and friend and looked at him. Then he rose and went to look for Tumulty. In a few minutes he was back.

"I've asked Tumulty to find the conductor and have the train stopped," he said, "I want to take you for a good brisk walk—I think it would make you feel a lot better. You've had almost no physical exercise in days." He did not admit that he was seriously alarmed.

Wilson nodded wearily, but said nothing. Some minutes later the train came slowly to a stop and backed into a siding. The President, Mrs. Wilson, Dr. Grayson, and two Secret Service men clambered down the steps and walked back a few hundred feet to a road crossing.

The sun had gone down. But above the mountains to the west were orange and yellow clouds that lit the narrow dirt road with grass between two hard-packed tracks. A little to the north of them was the Arkansas anastomosing down its broad, flat bed. Fresh-cut alfalfa in a field by the road spread its sweet heady fragrance through the air, and there was a faint odor too of sage and piñon. Tiny insects buzzed softly in the President's and Mrs. Wilson's ears and flew into their eyes. The evening air was cool and new, an invitation to take deep breaths.

The party went over a little rise in the road and then down toward the river, perhaps a mile away but looking closer. The train was out of sight.

"Extend yourself a little," said Grayson. "Run down as far as that curve in the road."

The President ran a hundred yards or so, then turned and came back. Grayson saw that he was breathing hard but normally.

"This was just what I needed," he panted. "Let's walk on a little way." He looked up at the darkening sky and filled his lungs with the American air. "God, it's beautiful!" he said.

They followed the road as it curved eastward along the edge of the river valley. Far ahead of them was a little farmhouse with a squeaking windmill turning lazily in the soft breeze. The windows were dimly lighted as by an old and feeble kerosene lamp. Now they came to a gate across the road. It seemed a good place to turn back to face the clouds that were becoming red and purple. Night was coming on, the high plains night, with its clear, fast-cooling air and bright early stars.

The walk back to the train was brisk, and the tired man entered the *Mayflower* greatly refreshed and ready for a hearty meal. His headache was eased and his circulation much better. Perhaps he would be able to sleep soundly this night and wake up in the morning ready to face his job at Wichita.

But toward midnight Mrs. Wilson found him sitting on the edge of his bed, resting his head on the back of a chair in front of him. She sent for Dr. Grayson, who knew at once, as she did, that the President was desperately ill. He could not force himself to lie down; he could not sit still; he had to dress and move out into the car. Nothing the doctor could do seemed to ease him. His face was drawn, lined, and not like the face they had known but somehow changed and strange to them. They worked over him until nearly dawn as the train clicked on, and at length, bolt upright on a hard seat, he fell asleep.

Two hours later he was awake again, and insisting that he would carry on. Mrs. Wilson talked with Tumulty and Dr.

Grayson, each knowing that he could not. As they were talking he came in, dressed and shaved and bravely pretending he felt better. But it was impossible; one look at him could leave no doubt. The tour must be ended.

They were already at the outskirts of Wichita. Tumulty gave out a statement together with Grayson's. The Presidential train would go straight to Washington over the shortest route, with as few stops as possible. There the President would have a long rest.

Tumulty and E. W. Smithers of the President's staff sat down with Thomas Lipsett of the railroad administration in the station at Wichita and burned the wires eastward, upsetting three great railroad systems, rerouting the train to Kansas City over the Santa Fe, from Kansas City to St. Louis over the Missouri Pacific, and from there to Washington over the Pennsylvania.

The Secret Service insisted that every switch and sidetrack in the 1,700 miles between Wichita and Washington be guarded or spiked down, that every mile of track be inspected before the train went over it, that every regular train be rescheduled and sidetracked if necessary. Yet in less than half an hour the arrangements had been completed and the train was on its way to make a record run.

And now began the long and hopeless illness that canceled Wilson's efforts. He was winning and yet he had not quite won. Some thought that if he had died that night as his train roared across the Kansas prairie, his martyrdom would have won what he had almost won. But he did not die. He lived, and living, could not muster strength to lead the final battles which had still to be fought and which still called for mighty leadership. His lieutenants in the fight, uncertain, confused, hopeful for the Chief's recovery that never came, were in the course of a few months disarmed and outdone. The fight was lost.

6

He had told it in St. Louis. He had told what he would do if he lost his fight, what he would say to the men who had suffered and bled for Democracy and Peace and Freedom.

"I would stand up before them and say:

" 'Boys, I told you before you went across the seas that this was a war against wars, and I did my best to fulfill the promise, but I am obliged to come to you in mortification and shame and say that I have not been able to fulfill the promise. You are betrayed. You fought for something that you did not get.

" 'And the glory of the armies and navies of the United States is gone like a dream in the night, and there ensues upon it, in the suitable darkness of the night, the nightmare of dread which lay upon the nations before this war came; and there will come sometime, in the vengeful providence of God, another struggle in which not a few hundred thousand fine men from America will have to die, but as many millions as are necessary to accomplish the final freedom of the peoples of the world.' "

12. Back to Normalcy

BEYOND Paris, beyond Berlin, east beyond the slopes of the Boehmerwald, a new flag flew over an old city. In the healing summer of the Peace, hope moved in the streets of Prague. In the evening silence, old men said they could hear the voice of Comenius ringing across the Týn square:

"By the Grace of God, when the storm . . . has passed, the government of thy affairs will return to thee, O Czech people."

But the younger men heard the voice of Alois Rašin which had spoken at the dawn of freedom:

"Keep thy escutcheon bright. . . . Belie not the faith of our liberators, Masaryk and Wilson, that they have won freedom for a people fit to govern itself."

There was not a Czech who could not feel the weight of the three centuries between the voices. From father to son the word had been passed on from Comenius. There were years when the Hapsburg hand had been lighter, when there had been a measure of home rule. Then the people had earnestly studied democracy. But the days of the free Bohemia before the battle of White Mountain in the Thirty Years War had not returned. Always over the horizon lay the Empire. If an enlightened Hapsburg left his throne to a tyrant Hapsburg, the cloud would come back over Prague and the long green valleys to the east. Now the Empire was dead.

Now in the summer of 1919, there were no more Hapsburgs. It was useless to mourn the thousand martyrs of

Prague executed during the war. Their children lived in a free nation. The children of the thousands of men and women who had been chained in trucks and driven through the streets to die in dark and nameless prisons would make their own laws tomorrow. They would be kindly laws, laws respecting the dignity of man, educating, guiding laws with malice toward none.

"But you will persecute the German minorities. . . ."

"Why? The Germans are people like ourselves except when there is someone to rouse them against us. We have had our revenge against their rulers."

"Russia will make you communist."

"No. Russian communism is not democracy."

"But what will protect you? You are a small state among old enemies. They may grow strong again."

"The war was fought to protect the rights of small nations. Now that it has been won, the League will protect us."

So the Czechs answered all the questions. The past was dead; there was no doubt of the future. There were dark places in the old town of Prague. Children still died in sunless, crowded rooms. Sewers still ran, open, in certain streets. These things would be changed. Commissions were already working for new social laws. Industry would bring prosperity. Sixty per cent of Austria's skilled workers were Czechs. Seventy-five per cent of Austria's industries were in Bohemia and Moravia. Now with eyes opened toward the west and all the barriers down industry would learn new ways from America. With the center of Europe made safe for democracy, the Czechoslovak Republic would march ahead into its longest dreams.

Many Americans came to Prague in the summer of 1919. They came for the American Red Cross which, in all parts of the world, was assisting the travail which bore the new era. They came for the American Relief Administration. There were social workers of the Y.W.C.A. and the Y.M.C.A.— men and women invited by President Masaryk's daughter to make a survey of health, education, recreation, and housing in Prague. "We have much to learn," said Alice Masaryk, whose mother was an American, "and much to forget." She had lived in a Hapsburg prison while her father worked for freedom. She knew much of sickness, hunger, darkness, and silence. Now she was head of the Czech Red Cross. Working with her, the Americans, whose habit was freedom, would be practical about frightened children, stumbling adolescents, undernourished adults; about ventilation, bathing, calories, exercises, clubs, schools, and the kind of organization which grips the fancy of people preparing to cope with liberty.

But the Czechs were proud. With them oppression had never bred servility. Perhaps it was the living tradition of the Hussite armies which had kept it out. Hus was a religious reformer who cleaned corruption and hypocrisy out of the Bohemian church. He was burned at the stake and his followers fought with angry crusading armies to keep their country free for straight thinking. The armies failed but the legend lived. "It is still true," said the Bohemians on the scaffolds. The Hus statues stood in the squares, in the churches. If the Hapsburgs tore them down, the cunning, tireless artisans worked in cellars to replace them. If the people had let the legend die, their lives might have been easier. But they were obsessed with the Hus ideals and applied them to the small businesses of daily life, keeping the continuity. It was not the Hus way to cringe before a lord for bread. Laughing, the Czech would stand on the gallows. His grave would be the rallying place for a thousand others.

So the Czechs were proud. Their businessmen did not go smiling and smirking after trade. They did not play golf with their customers or buy them champagne. "People buy my shoes," said Batya of Zlin, "because they are better shoes and cheaper."

So the Czechs of Prague scorned charity. It smelled of the Hapsburgs. They made careful arrangements with the Americans. Their eagerness to learn was like a frenzy, but only if their share of the work was greater than the teacher's. Their jealousy of their own plans for their own state was intense but it was dynamic. They knew that their leaders were masters of democratic theory and they itched to apply it. They would borrow on the materials of reconstruction from other democracies—the proved mathematics of experience—but the art must be all theirs. The republic would be fashioned the Czechoslovak way. The parliament might be on an English model, the party pattern half-French, the presidency half-American. Out of the mixture would come Czechoslovak laws, order, foreign policy, finance, commerce, and education.

The Americans, then, must watch their step. Their job was simply to guide the Czechoslovak workers. It was not difficult, for the mood was friendly. In the background was respect for a new legend which had been joined, somehow, without patch or splint, to the legend of Hus and Comenius. It was the story of a continuity of ideal. It was the story of revolution, of a break with tyranny, of separation from the kind of divine-right rule which once oppressed thirteen Atlantic colonies. It was the story of a fight for unity. There was no break in it.

Its living interpreters were Masaryk and Woodrow Wilson.

Americans in Prague could not easily forget this background. The city with its terraces rising from the river up the steep hill of Hradcany to the formidable medieval castle at the top; with its ancient statue-lined bridges, its brown baroque-faced buildings, the congested "old town" where the strange saints looked down from jammed-in churches on market stalls piled with cabbage and carrots and hung with necklaces of sausages—the city was far from an American city. Yet in the new spirit there was a kind of American sublimation.

The best of the American story was there, not the worst. Where Prague was sordid, it was with European squalor. But where it rose above its own darkness it was with an American impulse. Its folk looked westward, but not too closely. What they saw was the ideal America, its myths and its avatars. The Liberty Bell rang loud in their ears; they did not ask about its cracks.

So the Americans were able to see in Prague a purified America detached from its vices. They saw what might have been and what might yet be. They saw ideas which had been selected and seized from the ruck which obscured them at home. They saw something caught, crystallized, and eternally preserved from any shambles of politics which might clutter and confuse their own postwar society.

When curious and disturbing news came over the Atlantic the Americans in Prague found comfort in the symbols the Czechs had kept. In some dark chapel of every ancient church the American and Czech flags stood together. Between them was a portrait of Wilson. In the schools, in every shop window were two photographs joined together, Wilson and Masaryk, with the crossed flags above them. The great old railway station had been renamed the "Wilson Station"; the imperial arms in the corners of its concourse had been chiseled away and a simple "W" substituted.

Sometimes the tender consciences of the American workers were startled by the Czech demonstrations.

"Wilson has many enemies at home."

"All great men have enemies."

"But they say the people may repudiate his League."

"Nonsense! The League is an American concept."

"They say the people may defeat Wilson in the next elections. They say he is ill from his disappointments. Perhaps he will not live to be defeated."

"He will live here. In Czechoslovakia he will live a long time. You Americans do not understand how we feel. You have seen only Prague. But in almost every village of Moravia and Slovakia there is a street or a square named for Wilson. Even in Ruthenia (what was called sub-Carpathian Russia)—the children are studying the story of the League and the Fourteen Points and of how Wilson was converted against Austria and of his manifesto on our Republic. We do not examine his faults. It is likely Wenceslas had them too and Palacký and Father Masaryk. Faults and enemies. What do they matter to us? Self-determination, the concert of free peoples, revolution against an old order, the collapse of economic barriers—these are what count."

2

In Chicago in the heat of June, 1920, an American Senator stepped onto a platform and spoke. And the thousands who heard him could not help being impressed with this elder statesman and what he stood for as they watched and listened. Henry Cabot Lodge was more than a senator; he was a symbol and a tradition and an historic figure, and his hearers knew it.

The last of the Puritan grandees, [wrote one reporter in describing him] aged seventy and lithe as a boy of seventeen. . . . Aquiline, slim, sententious, distinction is in every physical contour and in every chiseled sentence of this Brahmin of the Boston Brahmins. Distinction is in the white and briefly curling locks of the man, in the pointed beard, in the black cutaway and white waistcoat. . . . Throw a cloak over Lodge's left shoulder and he would step into a Velasquez group in the Prado and be authentic—authentic to his finger tips.

"Mr. Wilson," said Lodge, "stands for a theory of administration and government which is not American. His methods, his constant if indirect assaults upon the Constitution and upon all the traditions of free government, strike at the very life of the American principles upon which our Government has always rested. The return of the Democrats to power with Mr. Wilson or one of his disciples still the leader and master of a great party, which before his advent possessed both traditions and principles, would be a long step in the direction of the autocracy for which Mr. Wilson yearns and a heavy blow to the continuance of free representative government as we have always conceived and venerated it.

"The peril inseparable from Mr. Wilson and his system goes far beyond all party divisions, for it involves the fundamental question of whether the Government of the United States shall be a government of laws and not of men, whether it shall be a free representative government, or that of a dictatorship resting on a plebiscite carried by repellent methods. Mr. Wilson and the autocracy he represents, and all those who believe in his doctrines and share his spirit represent, must be put aside and conclusively excluded from any future control. . . .

"We must be now and ever for Americanism and Nationalism, and against internationalism. There is no safety for us, no hope that we can be of service to the world, if we do otherwise."

The scene was a National Convention met for the purpose of nominating a candidate for President, and Mr. Lodge was sounding the keynote.

The platform had already been written. Senator Lodge had worked on it with the chairman, his friend Jim Watson, of Indiana. Medill McCormick had contributed his ideas. Senators William Borah and Hiram Johnson had expressed themselves. And at length the document had been issued, with a statement on the foreign relations of the United States as an important section.

The Republican Party [read the 1920 platform] stands for agreement among the nations to preserve the peace of the world. We believe that such an international association must be based upon international justice, and must provide methods which shall maintain the rule of public right by the development of law and the decision of impartial courts, and which shall secure instant and general international conference whenever peace shall be threatened by political action, so that the nations pledged to do and insist upon what is just and fair may exercise their influence and power for the prevention of war.

We believe that all this can be done without the compromise of national independence, without depriving the people of the United States in advance of the right to determine for themselves what is just and fair when the occasion arises, and without involving them as participants and not as peace-makers in a multitude of quarrels, the merits of which they are unable to judge. . . .

The keynote thus sounded, and the platform approved, it was time to nominate a candidate. And the hotels of Chicago's Loop, and the floor of the Coliseum where the delegates met, and the streets of the city were filled with talk about the choice that would be made.

"General Leonard Wood's the man," said some. "Teddy Roosevelt's old commanding officer. Great soldier. Strong personality. Pershing and Wilson wouldn't let him go to France, but he did wonderful work here."

"But the country's tired of war. We don't want a military man. Frank Lowden's the best Presidential prospect in years. Fine record in Congress, marvelous governor of Illinois. He's got a good personality, speaks well, and he's independent and uses his brains. Absolutely honest and honorable. Great man, Lowden."

"He's all right, but Gompers hates him. He's got organized labor against him."

"How about Hiram Johnson? He's putting on a great show. He'd make a clean-cut campaign against the League. No pulling of punches. The issues would really stand out with Johnson running!"

"Yeah, too much. But what about Hoover? He did fine work abroad."

"Nobody cares what he did abroad. The country's sick of abroad. But it really makes no difference who we nominate. The people are sick of war and Wilson. We could win with a yellow dog."

In the large, perhaps, it would make no difference, but to each candidate it made a great deal of difference. And the early ballots showed that none of them had any intention of giving up without a fight.

Colonel George Harvey was not a delegate to the Convention. He was not a senator. He had no party position. Some people who remembered that he had helped Woodrow Wilson become President in 1912 even doubted whether he was really a Republican. Yet he managed to make his Room 404 at the Blackstone Hotel a center of convention activity after the first day's indecisive vote.

It began with dinner that night. Colonel Harvey was host to Henry Cabot Lodge, Charley Curtis, and Frank Brandegee. The discussion started with an agreement that Wood and Lowden were deadlocked, a fairly obvious fact which had been noticed by the entire convention. It was clear, too, that the weather was hot, the hotel bills high, and the interest flagging. Above all, the delegates didn't want to be stuck in Chicago over Sunday. They wanted to get home.

Knowing well the ways of conventions and delegates, these four old hands were quite aware that under the circumstances the first candidate to show a substantial gain in strength the following morning was very likely to be stampeded into office. A "band wagon" reaction could definitely be counted upon. Deadlocks almost invariably worked this way. People who jump on a band wagon early have a better chance at patronage plums after the election, and this fact produces a sort of nervous tension that makes delegates bolt at the slightest sign of new or fast-building strength.

The job now was to select a candidate and then round up a good-sized batch of votes which would start him off on the next day's balloting with a considerably larger total than he had had the day before.

Whom should they choose? The three senators were inclined to want someone who would seek and listen to Senate advice and who would not show too much independence. A steady, reliable man, conservative and careful, one who would make a good campaign and a safe and sane President, and of course, a man who would have nothing to do with Europe.

Soon after dinner Senator Jim Watson, of Indiana, and Senator Reed Smoot, of Utah, dropped in. Senators McCormick, of Illinois, Wadsworth and Calder, of New York, and ex-Senator Grundy, of Pennsylvania, followed. They wandered in and out, bringing various leaders with them. The qualifications or lack of qualifications of each possibility were hashed over. The postponement of a decision until Monday was considered, but no one was willing to risk the wrath of the delegates, many of whom were already running out of funds. And many more were disgruntled by the realization that their favorite candidate could not win. No, Saturday was the day.

But who? Certainly not Johnson, with his wild-eyed radical followers—although they represented a fairly large block of votes. Certainly not Hoover—he was too close to the administration and had spoken in favor of the League. There was Charles Evans Hughes, but there was no enthusiasm for him, and his name had scarcely been mentioned during the convention. George Harvey kept suggesting Will Hays, which brought nothing but silence from Lodge and Brandegee. Governor Sproul, of Pennsylvania, would probably make a good candidate, but the backing of General William W. Atterbury, vice-president of the Pennsylvania Railroad, would antagonize too many voters. Senator Knox, of Pennsylvania—Penrose's candidate—had a weak heart. Nicholas Murray Butler was, of course, too much like Wilson. A university president would not do. Henry Cabot Lodge would not consider it for himself—because of his age. Governor Henry Allen, of Kansas, was too new in politics and only locally known. Coolidge was too far east.

Someone suggested Warren Harding. No one jumped to his feet and shouted eureka, but there seemed nothing very important against the man. He was good-looking and agreeable. He certainly would listen. He was safe and conservative. He always voted at his party's call. He had never introduced any radical program—nor any program at all, so far as most of the men in the room could remember.

Charley Curtis dashed around to get reactions from various leaders on the suggestion. On the whole they were good enough. It was clear that a fair number of delegates could be swung over to the Ohio man—perhaps enough to give him the appearance of a somewhat slow-starting steam roller. So it was decided.

What were Harding's views on important questions? Not many people knew, but some newspaper editors before Saturday morning had had hints that Harding would be nominated, and there were frantic searches in half a hundred newspaper morgues for copies of his speeches. Perhaps the most famous the hurried researchers found was:

America's present need is not heroics, but healing; not nostrums, but normalcy; not revolution, but restoration; not agitation, but adjustment; not surgery, but serenity; not the dramatic, but the dispassionate; not experiment, but equipoise; not submergence in inter-nationality, but sustainment in triumphant nationality.

On the League of Nations they found he had spoken thus:

It is my deliberate conviction that the League of Nations Covenant, as negotiated at Paris and signed at Versailles, either creates a supergovernment of the nations which enter it or it will prove the colossal disappointment of the ages. Though it would be vastly more serious as the former, I can not believe this republic ought to sanction it in either case. Why proclaim a promise that will embitter the world's disappointment?

On business:

American business is not big business. Wilful folly has been in those persons in distended power over our national affairs who have spoken of American business as if it were a large and selfish interest seeking special privileges, and who, on that basis, have put their bungling hands upon its throat and tried tinkering and experimenting with it, and abusing it and treating it with suspicion. Let us put an end to holding success to be a crime.

And again:

Conditions have been evolved where the tendency is to get away from the human side, when it ought to be more intimately considered. That is why business has been brought into closer contact with government, though business itself has inherited a freedom from the very beginning of civilization.

On Labor:

Life is labor, or labor is life, whichever is preferred. Men speak of the labor issue as paramount or imperious or critical—it is always the big thing because it is the process of all progress and attainment, and has been since the world began. The advocate of excessively reduced periods of labor simply proposes to slow down human attainment, because labor is the agency of all attainment. If by some miracle of agreement we could reduce the hours of labor to four per day—I speak of labor now in the sense of that which is employed for pay—the live, progressive, civilization-creating, progressive labor would have to go on working twice or thrice that time, because labor is the ferment of human development.

3

Another point of view was later expressed by the vice-presidential candidate of the Democratic party, Franklin D. Roosevelt. "In our world problems," Mr. Roosevelt stated at his home in Hyde Park, New York, on August 9, 1920, "we must either shut our eyes, sell our newly built merchant marine to more far-seeing foreign powers, crush utterly by embargo and harassing legislation our foreign trade, close our ports, and build an impregnable wall of costly armaments and live, as the Orient used to live, a hermit nation, dreaming of the past; or we must open our eyes and see that modern civilization has become so complex and the lives of civilized men so interwoven with the lives of other men in other countries as to make it impossible to be in this world and not of it. We must see that it is impossible to avoid, except by monastic seclusion, those honorable and intimate foreign relations which the fearful-hearted shudderingly miscall by that devil's catchword, 'international complications.' . . .

"Even as the nation entered the war for an ideal, so it has emerged from the war with the determination that the ideal shall not die. It is idle to pretend that the war declaration of April 6, 1917, was a mere act of self-defense, or that the object of our participation was solely to defeat the military power of the Central Nations of Europe. We knew then, as a nation, even as we know today, that success on land and sea could be but half a victory. The other half is not won yet. To the cry of the French at Verdun: 'They shall not pass!', the cheer of our own men in the Argonne: 'We shall go through!'—we must add this: 'It shall not occur again!'" "

4

Armistice Day, 1923. Warren Gamaliel Harding had lived and become President and died and been buried. America had made her separate peace with Germany, the peace Henry Cabot Lodge had helped to bring about, though two years earlier he had said, "It would brand us with everlasting dishonor and bring ruin to us also if we undertook to make a separate peace." Now America was at peace with Germany, and inside Germany on this armistice day the smoke had scarcely cleared from the Bavarian War Ministry in Munich where old General Ludendorff and the upstart Adolf Hitler three days before had barricaded themselves and been dislodged and smashed by the Reichswehr. An American correspondent had written:

The two leaders are down and out and thoroughly discredited. . . . The Ludendorff-Hitler putsch was all over this morning with no shouting. This Bürgerbrau coup d'état was the craziest farce pulled off in memory. . . .

In Washington early in the afternoon nearly 20,000 people, a great many of them ex-service men, converged upon a house on S Street. Not 5,000 of them could get close enough to catch a glimpse of the wan, black-clad figure that stepped forth flanked by alert and careful friends who would help him if he needed help. Senator Carter Glass spoke a few words of greeting while the form of Woodrow Wilson stood unassisted but far from steady, with hollow eyes staring at the pavement.

Now Senator Glass had finished, and the shape beside him struggled with pain and emotion and after a long pause began:

"Senator Glass, ladies and gentlemen, I am indeed deeply touched and honored by this extraordinary exhibition of your friendship and confidence.

"And yet, I can say without affectation, that I wish you would transfer your homage from me to the men who made the armistice possible. It was possible because our boys had beaten the enemy to a standstill. You know, if you will allow me to be didactic for a moment, 'armistice' merely means 'standstill of arms.' Our late enemies, the Germans, call an armistice 'Waffenstillstand'—an armed standstill—and it was the boys that made them stand still."

There were laughter and applause, and Woodrow Wilson managed to continue:

"I am proud to remember that I had the honor of being the Commander-in-Chief of the most ideal army that was ever thrown together—"

His eyes filled with tears; he struggled with himself for a long minute. . . .

"Pardon my emotion," he said, though there was no need to ask pardon of the stricken assemblage that faced him then. Suddenly stronger, he added—"though the real fighting Commander-in-Chief was my honored friend Pershing, whom I gladly hand the laurels of victory."

He seemed about to go on, but the words that came meant only that he could not.

"Thank you with all my heart for your kindness," he said, and those nearby heard him murmur under his breath, as though telling himself his strength was spent, "That's about all I can do."

A band brought there by his devoted Joe Tumulty struck up "How Firm a Foundation"—but after a few bars the old man's strength suddenly gathered and he raised his hand for silence.

"Just one word more; I cannot refrain from saying it.

"I am not one of those that have the least anxiety about the triumph of the principles I have stood for. I have seen fools resist Providence before, and I have seen their destruction, as will come upon these again, utter destruction and contempt. That we shall prevail is as sure as that God reigns. Thank you."

And he turned and went back into his house.

Appendix

THE TEXT OF THE FOURTEEN POINTS

President Wilson's Fourteen Points, as set forth in his address made before the joint session of Congress, on January 8, 1918.

1. Open covenants of peace openly arrived at, after which there shall be no private international understandings of any kind, but diplomacy shall proceed always frankly and in the public view.

2. Absolute freedom of navigation upon the seas outside territorial waters alike in peace and in war, except as the seas may be closed in whole or in part by international action for the enforcement of international covenants.

3. The removal, so far as possible, of all economic barriers and the establishment of an equality of trade conditions among all the nations consenting to the peace and associating themselves for its maintenance.

4. Adequate guarantees given and taken that national armaments will be reduced to the lowest point consistent with domestic safety.

5. A free, open-minded and absolutely impartial adjustment of all colonial claims based upon a strict observance of the principle that in determining all such questions of sovereignty the interests of the populations concerned must have equal weight with the equitable claims of the government whose title is to be determined.

6. The evacuation of all Russian territory, and such a settlement of all questions affecting Russia as will secure the best and freest co-operation of the other nations of the world in obtaining for her an unhampered and unembarrassed opportunity for the independent determination of her own political development and national policy, and assure her of a sincere welcome into the society of free nations under institutions of her own choosing; and, more than a welcome, assistance also of every kind that she may need and may herself desire. The treatment accorded Russia by her sister nations in the months to come will be the acid test of their good-will, of their comprehension

of her needs as distinguished from their own interests, and of their intelligent and unselfish sympathy.

7. Belgium, the whole world will agree, must be evacuated and restored, without any attempt to limit the sovereignty which she enjoys in common with all other free nations. No other single act will serve as this will serve to restore confidence among the nations in the laws which they have themselves set and determined for the government of their relations with one another. Without this healing act the whole structure and validity of international law is forever impaired.

8. All French territory should be freed and the invaded portions restored, and the wrong done to France by Prussia in 1871 in the matter of Alsace-Lorraine, which has unsettled the peace of the world for nearly fifty years, should be righted, in order that peace may once more be made secure in the interest of all.

9. A readjustment of the frontiers of Italy should be effected along clearly recognizable lines of nationality.

10. The peoples of Austria-Hungary, whose place among the nations we wish to see safeguarded and assured, should be accorded the freest opportunity of autonomous development.

11. Rumania, Serbia and Montenegro should be evacuated; occupied territories restored; Serbia accorded free and secure access to the sea; and the relations of the several Balkan States to one another determined by friendly counsel along historically established lines of allegiance and nationality; and international guarantees of the political and economic independence and territorial integrity of the several Balkan States should be entered into.

12. The Turkish portions of the present Ottoman Empire should be assured a secure sovereignty, but the other nationalities which are now under Turkish rule should be assured an undoubted security of life and an absolutely unmolested opportunity of autonomous development, and the Dardanelles should be permanently opened as a free passage to the ships and commerce of all nations under international guarantees.

13. An independent Polish State should be erected which should include the territories inhabited by indisputably Polish populations, which should be assured a free and secure access to the sea, and whose political and economic independence and territorial integrity should be guaranteed by international covenant.

14. A general association of nations must be formed under specific covenants for the purpose of affording mutual guarantees of political independence and territorial integrity to great and small States alike.

Notes

WE are indebted to many people for assistance in gathering the basic material for this book. We want especially to thank Dr. Charles Seymour of Yale University for permission to go through the collection of Colonel House's papers and to Mr. Russell Pruden for his assistance in this connection. Dr. Seymour also kindly gave us his own recollections of personalities and events. We thank the Council on Foreign Relations for access to its valuable library. We are grateful to Messrs. David C. Mearns and Donald G. Patterson of the Library of Congress and Miss Harriet Van Wyck of the Woodrow Wilson Foundation for valuable assistance in the necessary research. We are indebted to Milos Safranek and Josef Hanc of the Czechoslovak consulate in New York, and to Arthur Sweetser, S. T. Williamson, Denna F. Fleming and Jonathan Daniels for special assistance.

In certain scenes we have reconstructed conversations, basing them on the most authentic available accounts or upon documented statements or recorded opinions. Where possible we have used verbatim dialog.

Full titles and data on books mentioned in these notes will be found in the bibliography.

Chapter 1

The description of wartime Washington is made up from files of current Washington newspapers and from personal observations of people who were there at that time. The conference between Colonel House and President Wilson starting on page 5 is reconstructed mainly from Charles Seymour's *Intimate Papers of Col. House*, Vol. III, Chap. 11, "The Fourteen Points." The material on wartime America is taken mostly from newspapers of the period. The story of Mr. Wilson's campaign for the governorship of New Jersey beginning on page 12 is partly from Kerney, James, *Political Education of Woodrow Wilson*; partly from Tumulty, Joseph P., *Woodrow Wilson as I Know Him*. Matthew Josephson in *The President-Makers* also gives a vivid description of the grooming of Mr. Wilson for the convention and the campaign. President Wilson's domestic program is summarized briefly by Charles W. Eliot in "The Achievements of the Democratic Party" in *The Atlantic Monthly* for October, 1916. Mr. Henry Cabot

Lodge's encounter with Mr. Wilson on page 15 is described by Mr.
Lodge on p. 2 of *The Senate and the League of Nations*, and Mr.
Lodge's speeches in the Senate on page 16 are also in Mr. Lodge's
book, pp. 6 and 7. The remarks of Billy Sunday on page 19 are from
Washington papers of the time. The events in the House of Representatives and the President's Fourteen Points speech are taken from
the *Congressional Record* for January 8, 1918. The beginnings of
Mr. Lodge's opposition to the President are described in Chapters 3
and 4 of his book *The Senate and the League of Nations*.

Chapter 2

Background for the Russian section of this chapter are in Trotsky:
History of the Russian Revolution, Radziwill, *Nicholas II*; White,
Lenin; Gordon, *Russian Year*; Wheeler-Bennett, *The Forgotten
Peace*; Reed, *Ten Days*; the two books of letters from the Tsar and
the Tsaritsa; London *Times* and *Manchester Guardian* for November
and December, 1917.

Page 31, Germans stopped short of Petrograd, September, 1917,
because of demand for troops on Italian front, Hoffmann *Diaries* I,
196 and note. Page 32, description of first week of November in
Gordon, Chap. 18. For the Smolny incident, pages 32 ff., see Wheeler-
Bennett, pp. 67 ff., and Reed, p. 125. Page 33, quote from Decree of
Peace, we have used Cumming and Pettit, *Russian American Relations*,
Document No. 25, p. 41. Page 34, on John Reed, see Granville Hicks,
Chap. I. William Hard's book gives Raymond Robin's story. Pages
36 ff. are based on Sisson's book. The Wilson letter is from Sisson,
One Hundred Red Days, p. 9, quoted by special permission of the
publishers, Yale University Press. Page 38, Sisson's answers to Bolshevik
papers are described in Sisson, pp. 198, 199. For terms of Brest-
Litovsk armistice, see Wheeler-Bennett, p. 379, and *Proceedings*, p. 20,
passim, see *Manchester Guardian*, Dec. 19, 1917. Page 41, quote from
Sisson cable is from Cumming and Pettit, p. 67, by special permission
of the publishers, Harcourt, Brace & Company. Page 43, C.P.I.'s
activities described in Sisson, pp. 209, 210.

London section. Page 44 for July 4 ceremonies, see *Times*, London,
July 4 and 5, 1917. Page 44, quote is from *Times*, July 5, 1917.
Page 46, for opinion of British military leaders, see Seymour, *The
Intimate Papers of Colonel House*, III, 256 n. For conditions in
A.E.F., 1917, see Ayres, *War with Germany*. Quotes pages 46 and 47
are both from London *Times*, Jan. 10, 1918.

Paris section. Page 49, Ribot, French Premier in April, 1917, made
his statement after U. S. declaration, see William G. Sharp, *War
Memoirs*, p. 181. Page 49, see Pershing, *My Experiences in the World*

War, I, 92, on parade. "Nous voici, Lafayette" was said by Col. Stanton at Picpus Cemetery (Pershing, I, 93). Page 50, for reference to Painlevé, French War Minister in August, 1917, who became Premier in September, 1917, see Painlevé, *Comment j'ai nommé Foch et Pétain*, pp. 24 ff. Page 50, for Pershing references, see Paxson, II, 188; Pershing, I, 250. Pershing's first urgent request for "a million men by May" was made in July, 1917 (Pershing, I, 94). In December, he did not specify the number but asked for 24 combat divisions by the end of June in addition to rear forces which would bring the total to about one million.

Rome section. For Roman background, see Gino Speranza's *Diary*. For comment on Sonnino, see Mowrer, pp. 255-256. Page 52, the Treaty of London and events leading up to it are described in Albrecht-Carrié, Chap. 1. Trotsky's publication of the Treaty in *Izvestia* was on November 26, 1917.

Berlin section. Page 54. The House Collection at Yale which the authors studied with the kind permission of President Charles Seymour contains Ackermann and Herron correspondence. Page 55, on Reichstag Peace Resolution, see Lutz, *Fall of German Empire*, II, 282 ff., and Wheeler-Bennett, p. 100. Pages 56 ff. Data on strikes from Lutz, *Fall*, II, 234 ff., quoting documents, newspaper accounts, etc. Page 57, quote from Ebert speech, Lutz, *Fall*, II, 244, 245. Page 58 on Ludendorff, see Wheeler-Bennett, p. 197. Pages 57, 58, action to suppress strike, etc., described in Lutz, *Collapse*, p. 110.

Chapter 3

The reactions of Senator Lodge to President Wilson's Fourteen Points, as given on page 60, are those expressed by the Senator in *The Senate and the League of Nations*, p. 92 ff. The comment on Senator Knox is that of E. G. Lowry in his *Washington Close-ups*. Mr. Lodge quotes from his speech before the League to Enforce Peace (page 62), in *The Senate and the League of Nations*, p. 131. The quote from George Harvey's *North American War Weekly* on page 64 is from the issue of January 12, 1918. Herbert Croly's editorial is from the *New Republic* of January 12, 1918. (It is unsigned, but Mr. Daniel Mebane of the *New Republic* assures us that the paragraph quoted was written by Mr. Croly.) The reactions of the various senators and representatives to President Wilson's Fourteen Points speech (page 66) are reported in the New York *Times* for January 9, 1918. Senator Chamberlain's attack on the war administration was reported in the New York *Times* and other morning newspapers of January 20, 1918. The investigations of shipbuilding at Olympia (page 67) were reported by the New York *Times* of January 3, 1918;

the same newspaper carried an account of the grilling of Charles Eisenman. Colonel Theodore Roosevelt's journey to Washington and interview on page 70 were reported in the newspapers of January 23, 1918. Alice Roosevelt Longworth in her book of memoirs, *Crowded Hours*, has given an account of her father's stay in Washington. The conversation at the dinner is assembled and reconstructed from newspaper reports of the occasion and from Colonel Roosevelt's known attitude regarding the political aspects of the situation. Representative Longworth's speech on page 73 is from the *Congressional Record* for March 16, 1918. George Creel has written an account of the attacks upon him in his *How We Advertised America*. The remarks criticizing the administration on pages 74 and 75 by Senators Lodge, Johnson and Thomas are reported in the *Congressional Record* for March 26, 1918.

Chapter 4

The background for the Russian section is Wheeler-Bennett's *The Forgotten Peace*. Page 76, Edgar Sisson came into possession of documents in Russia which made a case for German influence on the Bolsheviks. When these (famous at the time as the "Sisson Papers") were published in the U. S. by the Creel Committee, there was much controversy as to their authenticity. Certain experts pronounced them genuine, others called them forgeries. They are published as an appendix to Sisson, *One Hundred Red Days*. Page 78, for detailed description of Brest-Litovsk dinner, see Hoffmann *Diaries*, II, 195; Czernin, 219 f. Pages 78, 79, for Soviet-German controversy on terms, see Hoffmann, II, 202. Page 79, *Täglische Rundschau* is quoted by Wheeler-Bennett, *The Forgotten Peace*, p. 122. Page 80, deputy's statement quoted by Wheeler-Bennett, p. 135. On Lenin's attitude, pages 78, 81 ff., see Lenin, *Twenty-one Theses* in Wheeler-Bennett, pp. 385-391.

The final evacuation of Kiev came on Feb. 8 (Jan. 25 old style), Hrushevsky, *History of the Ukraine*, p. 543. For Austria and the Ukraine peace, see Ludendorff, *General Staff*, II, 545, Czernin, Chap. X. Page 84. The Trotsky letter is quoted by special permission of the author from Wheeler-Bennett, *The Forgotten Peace*, pp. 185, 186. Page 87 for losses due to Brest-Litovsk treaty, see U. S. Dept. of State, *Papers*, Russia, 1918, I, 490. Page 88, on German training, Ludendorff, II, 200 f. Ludendorff references are to *Own Story* unless otherwise specified.

Western Front. Descriptions of the March 21 offensive vary considerably. See Cruttwell, pp. 506 ff., McEntee, Chap. LXVII; Buchan, IV, 190 ff.; Ludendorff, II, 229 ff. Pages 96, 97, the Doullens meeting variously described by Foch, *Memoirs*, p. 263; Chambers, *The War Behind the War*, pp. 490, 491; and Clemenceau, *Grandeur and Misery of Victory*, p. 40. (Clemenceau is in error as to the date.) The Pershing incident, pages 91-93, is described in Pershing, I, 363-365. Page 94. Ludendorff writes of the food looting, II, 245.

For Austro-Hungarian background, see Masaryk, *The Making of a State*, Chap. I. See also Chambers, Chaps. IX and XX. The Hungarian response to Wilson is shown in *Pester-Lloyd*, Budapest, Oct. 18, 1918. Page 98. Quotation is from Czernin, 189.

The Czechoslovakian background is from Masaryk, Seton-Watson, Baerlein, Graves, Dupuy.

Pages 102 ff. See Wheeler-Bennett, *Wooden Titan*, p. 157, on Hindenburg. Pages 103 ff., see Ludendorff, II, 279-296; Report of General von Kuhl in Lutz, *Collapse*, Chap. III. Page 104 on propaganda, Bruntz, Chap. V. The propaganda message quoted at the bottom of page 104 is from Bruntz, p. 151. It is probably of Russian origin though widely used in the German underground. Page 105. Quote from Ludendorff on March offensive, Ludendorff, II, 217; page 106, quote "Five times in this War . . ." from Hertling, *Ein Jahr in Der Reichkanzle*, p. 146. For Ludendorff's attitude on German behavior, see Ludendorff, II, 331. Page 107, on conference, see Ludendorff, *The General Staff and its Problems*, II, 580. Page 108 f. An interesting exposition of German thinking at this time is given by Prince Max of Baden in his *Memoirs*, Chap. IV.

Chapter 5

The meeting of Colonel Roosevelt and Mr. Taft was described in the New York *Times* of May 26 and May 27, 1918, and by other morning papers. The Independence Hall meeting described on pages 112 to 114 was reported in the London weekly, *The New Europe*, for December 5, 1918, by Elmer Davis. The Wisconsin Assembly's resolution (page 114) was reported in newspapers of March 7, 1918. The account of the Socialist meeting and subsequent defeat of the Socialist representatives on page 116 is derived from newspapers of March 2, 1918, and from *The American Yearbook* for 1918. The meetings and problems of the House Ways and Means Committee (page 117) were particularly well covered by the New York *World* on August 29, 1918. The political effect of the influenza epidemic was the subject of widespread Republican complaint. (The attribution of the epidemic to the Chinese coolies is from the *Medical Record* of October 22, 1918, according to Mark Sullivan in *Over Here*, p. 652.) The Springfield speech of Colonel Theodore Roosevelt (p. 119) was reported in the papers of August 27, 1918. The German notes (p. 121 and following) are given in *Preliminary History of the Armistice*, published 1924 by the Carnegie Endowment for International Peace. Colonel Roosevelt's statement at Oyster Bay on October 13 was reported by the New York *Times* of following date. The account of the bringing of the German note to President Wilson at the Metropolitan Opera House (p. 122) is mostly from the New York *Times* of October 13, 1918. Charles Seymour in the *Intimate Papers*, Vol. IV, page 81, gives an account which varies slightly. The discussion between Colonel House and President Wilson (p. 124) is described in the *Intimate Papers*, pp. 82-86. The Tardieu quote on page 125 is from page 54 of Tardieu's book *The Truth About the Treaty*. It also appears in the *Intimate Papers*, Vol. IV, p. 84. The description of the position of the Allies in the field (pp. 124 and 125) is derived from the *Intimate Papers*, p. 119 et seq., meeting of House, Foch, Weygand and others. This situation, which would have made it extremely costly in lives to continue the drive, and which might have made it impossible to go forward for many months, is very well described in considerable detail by John Buchan in his *History of the Great War*, Vol. IV, p. 416. Those who feel the Allies made a mistake to sign an armistice should study the evidence Buchan gives as to the difficulty of a "march to Berlin" at that time. (In fairness to Wilson's opposition it should be pointed out that this information was not available to them, and obviously could not be made available, for if a hint of it had been given, the Germans might have changed their whole course of action with serious consequences to the Allies.) Colonel Theodore Roosevelt's endorsement of Albert B. Fall (p. 125) is reported in the New York *Times* for November 2, 1918. The joint appeal by Colonel Theodore Roosevelt and Mr. Taft for the election of Truman Newberry (p. 126) is reported in David Lawrence's *The True Story of Woodrow Wilson*, p. 235. Mr. Lawrence also reports the identical telegrams sent to Senators Lodge, Poindexter and Hiram Johnson. The conferences between President Wilson and his secretary, Joseph P. Tumulty, are described by Mr. Tumulty in his book *Woodrow Wilson As I Know Him*, p. 322 ff. Dr. Denna F. Fleming, in his *United States and the League of Nations*, p. 45, also discusses these talks and their result— the so-called "Partisan Appeal." The scene in Senator Lodge's office (page 130) is reconstructed from newspaper accounts, which are fairly full, especially that of the New York *Times* of October 26, 1918.

Will Hays' statement on page 132 was reported by most newspapers of October 28, 1918; and the bulk of the text is also printed in *The American Yearbook* for 1918 (p. 32). The Carnegie Hall meeting, page 133, was reported in New York papers of October 29, 1918.

Chapter 6

The incident which begins this chapter is a personal reminiscence, recorded in letters written soon after.

The description of the armistice negotiations is based on Foch, *Memoirs*, pp. 466 ff. Some of the color is given in Lausanne's article in *National Review*. Page 138, for interview with House see Seymour, *Intimate Papers*, IV, 91. (The quoted reply to House is from Foch, p. 463.) For pre-armistice documents, see *Preliminary History of the Armistice*. See also Weygand article in *National Review*, L'Hopital *Foch*, and Mordacq *L'Armistice*.

The description of the armistice in Paris on pages 142 ff. is based on interviews, etc.

The Churchill-Lloyd George conversation, pages 147 ff., is based on Churchill, *The Aftermath*, pp. 4 ff.

Page 149. Quotation is from Churchill, *The Aftermath*, pp. 5 and 6, by special permission of the publishers, Charles Scribner's Sons.

The section on Colonel House is based on Seymour, Chap. VI, Vol. IV, and on interviews with friends of Colonel House. Pages 150, 151, Lippmann statement, Seymour, IV, 190; Lippmann to House, Seymour, IV, 189; page 151, Clemenceau note, Seymour, IV, 192. On Fourteen Points conversation, page 153, in which a few liberties have been taken with the wording of the dialog, see Seymour, IV, 164 ff., and Lloyd George, *Truth About the Treaty*, pp. 75 ff.

Chapter 7

The account of the false armistice is taken from newspapers of November 7 and 8, 1918; with bits from Mark Sullivan's *Over Here*. The part played by the Associated Press is told by Oliver Gramling in his *AP: the Story of News*, p. 277. *Current History Magazine* for December, 1918 (p. 361), carries an account of President Wilson's speech (see p. 159). The description of Armistice Day in San Francisco and the bay area on pages 160-161, is derived from newspapers of the time, especially the San Francisco *Chronicle*. Mark Sullivan in his *Over Here*, of course, gives a detailed description of the day all over the country. The story of The Inquiry which starts on page 164 is told by Dr. J. T. Shotwell in his book *At the Paris Peace Conference*, pp. 3-19. Dr. Shotwell's description of the transient visitors appears on page 11 of the same work. For parts of our reconstruction of the purposes and philosophy of the Inquiry we are indebted to Dr. Charles Seymour of Yale University, who kindly made the collection of Colonel House's papers available to us and also gave us some of his own recollections and impressions. Some of the local issues which resulted in the election of a Republican senate majority which we discuss on page 168 are described in *The American Yearbook* for 1918. It was an election in which local issues were of considerably greater importance than was usually recognized at the time. Colonel Theodore Roosevelt's statement on page 170 was reported by the newspapers of November 28, 1918. Dr. Denna F. Fleming in his *The United States and the League of Nations* gives a comprehensive account of the events leading up to the President's departure for Paris. The selection of Henry White as member of the American Peace Commission is discussed by Allan Nevins in his book *Henry White*, published by Harper & Bros., who kindly gave us permission to quote Lodge's letter to White on page 172. New York newspapers of December 4 and 5, 1918, were full of the President's departure for Paris (page 173). The meeting between President Wilson and the Inquiry on board the *George Washington* (p. 174) is described by Shotwell on p. 175 of his book, *At the Paris Peace Conference*. The conversation on page 175 between the President and George Creel on deck is reconstructed from p. 162 of Mr. Creel's book, *The War, the World and Wilson*, and partly from Mark Sullivan's *Over Here*, p. 452. The final paragraph of the chapter is taken direct from Creel, p. 163, by permission of the publishers, Harper & Bros.

Chapter 8

There is much background material on Wilson's welcome in France. We have used, mainly, the London *Times*, Jan. 14, 15 and 16, Shotwell, the *Echo de Paris*, the New York *Herald*, Paris edition, *le Temps* and Edith Wilson's *My Memoirs*.

Page 177. Quotation of placard is from James T. Shotwell, *At the Paris Peace Conference*, by special permission of the publishers, The Macmillan Company. The quotation from Clemenceau is from London *Daily Mail*, Paris edition, Dec. 15, 1918. Pages 180 ff. are based on Edith Wilson, pp. 180 ff. The statement by Wilson at bottom of page 181 is based on Seymour, IV, 243 n.

The London section is based on Edwards, *David Lloyd George*, 557 ff.; Lloyd George, *Memoirs*, pp. 157 ff.; Nicolson, pp. 18 ff.; Simonds, pp. 50-52; Birdsall, pp. 36-40; Creel, *The War, the World and Wilson*, pp. 165-167, and the London *Times*, Dec. 14, 1918.

Page 189. For Clemenceau's statements, see Temperley, *History of the Peace Conference*, III, 58, 59.

Page 189. The attitude of Americans about the delay is expressed

by Baker, *Woodrow Wilson and World Settlement*, I, 97 ff.; and
Creel, *The War, the World and Wilson*, pp. 164 ff.

The background of the Roman section is given in more detail in
Creel, pp. 168-170. Edith Wilson, Chap. 16, Speranza, *Diary*, Jan.
17, 1919, and Albrecht-Carrié, pp. 81-86. Page 191, see Hansen,
Adventures of the Fourteen Points, p. 12, on journalists.

Good Paris background for this period is given by Thompson, *The
Peace Conference Day by Day*.

For the opening of the Conference, see Miller, *My Diary* (Vol.
I), Nicolson, *Peacemaking*, Seymour, Shotwell. Page 196, for French
demands, see Miller, *Diary*, Dec. 9, 1918, also Document 58, Miller,
II, 255. The description of M. Pichon's room, pages 197, 198, is
based on Clive Day *The Peace Conference* in House and Seymour,
What Really Happened, pp. 17, 18. The resolution on page 199 is
from Temperley, III, 56, checked with Miller *Diary*, Jan. 25, 1919.

Much of the color of this chapter is based on personal memories
recorded in letters written from Paris.

Chapter 9

The conversation between Senators Lodge and Watson is reconstructed from Senator James E. Watson's *As I Knew Them*, published
by Bobbs-Merrill Co.; the direct quotations are used by special permission of the publisher. The speech on page 203 of ex-Senator Albert
J. Beveridge is from Claude Bowers' *Beveridge and the Progressive
Era*, p. 497, by permission of the publishers, Houghton Mifflin Company. Senator Knox's remarks on the League given on page 204 appeared in the *Congressional Record*, Vol. 57, Part 1, pages 603-5; and
Senator Lodge's December 21 speech is reported in the same volume
on page 724. Henry White's cable to Senator Lodge reported by us on
page 205 is given by Senator Lodge in his *Senate and the League of
Nations* on pp. 123 and 124. Senator McCumber's impassioned speech
on page 206 is in the *Congressional Record* for January 7, 1919.
Senator Hardwick's remarkable long list of questions appears in the
Congressional Record, Vol. 57, Part 5, p. 4704. The situation in
central Europe and the correspondence concerning it between Henry
White and Henry Cabot Lodge is given in Allan Nevins' *Henry
White*, p. 353, from which we have quoted by permission of the publishers, Harper & Bros. Senator Borah's position as given by us on page
208 is described in Ray Stannard Baker's *Woodrow Wilson and World
Settlement*, I, 91. See also Claudius Johnson, *Borah of Idaho*, p. 226,
for Borah's letter to the Chicago *Tribune*. Senator Harding's remarks
reported by us on page 208 are in the *Congressional Record* for Jan-

uary 21, 1919. Incidentally, George Harvey, in the *War Weekly* for Feb. 1, 1919, remarked that this speech suggested Harding was presidential timber—possibly one of the earliest of such suggestions. Senator Lodge's letter to Henry White on page 209 is from Allan Nevins' *Henry White*, and is quoted here by permission of the publishers, Harper & Bros. Mrs. Wilson's pleasant remarks about the Franklin D. Roosevelts appear in her book *My Memoir*, p. 240. The account of President Wilson's Boston visit and speech appeared in morning newspapers of February 25, 1919; the account in the New York *Times* being especially thorough. Most of the account of the White House dinner given on our page 212 is reconstructed from the New York *Times* of February 27, 1919. Senator Lodge in his *The Senate and the League of Nations*, p. 118 ff., describes the events leading up to the round robin of March 4, 1919 (see our pages 213-215). The account of the actual presentation of the resolution beginning on our page 215 is reconstructed from the *Congressional Record* for that day and from the accounts in the New York *Times* and New York *Sun* (the *Sun's* reporter observed the shaking hand that held the resolution). Vice-President Marshall's closing of the session on page 218 is reconstructed principally from the account in the New York *Times* of March 5, 1919.

Chapter 10

Personal memories and extensive interviews have supplied some of the atmosphere of this chapter. Pages 219, 220, description of Wilson's landing at Brest is based on account in the *Camp Pontenezen Duckboard* (a paper published by American troops at Brest), March 15, 1918, and the New York *Times*, March 14, 1918. From the account in Seymour, IV, 385 and 386, it is difficult to be sure how much of the conversation between House and Wilson was on the train and how much took place the following morning (March 14). The dialog has been constructed from the Seymour and House accounts, Seymour, IV, 385, 386. (Seymour is in error on the date of arrival at Brest, which was March 13th.) Page 222, statement on French reparations ($200,000,000) is from the House diary, Seymour, IV, 343. The quotation from the House diary, page 223, is from Seymour, IV, 362, by special permission of the publishers, Houghton Mifflin Company.

Page 229, the Norman Angell statement is from Hansen, *Adventures of the Fourteen Points*, p. 189. Page 231 on Italian story of Fiume, see Albrecht-Carrié, pp. 432 ff. For a spirited account of the April 23rd incident, see Hansen, Chap. IX. See also Albrecht-Carrié, Chap. V. The Wilson Manifesto is in Albrecht-Carrié, p. 498. The quotation on page 234 is from Harry Hansen, *The Adventures of the*

Fourteen Points (p. 157), by special permission of the publishers, D. Appleton-Century Co. Page 235. One account of the coolness between House and Wilson is given by Baker, *Woodrow Wilson and World Settlement*, I, Chaps. XVI and XVII. Seymour Appendix to Chap. IV, Vol. IV, disagrees with some of this.

A good summary of the German-Allied relations, April 21, 1919, to June 28, 1919, is given in Temperley, II, 2 ff.

For the Brockdorff-Rantzau incident, page 237, see Seymour, IV, 457, also Temperley, II, 2. Page 238, the Comments by the German Delegation on the Conditions of Peace and Counter-Proposals was printed in *International Conciliation*, October, 1919. Page 240, the reply of the Allies to the German Delegation was printed in *International Conciliation*, November, 1919. For a description of the signing at Versailles, see Shotwell and Temperley, II, 17, 18. Pages 243, 244, the quotation from the House diary, Seymour, *The Intimate Papers of Colonel House*, IV, 487, 488, is by special permission of the publishers, Houghton Mifflin Company.

Chapter 11

The account of the conversation between George Harvey (if it really was he) and Henry Clay Frick is reconstructed from George Harvey's *Henry Clay Frick; the Man*, p. 328 ff., and quotations from the book are by permission of the publishers, Charles Scribner's Sons. An excellent account of the precarious Republican control in the Senate and the reasons for it is given in William Dodd's *Woodrow Wilson and His Work*, pp. 379-381. The threat to filibuster reported by us on page 248 is to be found in the *Congressional Record*, Feb. 6, 1919, pp. 2808-2809. Fleming in his *The United States and the League of Nations* also analyzes the situation at some length. Spencer Ervin, in his book *Henry Ford vs. Truman H. Newberry, The Famous Senate Election*, gives a thorough background and a complete account of the whole affair. The net effect is pro-Newberry. On page 249, the remark of Senator Lodge is reported by Edith Bolling Wilson in her book, *My Memoir*, p. 242. The Republican attack upon Article II given by us on page 251 is from the *Congressional Record*, Vol. 58, Part 3, p. 2588, and was prepared by the Republican Publicity Association. The long and complicated Senate fight is described practically blow by blow in Dr. Fleming's *The United States and the League of Nations*. We have, of course, barely outlined it here. The conversation between President Wilson and Senator James E. Watson of Indiana, beginning on page 254, is reconstructed from Senator Watson's *As I Knew Them*, and quotations from it are by permission of the publisher, the Bobbs-Merrill Company. Senator Watson states that Mr.

Wilson told him a funny story, and the anecdote about the little boy
was in circulation in Washington at that time and may or may not
have been the one Mr. Wilson told. The scene between President
Wilson, Mrs. Wilson and Dr. Grayson beginning on page 257 is
reconstructed principally from Mrs. Wilson's book *My Memoir*, and
direct quotations from the book are by permission of the publisher,
the Bobbs-Merrill Company. The account of President Wilson's western tour beginning on page 259 is mostly from newspapers along the
route. Dr. Fleming discusses it at some length and in detail. Mrs.
Wilson and Joseph P. Tumulty in their books tell something of the
tour. Senator Ashurst's count of Democratic Senate votes on page 263
is reported by the New York *Tribune* of Sept. 7 and Sept. 8, 1919.
A description of the Borah-Johnson-McCormick meeting on page 264
is given in the Chicago *Tribune*. We have rearranged the speech
slightly for clarity. The quote on page 268 from David Lawrence's
syndicated piece is given by permission of Mr. Lawrence. The article
appeared in most papers carrying it on Sept. 22, 1919. We took the
text from the Salt Lake *Tribune* of that date. The call from Washington to Senator Johnson reported on page 268 was reported in the
New York *Times* of Sept. 27, 1919. The Salt Lake *Tribune* reported
Mr. Wilson's visit (page 269) in its issue of Sept. 24, 1919. Senator
Hitchcock's comments on the test vote described on page 270 were
reported in the New York *Times* of Sept. 25, 1919. The Rocky
Mountain *News* account of the President's Denver reception on page
271 is from the Sept. 25, 1919, paper, and on the same day the New
York *Times* under date line of Sept. 24, 1919, published the article
from which we quote on page 271 by special permission of the *Times*.
The journey from Pueblo to Washington is reconstructed mostly from
accounts of the newspaper men who accompanied the President on the
tour. Mrs. Wilson and Tumulty also describe it briefly in their books.
The quotation from Mr. Wilson on page 279 is from his speech at
St. Louis, Mo., on Sept. 5, 1919.

Chapter 12

For the background of the Prague section, we have used Masaryk,
Seton-Watson, Hanc, Hindus, Steed, Caldwell, Lowrie, the *Survey*,
June 11, 1921.

We have spoken of the voice of Comenius as "ringing across the
Týn square," as this was a place of execution in which Bohemian rebels
lost their lives. Page 280, the quote from Rasin is from Masaryk,
p. 347.

The newspaper accounts of the 1920 Republican convention in the
New York *Times*, the New York *Tribune* and the Chicago *Tribune*

are especially full of detail. Mark Sullivan in *The Twenties* (Vol. 6 of *Our Times*) and Samuel Hopkins Adams in *The Incredible Era* give colorful reconstructions of the proceedings. Harry M. Daugherty in *The Inside Story of the Harding Tragedy* tells the story of his tactics as Harding's manager. M. R. Werner's *Privileged Characters* contains many anecdotes of the convention; so does Ray Tucker's *Sons of the Wild Jackass*. The memoirs of Alice Longworth, Nicholas Murray Butler, C. W. Barron and Senator James E. Watson all contain recollections of the convention.

Harding's speeches have not been collected and published in one book as have those of many other presidents. On page 291, the speech beginning "America's present need is not heroics," was made at Boston on May 14, 1920, and reported in the newspapers of the following day. (It is also reprinted in *Rededicating America*, edited by Frederick Schortemeier, published by the Bobbs-Merrill Co.) The remarks on the League of Nations on page 291 were made from the Senate floor on Sept. 11, 1919, and may be found in the *Congressional Record* for that day. The speech beginning "American business is not big business . . ." is to be found in *Our Common Country*, by Warren G. Harding, p. 19, copyright 1921, and quoted here by special permission of the publishers, the Bobbs-Merrill Company. The speech on page 291 beginning "Conditions have been evolved . . ." was made at Providence on February 25, 1920, and reported in the newspapers of that city. (It is also reprinted in *Rededicating America*.) The remarks on labor on page 291 are from *Our Common Country*, and are quoted here by special permission of the publishers, the Bobbs-Merrill Company.

The Ludendorff-Hitler putsch item appeared in the New York *Times*, Nov. 10, 1923.

The account of Woodrow Wilson's last public speech, beginning on page 293, is reconstructed from newspaper accounts. Mrs. Wilson in her book *My Memoir* describes the occasion from her point of view, and most of Wilson's biographers mention it more or less briefly.

Bibliography

Adams, Samuel Hopkins, *Incredible Era. The Life and Times of Warren Gamaliel Harding*. Boston: Houghton Mifflin, 1939

Albrecht-Carrié, Rene, *Italy at the Peace Conference*. New York: Columbia University Press, 1938

Alexandra, *The Letters of the Tsaritsa to the Tsar, 1914-1917*. Translated by A. L. Hynes. London: J. Lane, 1929

The American Yearbook, 1918-1919

Anonymous (Gilbert, Clinton Wallace), *Mirrors of Washington*. New York: Putnam, 1921

Baden. *See* Maximilian.

Baerlein, Henry, *The March of the Seventy Thousand*. London: Leonard Parsons, 1926

Baker, Ray Stannard, and William E. Dodd, Editors, *The Public Papers of Woodrow Wilson, War and Peace* (Vol. III). New York: Harper & Bros., 1925-27

Baker, Ray Stannard, *Woodrow Wilson and World Settlement*, 3 Vols. New York: Doubleday, Doran, 1923

Barron, C. W., *They Told Barron* (edited and arranged by Arthur Pound and Samuel T. Moore). New York: Harper & Bros., 1930

Bassett, John Spencer, *Our War with Germany*. New York: Knopf, 1919

Beneš, Edward, *Democracy, Today and Tomorrow*. New York: Macmillan, 1939

Beneš, Edward, translated by Paul Selver, *My War Memoirs*. Boston: Houghton Mifflin, 1928

Berdahl, Clarence A., *The Policy of the United States with Respect to the League of Nations*. Geneva: Graduate Institute of International Studies; Publications, No. 6, 1932

Birdsall, Paul, *Versailles Twenty Years After*. New York: Reynal and Hitchcock, 1941

Bishop, Joseph B., Editor, *Theodore Roosevelt and His Time, Shown in His Own Letters*, 2 vols. New York: Scribner, 1920

Bolling, John Randolph, *Chronology of Woodrow Wilson*. New York: Stokes, 1927

Bowers, Claude G., *Beveridge and the Progressive Era*. Boston: Houghton Mifflin, 1932

Brest-Litovsk, Proceedings, *The Peace Negotiations between Russia and the Central Powers*, Nov. 21, 1917 to March 3, 1918. Washington: Government Printing Office, 1918

Bruntz, George G., *Allied Propaganda and the Collapse of the German Empire in 1918*. Stanford University Press, 1938

Buchan, John, *A History of the Great War*, 4 vols. Boston: Houghton Mifflin, 1922

Butler, Nicholas M., *Across the Busy Years*. New York: Scribner's, 1939

Bunyan, James, and H. H. Fischer, *The Bolshevik Revolution, 1917-1918*, Documents and Materials. Stanford University Press, 1934

Caldwell, R. J., *The Economic Situation in Czechoslovakia in 1920*. U. S. Dept. of Labor. Washington: Gov't Pr't'g Off., 1920.

Carnegie Endowment for International Peace, *Preliminary History of the Armistice*. Official Documents Published by the German National Chancellery by Order of the Ministry of State. Translated by Carnegie Endowment for International Peace. New York: Oxford University Press, 1924

Chambers, Frank P., *The War Behind the War*, 1914-1918. A History of the Political and Civilian Fronts. New York: Harcourt, Brace, 1939

Churchill, Winston, *The Aftermath*. New York: Scribner, 1929

Clarkson, Grosvenor B., *Industrial America in the World War; The Strategy Behind the Main Line, 1917-1918*. Boston: Houghton Mifflin, 1924

Clemenceau, Georges, *Grandeur and Misery of Victory*. New York: Harcourt, Brace, 1930

Cocks, Seymour, *The Secret Treaties and Understandings*. Text of the Available Documents. London: Union of Democratic Control, 1918

Crawford, Ruth, Director of the Social Survey of Prague (1919), *Pathfinding in Prague*. In *The Survey*, June 11, 1921

Creel, George, *How We Advertised America*. New York: Harper, 1920
—— *The War, the World and Wilson*. New York: Harper, 1920

Cruttwell, C. R., *A History of the Great War, 1914-1918*. New York: Oxford University Press, 1934

Crowell, Benedict, and Robert F. Wilson, *How America Went to War;
The Giant Hand; Our Mobilization and Control of Industry
and Natural Resources,* 1917-1918. New Haven: Yale University
Press, 1921

Cummings, C. K., and Pettit, Walter W., *Russian-American Relations.*
New York: Harcourt, Brace, 1920

Czernin, Count Ottokar, *In the World War.* London: Cassell and Co.,
Ltd., 1919

Daugherty, Harry M., in collaboration with Thomas Dixon, *Inside
Story of the Harding Tragedy.* New York: The Churchill Company, 1932

Davis, Forrest, *The Atlantic System. The Story of Anglo-American
Control of the Seas.* New York: Reynal and Hitchcock, 1941

Democratic Campaign Textbook, 1916, 1920, 1924. New York:
Democratic National Committee

Dodd, W. E., *Woodrow Wilson and His Work.* New York: P. Smith,
1932

Dupuy, Richard Ernest, Major, U. S. Army, *Perish by the Sword.*
The Czechoslovakian Anabasis and Our Supporting Campaigns
in North Russia and Siberia, 1918-1920. Harrisburg, Pa.: The
Military Service Publishing Co., 1939

Ervin, Spencer, *Henry Ford vs. Truman Newberry.* The Famous Senate Election. New York: R. R. Smith, 1935

Fleming, Denna Frank, *The Treaty Veto of the American Senate.*
New York: Putnam, 1930

—— *The United States and the League of Nations,* 1918-1920. New
York: Putnam, 1932

—— *The United States and World Organization,* 1920-1933. New
York: Columbia University Press, 1938

Foch, Ferdinand, *The Memoirs of Marshal Foch,* translated by Colonel T. Bentley Mott. New York: Doubleday, 1931

Forster, Kent, *The Failures of Peace;* the Search for a Negotiated
Peace during the First World War. Washington: American Council on Public Affairs, 1941

Gordon, Allan, *Russian Year.* A Calendar of Revolution. London:
Cassel, 1935

Graves, William S., *America's Siberian Adventure.* New York: J. Cape
and H. Smith, 1931

Groves, Charles Stuart, *Henry Cabot Lodge: the Statesman.* Boston:
Small Maynard, 1925

Guardian, Manchester: November and December, 1917

Hale, William B., *The Story of a Style*. New York: B. W. Huebsch, 1920

Hanc, Josef, *Tornado Across Eastern Europe*. New York: The Greystone Press, 1942

Hansen, Harry, *The Adventures of the Fourteen Points*. New York: The Century Co., 1919

Hard, William, *Raymond Robins' Own Story*. New York: Harper, 1920

Harding, Warren G., *Our Common Country* (Fred E. Schortemeier, editor). Indianapolis: Bobbs-Merrill Co., 1921

Harvey, George B., *Henry Clay Frick; The Man*. New York: Scribner, 1928

Hendrick, Burton J., *The Life and Letters of Walter H. Page*, in 2 vols. New York: Doubleday, 1922

Herron, George D., *Woodrow Wilson and the World's Peace*. New York: Mitchell Kennerley, 1917

Hertling, Karl, Graf von, *Ein Jahr in der Reichskanzlerei*, etc. Freiburg: 1919

Hicks, Granville, *John Reed*. New York: Macmillan, 1936

Hindus, Maurice, *We Shall Live Again*. New York: Doubleday, 1939

Hoffmann, Max, *War Diaries and Other Papers*. Translated from the German by Eric Sutton. London: M. Lecker, 1929

Holt, William S., *Treaties Defeated by the Senate; A Study of the Struggle Between President and Senate on the Conduct of Foreign Relation*. Baltimore: The Johns Hopkins Press, 1933

L'Hopital, Commandant, *L'Armistice et La Paix*. Paris: 1938

House, Edward Mandell, and Seymour, Charles (editors), *What Really Happened at Paris*. New York: Scribner, 1921

Houston, David F., *Eight Years with Wilson's Cabinet*, 1913-1920; *With a Personal Estimate of the President*. Garden City, N. Y.: Doubleday, Page & Co., 1926

Hrushevsky, Michael, *A History of the Ukraine*. Ed. by O. J. Frederikson. Published for the Ukrainian National Association. New Haven: Yale University Press, 1941

Jessup, Philip C., *Elihu Root*. New York: Dodd, Mead, 1938

Johnson, Claudius O., *Borah of Idaho*. New York: Longmans Green, 1936

Johnson, Willis F., *George Harvey, A Passionate Patriot*. Boston: Houghton Mifflin, 1929

Josephson, Matthew, *The President-Makers: 1896-1919*. New York: Harcourt, Brace, 1940

Kent, Frank R., *The Democratic Party, A History*. New York: The Century Co., 1928

Kerney, James, *The Political Education of Woodrow Wilson*. New York: The Century Co., 1926

Keynes, John Maynard, *The Economic Consequences of the Peace*. New York: Harcourt, Brace, 1920

Langsam, Walter Consuelo, *The World Since 1914*. New York: Macmillan, 1940

Lansing, Robert, *The Big Four and Others of the Peace Conference*. Boston: Houghton Mifflin, 1921

—— *The Peace Negotiations, A Personal Narrative*. Boston: Houghton Mifflin, 1921

Lasswell, Harold D., *Propaganda Technique in the World War*. New York: Peter Smith, 1938

Lawrence, David, *The True Story of Woodrow Wilson*. New York: George H. Doran Co., 1924

Lloyd George, David, *War Memoirs*, 2 vols. London: Ivor, Nicholson & Watson, 1933

—— *The Truth about the Peace Treaties*. London: Gollancz, 1938

Lodge, Henry Cabot, *The Senate and the League of Nations*. New York: Scribner, 1925

Longworth, Mrs. Alice (Roosevelt), *Crowded Hours, Reminiscences of Alice Roosevelt Longworth*. New York: Scribner, 1933

Loth, David G., *Woodrow Wilson, the Fifteenth Point*. Philadelphia: Lippincott, 1941

Lowry, Edward G., *Washington Close-Ups, 1921*. Boston: Houghton Mifflin, 1921

Ludendorff, Erich von, *The American Effort*. In the *Atlantic Monthly*, May, 1922

—— *The General Staff and Its Problems*. London: Hutchinson & Co., 1920

—— *Ludendorff's Own Story*, August, 1914-November, 1918. 2 vols. New York: Harper, 1920

Lutz, Ralph Haswell (editor), *The Causes of the German Collapse in 1918*. Official Report of German Constituent Assembly and of German Reichstag, 1918-1928. Stanford University Press, 1934

—— *The German Revolution, 1918-1919*. Stanford University Publications, University Series. History, Economics and Political Science, Vol. I, No. 1. Published by the University, 1922

Lutz, Ralph Haswell (editor), *Fall of the German Empire, 1914-18.* Stanford University Press, 1932

Marburg, Theodore, *Development of the League of Nations Idea.* Edited by John Latane. 2 vols. New York: Macmillan, 1932

Marshall, Thomas R., *Recollections of Thomas R. Marshall.* Indianapolis: Bobbs-Merrill, 1925

Masaryk, Thomas G., *The Making of a State.* London: G. Allen & Unwin, 1927

—— *Memories and Observations,* 1914-1918. Introduction by Henry Wickham Steed. London: George Allen and Unwin, Ltd., 1927

Maximilian, Prince of Baden, *Memoirs,* 2 vols. London: Constable, 1928

Miller, David Hunter, *The Drafting of the Covenant,* 2 vols. New York: G. P. Putnam's Sons, 1928

—— *My Diary at the Conference of Paris,* 20 vols. Privately printed, 1928

Mock, James R., and Larsen, Cedric, *Words That Won the War.* Princeton: Princeton University Press, 1939

Mordaco, Gen. H., *L'Armistice du Novembre, 1918. Recit d'un témoin.* Paris, 1937.

Mowrer, Edgar Ansel, *Immortal Italy.* New York: D. Appleton & Co., 1922

Munzer, Sdenka, and Jan, *We Were and We Shall Be.* New York: Frederick Unger, 1941

Nevins, Allan, *Henry White.* New York: Harper, 1930

Nicholas II, Emperor of Russia, *The Letters of the Tsar to the Tsaritsa, 1914-1917.* Translated by A. L. Hynes. London: J. Lane, 1929

Nicolson, Harold, *Peacemaking, 1919.* Boston: Houghton Mifflin, 1934

Nowak, Karl Friedrich, *The Collapse of Central Europe.* With an introduction by Viscount Haldane. London: Kegan, Paul, Trench, Trubner & Co., Ltd., 1924

Padover, Saul K., Editor, *Wilson's Ideals.* Washington: American Council on Public Affairs, 1942

Painlevé, Paul, *Comment j'ai nommé Foch et Pétain.* Paris: Felix Alcan, 1924

Paxson, Frederic L., *American Democracy in the World War*, 2 vols. Boston: Houghton Mifflin, 1936-39

Pershing, John J., *My Experiences in the World War*, 2 vols. New York: Stokes, 1931

Pringle, Henry F., *Life and Times of William Howard Taft*. New York: Farrar & Rinehart, 1939

—— *Theodore Roosevelt: A Biography*. New York: Harcourt, Brace, 1931

Radziwill, Princess Catherine, *Nicholas II: Last of the Tsars*. London: Cassel, 1931

Reed, John, *Ten Days That Shook the World*. New York: Boni and Liveright, 1919

Republican Campaign Textbook, 1920. Republican National Committee, 1920

Riddell, Lord, *Intimate Diary of the Peace Conference*, 1918-1923. London: Gollancz, 1933

Robinson, Corinne, *My Brother Theodore Roosevelt*. New York: Scribner, 1921

Roosevelt, Theodore, *Selections from the Correspondence of Theodore Roosevelt and Henry Cabot Lodge*. New York: Scribner, 1925

Salandra, Antonio, *Italy and the Great War*. London: Edward Arnold and Co., 1932

Salvemini, Gaetano, *Dal patto di Londra alla pace di Roma*. Turin: Bogetti, 1925

Schortemeier, Fred E., *Rededicating America. Life and Recent Speeches of Warren G. Harding*. Indianapolis: Bobbs-Merrill, 1920

Schultze-Pfaelzer, Gerhard, *Hindenburg: Peace, War, Aftermath*. New York: Putnam, 1932

Scott, James Brown (Editor), *Official Statements of War Aims and Peace Proposals, December, 1916, to November, 1919. Carnegie Endowment for International Peace, Division of International Law*. New York: Oxford University Press, 1925

—— *Preliminary History of the Armistice. Official Documents published by the German National Chancellory by order of the Ministry of State*. Carnegie Endowment for International Peace, Division of International Law. New York: Oxford University Press, 1924

Seton-Watson, R. W., *Masaryk in England*. New York: Macmillan, 1943

Seymour, Charles, *The Intimate Papers of Colonel House*, 4 vols. Boston: Houghton Mifflin, 1926-1928

Sharp, William Graves, *The War Memoirs of*. London: Constable, 1931

Shotwell, James T., *At the Paris Peace Conference*. New York: Macmillan, 1937

—— *What Germany Forgot*. New York: Macmillan, 1940

Simonds, Frank H., *How Europe Made Peace Without America*. New York: Doubleday, Page, 1927

Sisson, Edgar G., *One Hundred Red Days*. A Personal Chronicle of the Bolshevik Revolution. New Haven: Yale University Press, 1931

Smith, Arthur D. H., *Mr. House of Texas*. New York: Funk & Wagnalls, 1940

—— *The Real Colonel House*. New York: George H. Doran Co., 1918

Speranza, Gino, *Diary*. New York: Columbia University Press, 1941

Steed, Henry Wickham, *Through Thirty Years*, 2 vols. New York: Doubleday, 1924

Sullivan, Mark, *Over Here* (Vol. 5 of *Our Times*). New York: Scribner, 1933

—— *The Twenties* (Vol. 6 of *Our Times*). New York: Scribner, 1935

Tardieu, Andre, *The Truth about the Treaty*. Indianapolis: Bobbs-Merrill, 1921

Taylor, A. H. E., *The Treaty of Rapallo*. Balkan Review. London, 1920

Temperley, H. W. V., *A History of the Peace Conference of Paris*, 6 vols. London: Frowde, 1920-1924

Thompson, Charles T., *The Peace Conference Day by Day*. New York: Brentano, 1920

Thompson, Charles Willis, *Presidents I've Known and Two Near Presidents*. Indianapolis: Bobbs-Merrill, 1929

The *Times*, London: July 1917, November and December 1917, December 1918, and March 1919

Treaties of Peace, 1919-1923. Introduction by Lt. Col. Lawrence Martin, Geographer of the Institute of Politics, 2 vols. New York: Carnegie Endowment for International Peace, 1924

Trotsky, Leon, *History of the Russian Revolution*. New York: Simon and Schuster, 1932

Tucker, Ray T., and Fred R. Barkley, *Sons of the Wild Jackass.*
    Boston: L. C. Page Co., 1932
Tumulty, Joseph, *Woodrow Wilson as I Know Him.* New York:
    Doubleday, 1921
Tyrkova-Williams, Ariadna, *From Liberty to Brest-Litovsk.* The First
    Year of the Russian Revolution. London: Macmillan, 1919
United States Department of Labor, *The Economic Situation in
    Czechoslovakia in 1920.* Washington, 1921
United States Department of State, *Papers on Foreign Relations,
    Russia,* I, 1918
United States Department of State, *Papers Relating to the Foreign
    Relations of the U. S.,* 1918. Supplement I, The World War,
    2 vols. Washington, 1933
United States War Department, *The War with Germany.* A Statis-
    tical Summary by Leonard P. Ayres. Washington: Government
    Printing Office, 1919
Watson, James E., *As I Knew Them.* Indianapolis: Bobbs-Merrill,
    1936
Werner, M. R., *Privileged Characters.* New York: R. M. McBride &
    Co., 1935
Weygand, General Maxine, *Marshal Foch and the Armistice.* In
    National Review, London, December, 1938. Vol. III, No. 670.
Wheeler-Bennett, John W., *The Forgotten Peace, Brest-Litovsk,
    March 1918.* New York: Morrow, 1939
—— *The Treaty of Brest-Litovsk and Germany's Eastern Policy.*
    Oxford: Clarenden Press, 1940
—— *The Wooden Titan. Hindenburg in Twenty Years of German
    History,* 1914-1934. New York: Morrow, 1936
White, William Allen, *Masks in a Pageant.* New York: Macmillan,
    1928
—— *Woodrow Wilson.* Boston: Houghton Mifflin, 1925
White, William C., *Lenin.* New York: Harrison Smith & Robert Haas,
    1936
Wilson, Edith Bolling, *My Memoir.* Indianapolis: Bobbs-Merrill,
    1939
Wilson, Woodrow, *Addresses of President Wilson Delivered on His
    Western Tour, Sept. 4 to Sept. 25, 1919* (Senate Doc. 120).
    Washington: Government Printing Office, 1919
Wister, Owen, *Roosevelt: The Story of a Friendship.* New York:
    Macmillan, 1930

Index

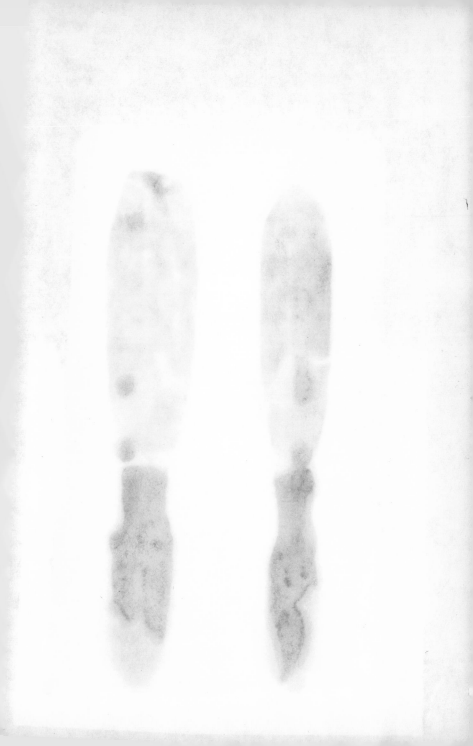